THE PROMISE OF
PROGRESSIVISM

HISTORY OF
SCHOOLS &
SCHOOLING

Alan R. Sadovnik and Susan F. Semel
General Editors

Vol. 45

PETER LANG
New York • Washington, D.C./Baltimore • Bern
Frankfurt am Main • Berlin • Brussels • Vienna • Oxford

James M. Wallace

THE PROMISE OF PROGRESSIVISM

ANGELO PATRI
& URBAN EDUCATION

PETER LANG
New York • Washington, D.C./Baltimore • Bern
Frankfurt am Main • Berlin • Brussels • Vienna • Oxford

Library of Congress Cataloging-in-Publication Data

Wallace, James M.
The promise of progressivism: Angelo Patri and Urban education /
James M. Wallace.
p. cm. — (History of schools and schooling; v. 45)
Includes bibliographical references and index.
1. Patri, Angelo, b. 1876. 2. Educators—United States—Biography.
3. Progressive education—United States—History. I. Title. II. Series.
LB875.P29W35   370'.1—dc22   2004006749
ISBN 0-8204-7142-9
ISSN 1089-0678

Bibliographic information published by **Die Deutsche Bibliothek.**
Die Deutsche Bibliothek lists this publication in the "Deutsche
Nationalbibliografie"; detailed bibliographic data is available
on the Internet at http://dnb.ddb.de/.

Cover design by Joni Holst
Front cover image: Maria Montessori visiting Patri's Public School 45 in 1915
Back cover image: Patri and his most famous graduate,
film actor John Garfield, 1941

The paper in this book meets the guidelines for permanence and durability
of the Committee on Production Guidelines for Book Longevity
of the Council of Library Resources.

© 2006 Peter Lang Publishing, Inc., New York
29 Broadway, New York, NY 10006
www.peterlang.com

Printed in the United States of America

To Mary with love

CONTENTS

PHOTOGRAPHS

Photographs provided by and reproduced by permission of James Wallace, Frank Merolla, Jr., Muriel Sherlock, and Marilyn Shea. Photographs from the Patri Papers are in the public domain

Series Editors' Preface

JAMES WALLACE'S *THE PROMISE OF PROGRESSIVISM: Angelo Patri and Urban Education* provides a needed addition to our History of Schools and Schooling series. Although the series has published a number of important books on the history of early twentieth century progressive education, including school histories and biographies of significant and often forgotten schools and leaders, most of these have been on the independent school sector. Certainly schools such as Dalton, City and Country, the Organic School, and others profiled in *"Schools of Tomorrow," Schools of Today: What Happened to Progressive Education* (Lang, 1999) and leaders such as Helen Parkhurst, Caroline Pratt, and Marietta Johnson profiled in *Founding Mother and Others: Women Educational Leaders During the Progressive Era* (Palgrave, 2002) are important. They also support our argument that many of the child-centered progressive schools of the period failed to live up to the democratic principles of equity and access central to progressivism. Nevertheless, there were important progressive reforms and leaders in the public sector, including the Gary Plan, Carleton Washburn's individualized system in Winnetka, Illinois, and the work of Ella Flagg Young and Margaret Haley in Chicago. Jim Wallace's biography of Italian-born, New York City progressive educator Angelo Patri adds to this list.

Angelo Patri was an important figure in New York City public education for over a half century. As a school principal and educational writer Patri exemplified the role of the New York City public schools in providing opportunity for generations of immigrants. Although the New York

City schools in particular and large urban systems in general have right-fully been criticized by revisionist historians as often reproducing exist-ing class and racial inequalities rather than providing significant avenues for mobility, this critique underestimates the significant successes of the New York City public schools in opening opportunities. Patri's success with immigrant students, his participation in the Gary program in New York, his thoughtful essays on progressive education are emblematic of how individuals within the city schools struggled to ensure access and op-portunity to working-class and immigrant children. That the system has not been as successful as we would like, especially for children of color, does not erase its successes or tarnish the efforts of thousands of teachers and administrators like Patri who worked tirelessly on behalf of the city's millions of children.

It is especially pleasing to us, one a graduate of CUNY (Sadovnik, Queens College, '75) and the other currently a faculty member at Patri's alma mater (Semel, CCNY), that this book celebrates the enormous con-tribution of these institutions to the lives of New York City's children. Often unfairly maligned since Open Admissions in 1969, CUNY in gen-eral and CCNY in particular represent the successes of public higher education in providing access, opportunity, and achievement to working-class, minority, and immigrant students. Patri's graduation from CCNY after coming to the United States as a child is representative of the experi-ence of thousands of immigrants of his time. That he stayed and affected the lives of New York City children as a teacher and principal calls atten-tion to CCNY's and CUNY's continuing roles as the largest producers of New York City teachers. From Patri's time to the present, the City on the Hill on Convent Avenue remains the best hope for each new genera-tion of working-class and immigrant students. As David Lavin and Paul Attewell's forthcoming book on the lives, thirty years later, of women CUNY graduates who began college during the first three years of Open Admissions poignantly demonstrates, CUNY continues to have long-last-ing positive effects on its students, their children, and the city. This tradi-tion is aptly illustrated by Wallace's biography.

Finally, it gives us pleasure to see this book come to completion. We have been involved with Jim in numerous panels over the past decade at the History of Education Society, American Educational Studies Association, and American Educational Research Association, where he presented parts of the Patri story. Having watched it evolve from initial fascination, to the idea for a biography, and then unfolding as a book, reminds us of the long and painstaking work required for good history and biography. Like all good historians, Jim mined the archives, interviewed living subjects, and traveled the country in search of new data. Such work does not quickly become translated into publishable articles and a book. Like good wine, historical scholarship takes love, respect, and time. And in the end, like a great bottle of wine, this book has been worth the wait.

Alan R. Sadovnik
Susan F. Semel
May 2005, New York City

Foreword

by David Tyack

THE PROMISE OF PROGRESSIVISM IS AN ENGAGING AND reflective account of Angelo Patri, an impoverished Italian immigrant who became one of the best-known and best-loved teachers in America. Even though there have been many millions of teachers, there are only a few rich biographies and autobiographies that deal vividly and complexly with their lives. This book is a welcome addition to that number.

In this study of Patri's life and times James Wallace presents some fascinating puzzles: How was Patri able to create child-centered schools within the huge and hidebound New York school system of a century ago? Amid wars and depression, shifting currents of educational reform, and political turmoil, how was Patri able to maintain a steady course for his forty seven years as teacher and principal, during which he managed to preserve reforms that worked and to sabotage misguided efforts to fix what was not broken? To what degree was Patri's version of child-centered education connected with the larger political and social movement called Progressivism?

Throughout the nearly half-century that Patri worked in schools, he sought to build bonds between his schools and their constituencies. He cultivated support with colleagues both inside and outside the school bureaucracy (becoming friends with Mayor Fiorello La Guardia, for example). He worked to build parks and social services in the school neighborhood and believed that the community-centered school was linked to child-centered education.

On a number of issues on which enthusiasts demanded either-or choices Patri took what today seems to be a moderate position. He strongly supported progressive pedagogy *and* the learning of traditional academic subjects. As an early advocate of multiculturalism he wanted immigrant children to celebrate their own cultures *and* to become incorporated into American society (no need to choose between Garibaldi and Lincoln). Patri is not easily categorized as liberal or traditionalist since he sought both to innovate and to conserve in education.

Like Leonard Covello, another Italian immigrant and educational pioneer, Patri was a superb storyteller. He attributed this talent to his father and to Italian folk tradition. These narratives were his favorite form of teaching, whether in a rowdy classroom, in a neighborhood meeting, in his autobiographical memoir, or in his advice columns on childraising in popular magazines.

Wallace weaves together many kinds of evidence to create a rich sourcebook on urban Progressive education. He works with the ninety boxes of Patri papers in the Library of Congress, oral histories given by his friends and relatives, reactions of students and teachers today to Patri's ideas and stories, and even home movies. The result is a broad array of perceptions of the man and his work. The alternation of Patri's autobiographical voice with that of historian Wallace gives an immediacy to the account that makes the biography seem more a conversation than a monograph. This is a book to savor.

Acknowledgments

GRATITUDE WAS ONE OF ANGELO PATRI'S MOST CONSIS-
tent characteristics. His writings expressed in many ways his intense
appreciation for his life in Italy and America, for his family, friends,
and education, and for the opportunity to do useful work. In acknowl-
edging the assistance of those who helped me write his biography, I feel
that same sense of gratitude, first of course to Patri himself for living
and recording such an interesting and productive life. I thank another
deceased person, the unknown Sara B. Graves, for preserving her copy
of Patri's *A Schoolmaster of the Great City*, which initiated my interest in
him. I think of her as representative of the many teachers and others
who have been enlightened and sometimes inspired by that book.

I particularly appreciate my friends and colleagues at Lewis and
Clark College who responded to my discussions of Patri. I thank Wanita
McPherson for her continued interest and friendship. Three colleagues—Andra Makler, Ruth Shagoury, and Clayton Morgareidge—
give their responses to Patri in chapter 13. I thank representatives of
several organizations for providing opportunities for me to discuss my
emerging work on Patri: the American Educational Studies Association
in 1996, 1997, and 1998; the American Educational Research Association
in 1998; the History of Education Society and the American Italian
Historical Association in 1999; and the Associazione Italiana Maestri
Catolici in 2002 and 2003. I am grateful to several people who at these
meetings contributed to my interpretation of educational biography

and history: John Beineke, Peter Carbone, Michael James, Craig Kridel, Kate Rousmaniere, Wayne Urban, Alan Sadovnik, and Susan Semel. Alan and Susan have also served as my Series Editors and have contributed in many ways to the development of the book.

I am grateful to the editors and reviewers of several journals and yearbooks for their comments and suggestions on my Patri articles and essays, and I appreciate having permission to quote from them: *Vitae Scholasticae*, 1994 and 1997; *Educational Studies*, 1997; *Italian Americans in the Twentieth Century*, 2001; *Atti del Convegno, AIMC*, 2002; and *History of Education Quarterly*, 2005.

I have had unfailing and interested assistance from present and former librarians in the Watzek Library at Lewis and Clark College: Louise Gerity, Joanna Haney, Elaine Heras, Elaine Hirsch, and Betty Smith; also from Kelly Wainwright and Melinda Carney-Morris in Information Technology.

I have also been helped, in person and by correspondence, by library staffs at the following institutions and organizations: Portland State University; Teachers College, Columbia University; City College of New York; Antioch College; Indiana University; Hebrew Union College; Southern Illinois University; and Tufts University. I appreciate the knowledgeable assistance of staff at the Library of Congress, including Jeffrey Flannery, Patrick Kerwin, Mary Ison, and Stephen Ostrow. I was assisted also by staff members at the Center for Migration Studies and the Immigration History Research Center. I have made substantial use of the Multnomah County Library, and thank its librarians for their help and the citizens of my city for supporting this marvelous public treasure. One of the many pleasures of this project has been the process of collecting all of Patri's published books. With the help of electronic searches I have enjoyed finding the books in various obscure small bookstores throughout the country.

Archivists at several institutions have been particularly helpful: Scott Sanders, Archivist at Antioch College has written me helpful letters and granted permission to cite materials from the Arthur Morgan Papers, (Series V, Antioch College, Box V A 1, General Correspondence); Kyna Hamil, of the Digital Collections and Archives of the Tisch Library at Tufts University has provided information concerning Patri's honorary doctorate in 1923 and granted permission to quote from those materials; Paula Anders McNally has provided materials and granted permission to quote from Dewey and

Patri letters in the John Dewey Papers, Special Collections, Morris Library, Southern Illinois University; David Ment, former librarian at the Milbank Memorial Library, Teachers College, Columbia University, sent a copy of Patri's thesis and answered my questions; Barbara Dunlap, Archivist at City College of New York, guided me through complex materials there. Sydney C. Van Nort, Chief of the Archives and Special Collections at City College, granted permission to quote from those materials. (Archives, The City College of New York, CUNY).

The Spencer Foundation gave me a small grant when I needed to interview Patri's surviving relatives. I appreciate the Foundation's support, which enabled me to fly around the country, talk with the relatives, and have the interviews transcribed. I thank these relatives for their interest and for sharing memories of Patri: Jeanne and Donald Greco, Richard and Marjorie Bause, and Frank, Jr. and Marybeth Merolla. Frank has been immensely helpful in a variety of ways and has been one of my best informants. I thank his daughter-in-law, Antonella Merolla, for translating some materials for chapter 5. I appreciate the help of my daughter-in-law, Lila Guenther, in transcribing interview tapes and for computer searches. And I am grateful to my father-in-law John McDonald, now deceased, for his translations of some Italian texts.

I have enjoyed corresponding with new e-mail friends on Dora Caterson Patri's side of the family. Muriel Sherlock in Northern Ireland sent census data, ship manifests, and photographs related to Patri and his wife Dora. Marilyn Shea sent census data, clippings, and photographs. When I tried to introduce Muriel and Marilyn I was pleased to learn that they already knew each other and that both were Dora's grandnieces.

I am grateful to my new friends and colleagues in Italy for their interest in Patri and for the different perspectives they inevitably have on his life. Giuseppe Pepe was my first contact with Italians interested in Patri; he and Ambrogio Ietto and others organized the two Patri seminars in Salerno and Piaggine. I appreciate the scholarly contributions of panelists Giuseppe Ancone, Luciana Bellatalla, Francesco D'Episcopo, Aula Magna, Sebastiano Martelli, and Antonio Vairo. I have enjoyed assembling chapter 5 with G. Pepe, and working with Luciana Bellatalla as she wrote chapter 12. I am particularly grateful to Marilena Risi who has written a piece for chapter 13, translated several documents for me, answered many questions, and maintained with me a long-distance cultural friendship. I have warm memories of my visits to Salerno and Piaggine, and thank the many people who extended their friendship to me. I have space only to mention the Marra family, Angelo Pipolo, Francesco and Chiara Domini, and Francesca Pricolo and Paolo Somma. Anna Ferrara kindly made me a copy of the Italian edition of *Biondino*. Merrie King kept me informed about her own trip to Salerno and her studies of Patri and Montessori.

I thank Patri's former students for sharing their memories with me. After I had talked about Patri at a meeting of the Italian American Historical Association, I was delighted when a cheerful elderly man stood up and announced proudly "I'm Joe Dongarra, and I attended Patri's PS 45." We talked after the meeting and then corresponded until his death. He was the first of Patri's former students whom I had found, and I treasure my too-brief relationship with him. Dongarra's colleague, Paola Sensi-Isolani, told me that Dongarra had a sister, Catherine Strobel, and she kindly shared with me her own experience at PS 45. I thank her daughter, Lois Fiester, for helping with our correspondence.

The American Italian Historical Association connection has been very useful. I sent e-mails about Patri to the AIHA membership and thus began a fruitful correspondence with Teresa Cerasuola; she interviewed family and friends who attended PS 45 and gave me helpful responses to several chapters of this book. She also told me about Richard Renoff, who gave me helpful information on Patri and introduced me to Rocky D'Erasmo, who sent me one of his books on Patri's Bronx neighborhood and who has connected me with other helpful people.

I am grateful to my new colleagues at Peter Lang Publishing for their consistently helpful and professional assistance: Chris Myers, Lisa Dillon, Bernadette Shade, and Ian Steinberg. I enjoyed translating *Biondino* with Betty Schmidt, my patient Italian tutor. My thanks to Christine Woyshner, Mary Bischoff, and others who have assisted in various ways and my apologies to helpful people whom I have overlooked.

I am pleased to acknowledge the assistance of my good friend, Charles Stones, now deceased, who gave me substantial help with computer research. David Tyack deserves special thanks for his advice, encouragement, and editing, and for writing the Foreword. Finally, I give my greatest appreciation to my wife, Mary Guenther, for her computer assistance, insightful editing, interest, support, and love.

Patri visits a book-binding workshop in PS 45
(Frank Merolla)

Introduction:
My Search for Angelo Patri

THIS BIOGRAPHY OF ANGELO PATRI HAD ITS BEGINNINGS in 1966 at a yard sale in New Hampshire, where I bought a copy of Patri's 1917 book, *A Schoolmaster of the Great City*, with "Sara B. Graves, Newport, NH." written in pencil on the flyleaf. Because of her clear, neat handwriting, I assumed that Sara Graves had been a teacher, and speculated that she might have been assigned the book for a course at Keene Normal School, an hour's drive from her home. I read and enjoyed the book and admired the author, and couldn't help wondering what Sara Graves, from the small town of Newport, had thought of this story from the immense, overwhelming "Great City."[1]

From time to time over the years I reread *Schoolmaster*, seeing it as a case study showing that innovative schools could thrive and survive within public school systems. However, I didn't think of writing about Patri until 1994 when a representative of the new reference work, American National Biography (ANB), solicited authors for articles on various educators, including Angelo Patri. Remembering my admiration for *Schoolmaster*, I volunteered to write a short article about him. That led to other articles that focused on Patri as immigrant, as educator, as multiculturalist, and as writer. After further study and more articles, I decided that it was time to write Patri's biography.

Patri's life experiences were rich, complex, and varied. Among the influences shaping Patri were his profoundly different childhoods in Italy and New York; his years as a student, from primary school through a master's degree; his career as a teacher and principal in New York City schools, from 1897 to 1944; his work as a columnist for newspapers and magazines from 1922 to 1962; his success as author or translator of eight books for children and ten for parents, teachers, and other adult readers; his years as a childless family patriarch and as a country gentleman in retirement.

I present this book not primarily as social science, but as a collection of narratives by Patri, me, and others, with occasional pauses for context, interpretation, and possible application to current issues.[2] I survey Patri's life chronologically in the first seven chapters and in the last six interpret his life through several themes. Patri's skill as a storyteller was central to his career. Patri used stories to give context to life situations and to bring to them his practical progressive viewpoint. I attempt something similar here in varying the contexts and narrative approaches in each chapter. Jonathan Mahler recently wrote that "it's virtually impossible to know what shape a book will take when one first embarks on it." That is certainly the case with this biography, and I can only hope that the varied shapes of the different chapters faithfully reflect some facets of the life of this complex man.[3]

The title, *The Promise of Progressivism*, derives in part from a statement in which Patri presents the promise embedded in the histories of his and other schools. "We should not be as confused as we are, for we know from the experiences of many schools, of many laboratories, what children need to grow and feel fit. Why not use the knowledge we have found to be true? . . . There is a touch of this promise in my story and that is why I tell it."[4]

I wish that Patri had written a complete autobiography. His only extended piece of published autobiography was his 1917 *Schoolmaster of the Great City*, issued when Patri was forty-one years old. However, his school reader *Biondino* is so consistent with other verified information about his early life that I begin with three chapters from it. Patri wrote *Biondino* in English but had it translated into two Italian versions published in Italy and the United States in 1950 and 1951. Although details may have been fictionalized, the stories present believable descriptions of Patri's earliest years.[5]

Recognizing the ambiguity in all this, and in the absence of a complete autobiography, I have tried to present some of the materials that I think Patri might have included had he written one. I have come to know Patri primarily through his own writings and assume that this will also be the case with the readers of this book. In retirement Patri wrote an extended memoir that covered his school life through 1944, and his editing of the manuscript suggests that he hoped to publish it. There are also occasional bits of autobiography scattered throughout his articles and books. In several chapters I have quoted heavily from these sources, trying to present an account of those years and events as much as possible through Patri's own words. Here and elsewhere I found useful a reminder from Gabriel Garcia Marquez: "Life is not what one lived, but what one remembers and how one remembers it in order to recount it."[6] This is certainly the case with the chapter section titled "The Last Day" in which Patri describes the process of moving out of his office after forty-seven years in the schools. This is presented as a slice of autobiography nearly as Patri wrote it. Some chapters include sections like Frank Merolla's writings about "Uncle Angelo," that might best be classified as informal memoir. Others include traditional narrative biography with my occasional commentary from the perspective of educational history. The section on Patri's students and the chapter on Patri as the "childless patriarch" are presented as two small examples of the process of learning and writing family history and educational history as well as some of the outcomes of that process.

I had intended to write on Patri's visit to Italy in 1927, but found that an Italian colleague, school inspector Giuseppe Pepe, had already begun such a study, so I am pleased to have collaborated with him on chapter five. Similarly, I had hoped to interpret Patri's ideas on childhood while describing his career as a writer, but when I read Professor Bellatalla's article I realized that she had already done even more on this than I had planned, so I include her thoughts as a separate chapter.

The least conventional chapter is "Back to the Future: Contemporary Perspectives on Patri."[7] This grew out of informal discussions about Patri that I had with family and friends over a period of several years. At various gatherings people would tell what was happening in their lives and would ask what I was doing. My responses often included stories about Patri and his work, and discussions of his experiences and ideas then intertwined with those of my many friends who are progressive teachers. I began giving them some of Patri's books and articles and soliciting their responses. I hope that readers will enjoy the variety of approaches and voices in that chapter. My fellow writers and I can't help bringing our own perspectives to Patri. As Anaïs Nin said, "We don't see things as they are, we see things as we are."

As I pursued my studies through Patri's books and articles, his ninety boxes of papers in the Library of Congress, and other sources, the positive image of Patri that I had derived from *Schoolmaster* remained. Part of this may be because I have been heavily dependent on the Library of Congress papers, which Patri himself saved. Although he preserved at least one critical letter, it is possible that he discarded others. So, with this benign picture of Patri I have consciously sought out anything that might present a more balanced picture. I have found only a few items suggesting that he may have been somewhat vain and attentive to his reputation. Thus my positive depiction of Patri remains; I mention this now only to note that I cannot call this a "critical" biography.

Harry Golden wrote that "America is always absorbing the immigrant only to reproduce the pioneer."[8] Patri, a pioneer in public progressive urban education certainly exemplified this pattern. As I describe Patri's ground-breaking work I will provide occasional comments, quotations, and interpretations so as to place Patri in the context of scholarship on education, immigration, and social history, and will begin with some examples here. In a foreword to Pedro Noguera's *City Schools and the American Dream*, James Banks wrote in 2003: "American classrooms are experiencing the largest influx of immigrant students since the beginning of the twentieth century." In that context Noguera's book "reminds us that urban schools are desperately needed by the communities they serve, and consequently are essential for the realization of the American dream of social justice and equality for all."[9] Patri's life and work in linking school and community may also remind us that this is a never-ending struggle, as important in the previous millennium as in this one. In telling Patri's story I have tried to be consistent with the approach of a recent article titled "New Directions in American Educational History." The authors propose educational history that gives "greater attention to how life and community experiences shape behaviors and choices and draws upon personal life rather than viewing schools as separate and personally neutral institutions."[10]

Adam Gopnik recently asked a succinct version of the ancient question, "Are there lessons in history, or just stories, mostly sad?" and answered his own question: "History does not offer lessons; its unique constellations of contingencies never repeat. But life does offer the same points, over and over again."[11] I present here a collection of stories by and about Angelo Patri, with points that he and I occasionally choose to make. From this material readers may generate their own versions of these stories, create their own "points," and perhaps construct some usable lessons about life and learning.

Bridge over brook near Patri home in Piaggine
(J. Wallace)

ONE

Biondino Comes to America, 1876–1881

by Angelo Patri

*P*ATRI HAD VERY BLOND HAIR AS A CHILD, AND WAS NICK-
*named "Biondino" ("Blondie"). At the age of seventy-four, six years after he re-
tired, he wrote a small book titled* Biondino. *He wrote the book in English, but
had it translated into Italian and published in Italy as* Biondino L'Emigrante
*(1950). The next year Maria Piccirilli retranslated it into Italian for S. F.
Vanni, an Italian-American publisher in New York City, and it was published as*
Biondino: A Reader. *Ms. Piccirilli added a glossary, making the book usable by
classes in intermediate Italian. Patri's original text in English has not been found,
so my Italian tutor and I translated the Vanni edition back into English.[1]*

As we translated the text line by line, I realized that many of the stories in
Biondino *were consistent with anecdotes that Patri had told in* Schoolmaster *and
elsewhere. Patri's goddaughter, Valentina Pugliese Perrone, who knew Patri for
nearly sixty years, was familiar with* Biondino, *which she described as a "largely
autobiographical" book. So, in the absence of other detailed sources about Patri's
childhood in Italy, I include here the last three chapters of* Biondino. *I changed the
sequence of two of the chapters in order to keep the emigration story intact. The
first section tells about Biondino's brief and painful visit to the village school. Patri
had mentioned this visit in* Schoolmaster *and elsewhere, and this version of the
story may partially explain his extreme sensitivity to schools and teachers and his
horror of corporal punishment. He did not want others to experience the hurt and
humiliation he describes here.[2]*

*The other two chapters tell about the family's preparations for and emigration
to America, ending with the tragic death of Patri's beloved little sister. This event
too may help explain Patri's deep empathy and concern for the difficult lives of his*

students and their families. No doubt Patri created dialogue and embellished some events here, but the basic story is consistent with what we know about him and his family from other sources. With those reminders I present these chapters as a plausible, readable, personal, and occasionally funny account of Patri's early life in Italy and his family's transition to America.

———— ———— ————

Time passes and never stops. Each day brings something beautiful and something ugly; what happened yesterday we forget today, and we need to accept what comes. And so Biondino did. One day he saw the boys who were going to school and followed them. If other boys were going to school, he wanted to go there too. He approached one of the bigger boys and said, "I'm coming to school too." "You are too small," said the larger boy, "you have to stay home and wait." "I am too small?" exclaimed Biondino. "I am not too small. I know how to stay on the back of a donkey better than you."

"So stay there. It is easier than going to school. You are too small to go to school."

"But I found the lost sheep," said Biondino.

"It was a rabbit, and it wasn't lost. It fell into a hole and didn't know how to get out. You are too little to go to school."

"No! It is not true! I have gone up the mountain to the cave of the bandits and rescued the Mayor. Take me with you!"

"So come, if you really want to. It's just one way to learn. Follow right behind me, but don't say that I let you in. And no whining, whatever happens." Biondino followed the boy all the way into the schoolroom, and the teacher let him stay. If a boy wants to go to school, so much the better; it's never too early to begin.

Biondino was placed on a bench in the back row where the biggest boys sat. It was a high bench and Biondino's feet didn't touch the floor, but he was proud to sit with the big boys. He could see easily over the heads of his friends; he could see the teacher, the blackboard, and the charts on the wall. On the right, the teacher had a long switch handy. Some boys were reading and some were writing. One said his lesson while standing near the teacher. The teacher looked here and there to see if all were doing their work.

Biondino looked around the room quietly, and thought that school was a very boring place. He thought he had been foolish to come and that it would be better to return home to his little sister and Grandpa. Exactly at that moment the teacher hit the bench with his switch and everyone paid attention to him. The boy who was saying his lessons went to his place.

Those who were studying closed their books. Those who were writing put down their pens. Silence. Absolute silence. Everyone had their eyes fixed on the master, who went to the blackboard and made certain marks with his chalk.

"Ah," thought Biondino, "now the teacher studies and the boys watch." And that seemed good for everyone: for a little while nobody did anything wrong. When the teacher had covered the blackboard with marks he turned to the class, pointing to the marks that they were to write, and all the boys began to shout together. Biondino thought: "This is what pleases me. If everyone can shout I can shout too. I am good at shouting," and while the class spelled the letters of the alphabet:

    a e i o u
    ba be bi bo bu
    ta te ti to tu . . .

Biondino opened his mouth wide and joined the chorus. Over the singsong of everyone who spoke, they heard a voice that went:

    a i o a e
    uuu aaa iii eee

The class turned with open mouths. The teacher watched intently. Biondino stopped singing. Things were not going well. Everyone was looking at him. The students wanted to laugh, but didn't dare to. The teacher stretched out his hand, took the long switch, and bang, gave Biondino a blow on the ear. What a blow that was! It seemed like his ear was cut from his head! With a cry of agony, Biondino got down from the bench, began to run, and didn't stop screaming until he got to Grandpa's house.

"Too small for school," grumbled Grandpa while he washed Biondino's ear with cold water. "A mule-driver shouldn't be a teacher." His sister boiled with rage. "I want to go to the school and tell that teacher what a cruel man he is!" Grandpa had a hard time quieting her and restoring peace. He told his grandchildren that they could walk to the church instead. There would be no benches or mule-drivers there.

The next day Biondino and his sister walked to the church. There were only a few old people kneeling and saying their prayers. Hand in hand the two walked around the church looking at the saints and the altars. A woman raised her head and saw them, and in fun began to chant: "aaa . . . oooo . . . uuuu . . . iiii . . . ." The story of his first day of school had been told in the homes of the boys, and all the village knew it. Biondino's ears became very red. He felt such humiliation that he couldn't move, but his sister immediately flew at the woman and gave her a push that sent her suddenly sprawling on the floor. "Ugly monkey!" said the woman. "You are a monkey!" replied the girl. And the two children escaped from the church and ran home to tell Grandpa what had happened. "Good heavens!" he said, "There's always something, one thing after another. Fools and children don't mix well."

One day his Grandpa called to Biondino and said to him, "Take this letter to the Mayor. Don't stop to play. Don't stop to dream. Take care of the letter. Carry it to the Mayor, wait for his response, and return home immediately."

"Yes, Grandpa. I will take the letter to the Mayor and return right away with his answer." Biondino was all excited. He had heard talk about a trip, about his father, about America. "Can it be that this letter has to do with the trip?" he thought as he knocked on the Mayor's door. "Ah, here you are," said the Mayor. "I have been waiting for you to bring the letter. Do you have it?" Biondino replied, "Grandpa sent you this letter." "Very good, tell your Grandpa that all is in order. Next month it will be ready. Tell him not to worry." "And next month all will be ready," repeated Biondino.

"Exactly right. Next month."

Biondino turned to leave but he went very slowly, as though he expected something else. "Ah, a moment." said the Mayor, "A moment, I almost forgot something. Something for you." Biondino knew what it was. "Sugar," he said, "I like sugar."

"Here are two pieces; one for the boy who helped free the Mayor from the bandits, and one for the little sister that you like so well. Remember: a piece for each one. This big piece is for you and this smaller piece is for your little sister. Put the big piece in your right hand and the other in your left hand. Run along."

Sugar was scarce, and even a piece of brown sugar was welcome. "Sugar, sugar. I like sugar," Biondino said. He looked at the piece in his right hand saying, "This is mine." He looked at the piece in his left hand. "This is my sister's. I can eat mine, but not my sister's. This is mine and I can taste it." And how good it was! And he tasted it again. He walked slowly and with each step took a lick of the big sugar. And he smiled with each lick.

"How small my piece is," he said, stopping his two feet. "My sister's piece, instead, has become a little bigger. The Mayor said that the bigger piece is mine. I will change the two pieces." And that is what he did. And then it was possible to lick the larger piece. And as soon as he said that, he began to lick. One lick after the other, and finally he saw that the piece in his right hand was becoming a little smaller than the one in his left hand. Soon he made another change of the piece in his right hand for the one in his left hand. Now all was well and he resumed walking.

Biondino had lost his nice smile, knowing that what he had done was not good. But he continued to change the small and large sugars and when he arrived at the door of his house his right hand had almost nothing and the other had only a tiny chunk so very small that it could no longer be called a piece of sugar.

"I have a piece of sugar," he said to his sister when he saw her come to meet him. "Give it to me! Give it to me!" she exclaimed, running toward Biondino. "I'll let you lick it," said Biondino, and the two children began to lick, taking turns until there wasn't any left. The sister was happy but Biondino was not. Now that the sugar was gone Biondino knew that he had been deceptive. He had not done it on purpose, but he certainly had not done what the Mayor had told him to do. Biondino was sorry and promised himself not to do it anymore.

"What did the Mayor say?" asked Grandpa.

"He said that next month all will be ready. He said not to worry. He will take care of everything."

"Good. Now your father can leave for America."

"America?"

"Yes."

"And where is America?"

"Far, far away, on the other side of the sea."

"Am I going too?"

"No, your daddy will go alone. You will stay with your sister, your mother, with me and Brother Felice. Then we will wait until he returns."

For Biondino, his father's departure did not mean much, because his father always left and always returned. This time it would be the same thing, he thought. But it was all different, very different. They were packing trunks and suitcases, saying goodbye and crying. Mother and Grandpa wept. They were all kissing and saying goodbye without happiness and without laughter, and this had never happened before. To go to America must be a different thing, but Biondino did not know why.

Father had been in America a year when the letter came that threw the family into the greatest excitement.[3] Biondino, his sister, his mother, and an uncle whom they scarcely knew had to prepare to go to America, because Father had sent for them. It was time to sew clothes, time to prepare the trunks. It was time to go see friends, to get letters and gifts to take to their relatives who lived in the city where Biondino's father had found a new home.

On the day set for departure a cart stopped before the door of the house. The trunks, the suitcases, and the travelers were loaded onto it. Brother Felice was with them. He was on his way to Rome and would go with the emigrants as far as Naples. He shouted a goodbye, and the cart began to sway onto the rough road.

After many hours, hours long and boring, they arrived at Naples. The trunks and the suitcases and the travelers were unloaded before a house where they would spend the night. They were put all in one room to eat and drink and to sleep a little until the following morning. A little cart took the baggage, and Biondino, the mother, the little sister, the uncle, and Brother Felice followed on foot to the pier. Outside, in the blue waters of the wide bay, a large steamer lay at anchor, larger than all the houses that Biondino had ever seen. Little rowboats went back and forth, carrying people and baggage to the steamer which was waiting to take them to the other ocean, to America.

When their turn arrived, Brother Felice said goodbye and gave his blessing to each one of the small group. "Goodbye, children. Now you go to your father in America. It is a great country, a country where everything grows well. May God guide you," he said, putting his hand on the boy's head. The rowboat took them to the steamer from which hung a rope ladder that reached down to the water. The men and the women climbed the shaky ladder, and the children and trunks and suitcases were carried on board by the sailors.

On the deck of the ship the little family, so small and sad, saw so much water, so many dreams of home, the good grandfather, the brook, the church, the monastery, the Mountain of Snow. The steamer started to move, the people raised their arms, waving their handkerchiefs and their hats, shouting, crying goodbye. The shore was receding; the sea was getting bigger, and the big ship was getting smaller. Soon the earth disappeared and there was nothing but water, water, the motion of the ship, the dark sky, and the musty smell. When there was a storm the emigrants went below decks. The ship rocked, pitched, and bowed. Everyone was seasick. The little sister was the only one always alert and smiling. It pleased her to be on the ship and everyone wished her well, passengers and sailors alike.

The long boring voyage, more than thirty days of bumpy seas, finally came to an end. The ship dropped anchor in a port where the water was rough, the air frozen, the sky obscured and sad. They waited on deck to disembark, waiting for many long hours. Each minute seemed an hour, each hour seemed an eternity. Wrapped up in shawls and cloaks, the emigrants crowded together on the deck, one next to the other on that cold December day. For the first time Biondino's little sister did not feel well. In her mother's arms she stayed very quiet, not interested in anything, in anyone.

Finally the family could disembark onto the pier. The mother shouted, "Here's Daddy!" Biondino looked where his mother pointed and saw a stranger with a black beard. That could not be his father, but it was his father, just the same, because when he heard him talk he recognized his voice at once. There was no other voice like that in all the world, so confident and sweet, so rich and harmonious.

After retrieving from the big pile the baggage that belonged to his family, the father, with some of his friends, led the little procession to their new home. It was only a few days before Christmas and everyone rejoiced to think about it, while unpacking the trunks and suitcases and putting the house in order in the rooms the father had prepared for them. The happiness did not last long. The neighbors came to visit the new arrivals, but without cheer; they talked very quietly with much sadness. They gave the girl medicine that would help her get well. The doctor came, but the sister died on Christmas day. Candles were lighted, not for baby Jesus, but for the child whose life was extinguished. This is how Biondino spent his first Christmas in America.

The day after the funeral, Biondino watched his father and saw him cut off his beard. When he had shaved, the father seemed again to be the young man with the broad shoulders and the strong face that Biondino remembered well—the head of the family, the fountain of strength and security, and a wave of courage returned to Biondino's heart. All was well. The father was with him in the new country, in the new house

The years passed and Biondino let his childhood and his memories go by. Now he was an American boy who was called Angelo. He went to school and then to the university. He became a teacher and was made director of a school which was attended in large part by the children of the families who came from his native land. After many years passed happily in the school, his work completed, he retired to live in peace among the hills, far from the big city, to cultivate his land. One day the postman brought a letter written by the teacher of the village where Biondino was born. The letter said:

"We are building a new school in the village and want to call it THE ANGELO PATRI SCHOOL in your honor, if this pleases you."

To me, Angelo, who many, many years ago was Biondino, the thought of living again in that small village in the mountains gives me pleasure; the thought of participating in the fun and the studies of the children, reliving with them my fancies. Thanks for thinking of me, as I respond to you with all my affection.

Photograph by Jacob Riis of a New York elementary school class, 1889
(Reprinted with the permission of the Museum of the City of New York)

TWO

Becoming American:
Becoming a Teacher,
1881–1907

FROM THE SMALL BEGINNINGS DESCRIBED IN *BIONDINO*, Patri went on to become one of America's best-known and most beloved educators during the first half of the twentieth century.[1] He grew up in Manhattan's Little Italy, listening to his father's lively, imaginative stories.[2] As Patri lived his adult life as teacher, administrator, lecturer, and writer, he continued his father's practice of telling stories intended both to entertain and instruct. Patri became a Deweyan educational progressive widely known through his leadership of two New York City Public Schools 4 (1907–1913) and 45 (1913–1944), and through his radio program, newspaper columns, magazine articles, and eighteen books. He was the first Italian-American school administrator in the United States, and one of the first to develop a community-oriented school.[3]

This narrative of Patri's childhood, youth, education, and career as educator and writer indicates that, while Patri became a successful American educationally and occupationally, he remained in many ways proudly Italian. I will tell Patri's growing-up story with occasional interpretations related to issues of urban, progressive, and multicultural education,

Patri was born in Piaggine, Italy, on November 27, 1876, the son of Carmela Conte Petraglia and Nicola Petraglia. This small bambino was weighed down with many names: Angelo Antonio Teodoro Petraglia. (The name Petraglia was later changed to Patri.)[4] Piaggine is a small town in the mountains of Salerno province in the Campania region of southern Italy. During Patri's first five years the family lived part of the time in Piaggine, and at other times on a small hillside farm in Piaggine Pruno, several miles from the town center. Patri had warm memories of his childhood: "I remember sitting with the family and the neighbors' families about the fireplace, while father, night after night, told us stories of the Knights of the Crusades or recounted the glories of the heroes of proud Italy." Patri revered his parents, and partly because of his father's stories, grew up with positive memories of his birthplace.[5]

Patri's father made several trips to New York in the 1870s and found work as a hod carrier and general construction laborer. In the late winter of 1881 he left for New York on the steamer Macedonia, arriving on March 17.[6] He found work and rented an apartment, and his family joined him that December, when Angelo was five. Thus they came to New York right at the beginning of what Andrew Rolle has called "one of the greatest migrations of all times"—that from southern Italy to America during the years 1880 to 1924.[7] In 1943, seven years before writing *Biondino*, Patri described the trip: "I remember a long time ago, standing on the deck of a steamer with my mother, my small sister, and my uncle. All about us on the deck there were crowds, a great mass of people. They were our friends. . . . Some were in tears, some smiled bravely and held the babies aloft in their arms. Some looked up in silence. The ship gong clanged, the whistle blew, the engines began to move, the propellers to turn. Gradually the steamer pulled out. That steamer with its precious cargo of young lives was bound for America. They, the young, the venturesome, came to America to try their fortune. In their lives were bound the hopes, the ambitions of their friends and relatives who were left behind."

Patri saw these events in a long historical perspective: "For years and years this scene was repeated. A chain of ships across the waters from Europe to America. It was the march of progress. Each steamer emptied its precious freight into American docks, American streets, American factories, railroads, farms, schools. They all came. They worked, they lived, they learned, they stayed. They forgot to go back. They began to say, 'America,' 'my' country, 'my' people. But always as they said this, they never forgot the dreams, the hopes, the ambitions of their friends across the water."[8]

The Patri family sailed from Naples, then Italy's largest city, to New York at a time when passage in steerage cost about $15.[9] They came too early to have the stereotyped immigrant experience of seeing the Statue of Liberty (1886) and of landing at Ellis Island (1892), but entered America through the Emigrant Landing Depot at Castle Garden.[10] When they arrived there were in New York City only 12,000 people who had been born in Italy, but 4,000 of them lived in Little Italy, the Italian section of East

Harlem in Manhattan where the Patri family settled.[11] The family was all too soon saddened by the death of Patri's young sister, Maria.

Patri's uncle Gaetano (Patri's mother's brother) helped Patri learn to read and write Italian, and he became proficient enough so that by age seven he was able to help neighbors write letters to their families in Italy. The family spoke Italian at home and, as Patri said in his 1917 book, *A Schoolmaster of the Great City*, all the English he knew "had been learned in the street."[12]

Many immigrant children began school late, and true to form, Patri did not enroll until, in 1887, he was eleven years old.[13] He reflected on this period in *Schoolmaster*: "When my family came to New York, I lost the companionship of open fields, grass, trees, flowers, sheep, streams, dark castles on the mountainsides. In their places were flats, dark stairs, and streets—paved streets with trucks and boys running wild, empty lots, waste heaps." There were losses and gains. "What a change, from the sunshine, the open fields, the folk stories, the friends, to this crowded city life! And yet what a wonderful place is a city. Here life is seething, moving, searching it knows not what—fellowship? Common ideals? . . ."

Following the path of least resistance, Patri became a street kid. "I wandered about with the rest of the children doing what we saw the older boys doing. . . . We used bad language because the older ones used bad language. We smoked for the same reason." They cheated, stole, and fought. "The streets and the boys who owned the streets were our masters. They did the training. Our parents worried and wondered. They punished us when they caught us. . . . Through all this there was never a word of school. School had nothing to do with living and we were busy living."[14]

Years later Patri wrote about his childhood in the third person: "Angelo Patri came to this country from Italy when he was five years old. For six years he roamed about the streets of New York, now and then picking up an English word. At eleven, and poorly equipped, he entered an American school and settled down to routine methods of study." He learned right away that the school did not fit the child. "A sickly boy, what he really needed was a chance to be active, to talk, to learn by guidance rather than by force. His father was ambitious to have him get a good education and all the money that could be spared, from the bare necessities of the family, was put forward to this purpose."[15] In *Schoolmaster* he gave additional perspective on his introduction to school. "My uncle from whom I had learned Italian went back to Italy, and I was left without a teacher, so one day I attached myself to a playmate and went to school: an 'American' school." [16] In school he was punished for being overactive, so he learned to sit still and recite the memorized lessons.

Patri's goddaughter, Valentina Pugliese Perrone, was the daughter of his life-long friend, Anthony Pugliese. Valentina was born in 1906, knew Patri until his death in 1965, and had clear memories of him.[17] In a short memoir she wrote that Patri and her father "were boyhood friends drawn together by their mutual heritage—their trip from Italy to America, attendance at public schools in the East Harlem section of New York City, at that time predominantly Italian. Both boys were of concern to their principal, Dr. Hess, who invited the boys to spend weekends with him and his family on Staten Island. He saw promise in these two and gave them the opportunity to live with English-speaking people, under the pretense of needing them for mowing and weeding, innately respecting their fierce Italian pride."[18]

This pride did not prevent Patri, when finishing his public schooling in 1892, from requesting a recommendation from Charles Holden, one of his teachers. Holden wrote: "This is to certify that Angelo Patri, a graduate of G.S. #39, has been a member of my class during the past year, that he has been a punctual, attentive, diligent scholar, showing marked ability, and excellent disposition. He has shown himself entirely trustworthy."[19] These qualities enabled Patri, in the ten years after he began formal education in 1887, to complete five years of public school and five years of study at the City College of New York, from which he graduated with an AB degree in 1897.

Psychohistorian Andrew Rolle asks: "Why did some immigrant children rise to the challenge of American life whereas others did not? The quality of the parent-child attachment was the factor that powerfully determined whether a child had a negative or positive life experience." Patri's immigrant parents were clearly among those described by Rolle who "showed tenderness and healthy strength in support of their progeny."[20] Intelligent and hardworking, Patri had acquired a rich informal education from his relatives and neighbors as well as necessary support and encouragement from his family.

Dominic Candeloro provides a broad context into which we may place the Patri family experience: "Italian immigrants were not helpless entities filtered, Americanized, socialized, and homogenized into squeaky clean middle Americans. Though many of them were illiterate, they brought with them a richly textured and time-tested folk culture based upon the institution of the family. . . . Italians brought with them a lively rural-paesani culture that, though imbued with class distinctions, lent itself to cooperative survival strategies in their new world."[21] Investment in the education of children was the major strategy used by the Patris and their friends, the Puglieses.

Selma Berrol has described the school arrangements that Angelo and Anthony experienced: "Until 1897, there were no public high schools in Manhattan (which was then the entire city of New York), and free secondary schooling was available only at the highly selective preparatory divisions at City College and Hunter."[22] Sixteen-year-old Angelo and Anthony entered the City College of New York (CCNY) in the fall of 1892 as "Sub-freshmen" in the classical course of study. This was, according to a college archivist, a "rigidly lock step" program, permitting only "a couple of senior year electives."[23] A review of the required courses in the program shows how classical the curriculum was. Becoming a liberally educated American called for a program heavy in Greek, Roman, and British classics, with only a smattering of American authors. It is fair to say that these Italian boys from peasant backgrounds received an essentially Victorian education at CCNY.

During the "Sub-freshman" year Angelo and Anthony studied English Language, Latin, Algebra, Geometry, Anatomy, Drawing, Botany, and Physics and read some works by Washington Irving and Henry Longfellow. Each year a few subjects were dropped and others added. New subjects during the freshman year were Greek, History, Descriptive Geometry, Compositions, and Zoology. In addition to textbooks the young men read Sallust, Scott, Cicero, and Xenophon. In the sophomore year they studied English Literature, Rhetoric, Logic, Chemistry, Trigonometry, and Declamations, and read from Shaw, Shakespeare, Virgil, Plato, Livy, Xenophon, and Arnold. During the junior year the new subjects were English Poetry, Mechanics and Acoustics, Chemical Physics, Anthropology, English Prose, Optics, Astronomy, and Political Economy. Readings included Arnold, Burke, Horace, Tacitus, Demosthenes, Macauley, Carlyle, Cicero, and Homer. In the senior year the new subjects were Foreign Language, Psychology, Pedagogics, Geology, Mineralogy, Paleontology, History of Art, History of Philosophy, and Ethics.[24]

In spite of this daunting academic load, Angelo and Anthony found time for some extracurricular activities. Both became members of the Clionia Literary Society, and during their senior year Anthony was president and Patri was vice-president of the group. They were members also of the YMCA and the Sound Money League.[25] This latter membership is a first hint of Patri's politics. The "Sound Money League" was an urban progressive group organized to resist the "soft money" associated with Bryanism.

Anthony and Angelo were among the earliest Italian-American graduates of CCNY, and theirs are the only clearly identifiable Italian names in the class list for 1897.[26] The students who edited the yearbook paired them humorously together. In a section titled "Why '97 Came to College," they have Patri say that he came "To admire Pugliese," and Pugliese immodestly say, "To do the same as Patri."[27] Further testimony to their close relationship was a joint recommendation written for them by Alfred G. Compton, Professor of Applied Mathematics. He wrote: "I take very great pleasure in testifying to the excellent character, as students, of Mr. Angelo Patri and Anthony Pugliese, members of the Senior Class of this college. They have great ability and industry, and it has been a pleasure to me to instruct them."[28]

Angelo and Anthony carried heavy academic loads during their five years at CCNY, usually taking about ten courses each semester. Patri was fortunate that his parents were able to support him while he completed the program. Years later he wrote: "I don't believe a boy or girl ought to earn his way through college. It is a waste of energy and power. It is unfair to put a double burden on unseasoned growth. . . . What would have happened to me if my parents had not paid my way through college by saving and sacrificing? I dread to think of it. My gratitude to them for the gift of a college education is beyond words to express."[29]

The gender confusion above ("boy or girl . . . his") calls for a brief comment. Patri, following the practice of his time, usually wrote in masculine terms. Here he starts to be inclusive of girls, but three words later reverts to masculine terminology. This confusion raises the broader issue of the Patri family's commitment to education. Patri's parents supported Patri through college, but his three sisters did not get comparable educational opportunities. Josephine, born in 1882, married and had a daughter by 1901, when she was nineteen. Rose, born in 1889, received enough education to become a special education teacher, and married at age thirty. Jane, born in 1891, studied office work and became a secretary in DeWitt Clinton High School. So, although the sisters did not have Angelo's extensive education, they acquired enough schooling to have productive careers. Patri left a fairly clear record of his own education, but says little about the education of his sisters. The family invested more heavily in the son's education, as was the common pattern among his countrymen. Kessner, writing about Italian immigrants, wrote that in "cases where parents did value education the son came first."[30] (Of course, this was true among the larger population as well.)

Angelo's education brought one immediate benefit to his parents. As a college senior Angelo was well able to help prepare his father for the naturalization examination. Nicolas passed the test, and on January 23, 1897, at the age of forty eight, became a citizen of his adopted country.[31]

The strong support of education in the Patri and Pugliese families was in contrast to the widely reported resistance to schooling of Italian-Americans, particularly those from Southern Italy.[32] Stephen Lassonde explains that this resistance was based in part on the realization that schooling often alienated children from their families and native language. These two families, however, came early in the great Italian immigration and either brought with them or acquired here the more "American" assumption that education could be a source of social mobility and family pride.[33] Another reason Lassonde gives for resisting education was the loss of income that the children might otherwise be earning. But Patri was apparently permitted to be a "street kid" until age eleven, and his parents then supported him through ten years of school and college. We can only assume that the parents, who were clearly intelligent and perceptive, came to see the value of schooling in American society.[34]

After Patri graduated, disaster struck. Patri's father "fell fifty feet down a ladder and was ill for a whole year . . ." [35] Nicolas was at various times a hod-carrier, whose job it was to carry heavy loads of mortar and bricks up ladders to the bricklayers. This is an exceedingly dangerous occupation, and he was one of many such victims.[36] So to support the family, in September 1897, Patri took a teaching job, thus beginning a distinguished forty-seven year career in education. His friend Anthony Pugliese began teaching that same fall. They later "told a story that on their first payday, they felt ashamed to accept their checks because they felt that to be with children was a sacred trust, not to be associated with anything as material as money."[37] In joining the ranks of teachers Angelo and Anthony took further steps toward inclusion in the larger culture by becoming employees of the New York City school system, already an avenue to mobility for earlier immigrants.[38] The opportunities provided by school jobs benefited the entire Patri family. Patri, his wife, her sister, two of Patri's sisters, and other relatives all worked for the New York City school system. Patri and Pugliese were among the first Italian-Americans to be employed as teachers in the New York schools. Kessner cites data showing that in 1904, seven years after they began teaching, out of a total New York Italian population of more than 219,000, there were only fifteen teachers.[39]

In 1955, almost fifty years later, Patri reflected on his first teaching experiences: "This is a story of myself at work in the public schools. It began in 1897 when I graduated from City College with a B.A. degree and started out to find a job. That was a year of financial depression and jobs were scarce, but then, as now, there were plenty of vacancies in the public schools, even though classes ranged from forty to fifty pupils." Requirements were simple: "All a college graduate needed to do was pass a thorough examination in the subjects of the school curriculum, get a teacher's license, present himself to a school and go to work as a substitute teacher at a salary of $1.20 per day."[40]

In spite of the economic depression, 1897 was in some ways an auspicious time to begin an educational career in New York City. The previous April, after a major political struggle, Mayor William Strong had signed a bill that abolished local ward school boards and centralized the school system. Then, as Sol Cohen recorded, "On May 3, 1897, by the stroke of a pen, New York City was trebled in size and more than doubled in population. The state legislature and the Governor had signed the 'Greater New York' bill enlarging the city to its present boundaries."[41]

Patri was assigned to a school where he had a room packed with sixty-six children, aged eight to fifteen—an unruly group that had driven out a series of substitute teachers. According to Patri, "discipline was the thing, I would discipline, and I did. I oppressed; I went to the homes; I sent registered letters. I followed up each infraction of rules relentlessly. There was no getting away from me. I was making sure that the children were punished for their misdeeds. . . ."

Within a month Patri had the class under control. "My discipline of the class and the promptness with which I followed up the absentees gained recognition." He was promoted to a fifth-year classroom, "composed of all the children that other teachers in approximate grades did not want. They were fifty misfits." In this situation discipline failed. "What was I to do? I began to tell over again the stories I faintly remembered having heard in the days when father sat and talked and we listened, not daring to move lest we lose a syllable of what he said. I told them about my own childhood in the mountains of Italy. . . . I told them about a wolf that attacked the sheep at night until my father seized and killed it barehanded."[42]

Storytelling worked, the students listened and learned, and discipline was restored. (Patri's disciplinary power certainly did not depend on his size. In 1900, at the age of twenty three, he was just over five feet three inches tall, and weighed only 109 pounds.)[43] But Patri's school was then apparently subjected to the efficiency craze which struck so many schools about that time.[44] Specific methods were imposed, supervisors snooped, routines flourished, procedures dominated. After his second year in the schools Patri, realizing that his one City College course in Pedagogics had provided meager preparation for his work, enrolled part-time at Teachers College, Columbia University, seeking to learn better ways of teaching.[45] His first year there was disappointing, but the next year he took a course with Dr. Frank McMurry which helped him find a sounder approach. McMurry was a progressive educational theorist who was teaching a pragmatic, "functional" psychology and methodology.[46] He had his students read John Dewey's 1897 essay, "Ethical Principles Underlying Education," where Patri learned that "conduct, not ability to recite lessons, was the real test of learning and the sign of culture."[47] Equally important, "Conduct always carried the idea of some one else; no isolation, no selfishness." With new ideas from McMurry and Dewey, Patri learned to spend less energy controlling children and more time observing them. "The God of Discipline was replaced by the God of Watchfulness."[48]

Patri's thinking as he completed his studies at Teachers College was clearly expressed in his master's thesis, titled "Educational Forces Outside of the Public School, Considered from the Standpoint of School Administration."[49] Patri listed the books and reports which he had read, including *Democracy and Social Ethics* by Jane Addams and *American Ideals*, by Theodore Roosevelt. He had studied the reports of many organizations, including the College and University Settlements, University Extension, Board of Education, Educational Alliance, Young Men's Christian Association, Children's Aid Society, and the Tenement House Commission. He began the thesis with a preface that shows how American he now felt. He hoped that the school might "become as it should be—the most potent factor for the uplifting of the race, the Americanizing of the foreigner, the perpetuation of our American traditions and ideals."[50]

In a section titled "The Problem" Patri reported that "New York below the Harlem River has a greater density of population than any city in the world," and that only one sixth of the population had been born in the United States. He then asked: "How Americanize this foreign element? What is there in each of these elements which can serve as a basis for us to work upon? What are their characteristics?" Patri then gave brief stereotyped descriptions of the various nationality groups in language reminiscent of that of the earlier immigrant, Jacob Riis, whose *How the Other Half Lives* (1890) was another of his sources.[51] "The Jew . . . whether poor or rich, knows that knowledge is power, and power as the means of getting on in the world is what his soul yearns for. . . . The Italian, numbering three hundred thousand of our population, is next in importance to the Jews, whose numbers are more than twice as great. . . . The Italian is proud, liberal, frugal, emotional, revengeful, ambitious," but has become "careless of his religion . . . . The Chinaman . . . is so secluded, and his Eastern ways are so different from ours that it is as hard for him to be assimilated as it is for us to find grounds upon which to Americanize him."

Patri recognized the pattern of urban white flight: "Where the negro congregates, thence the white man flees. No matter how much we talk about negro rights and privileges, as long as inherent prejudices hold sway the negro will be compelled to live by himself. . . ." But this new American felt free to make unsolicited recommendations for this descendant of slaves. "He must be taught the art of work through the institutions of Free Labor, Free School, and the Christian Religion. Through these he must learn the lessons of self-help, self-advancement, self-respect. Our public schools do but a small part of this work. Cannot the activities of the school and its co-operation with outside forces be so increased as to accomplish more for him?" (Patri does not capitalize "negro" here, but does so later in the thesis.)

The wording of Patri's next comment suggests that he shared in the well-known animosity between Italian and Irish immigrants: "In our very poor East and West side districts . . . we find another very dangerous and ignorant element . . . the poor Irish. Here ignorance and poverty are the result of drink. . . . The schools in what are known as the Gas-house District, the Slaughterhouse, Hell's Kitchen, present more problems of school management in a day than other schools do in a month. . . . " [52]

Patri then moved from description to analysis, exploring the causes of poverty and degradation. Crowded housing, sordid entertainment, the saloon, cheap novels, escapist newspapers, low wages, the high cost of living, and the need for mothers to work all exacerbated the problem. Patri reminded successful earlier immigrants of their responsibilities. "Of the better classes, it is scarcely necessary to speak. They have been here long enough to have absorbed the spirit of American freedom. In their hands lies the administration of the schools and we trust of the government. They should therefore be thoroughly acquainted with the great social problem before them and go about its solution consistently and without faltering. . . ." [53]

Patri knew the limitations of schooling: "The child attends school from nine to three o'clock and then he goes back to his other environment. . . . What can we do to assimilate the great mass of foreigners?" [54] Patri's answer is that it is not enough to educate the children; the adults must be educated as well, and the public schools must take the lead in providing and coordinating currently scattered adult education efforts. Schools already supported university extensions, clubs, adult education, libraries, and similar activities. "Cannot the work however, be extended to the ever growing foreign element of our city? . . . The idea taken up by the Public School System in its lectures and evening schools, and carried out by the Hebrew Educational Alliance, and the Italian Educational Alliance recently organized, can easily utilize University Extension courses." Patri had high expectations for the overworked schools: "The schools could reach the masses in a very direct manner, and succeed in doing for the adult what they are trying to do for the child, i.e., the bringing of higher ideals to the masses, the development of civic intelligence, the increasing of patriotism, the making men worthy of the trust which a democratic government has placed upon them."[55]

Patri was critical of the boss-dominated political system of America's cities, and his only word of political praise was for the socialists. "Municipal socialism" was popular among progressives at this time as an alternative to Democratic "bossism" and Republican conservatism. Patri's positive response to socialism shows that he strongly supported increased public involvement in education and reform, and that he saw private enterprise and voluntarism, however helpful, as inadequate responses to immense urban problems. In the final section of the thesis, "The Public School of the Future," Patri proposed the development of an institution which would provide sound schooling for children, while coordinating and integrating education and other services for families and communities. Here Patri sketched out many of the ideas and practices which he gradually introduced into his own schools just a few years later.[56]

Patri's seventy two-page thesis, based on extensive reading and on personal experience in public schools and other social and educational institutions, is not a dry academic report. It is an authentic progressive document that demonstrates Patri's impassioned commitment to improving the lot of children and families. One can see here early evidence of Patri's long interest in adult and parent education. He was impressed with the potential power of public schools, which reached most children in the city, and was hopeful about the educational impact of settlement houses, boys' and girls' clubs, churches, libraries, and other organizations which assisted children and families to deal with the challenges of urban living. But his basic and recurrent message was that the public schools should assume responsibility for coordinating, integrating, and promoting social and educational services for families and communities. The schools did what they could with students during their few years in classrooms, but continued education was essential for youth and adults as they left school and pursued their careers as workers, parents, and citizens. Out of his own experiences and studies, Patri was stating a message that would recur in each generation, and which historian Lawrence Cremin reiterated in book after book from the 1960s to the 1990s: education is too important to be left solely to the educators; a whole range of institutions and agencies must work together to develop the broad, deep, and effective education which democratic life demands.[57]

A half-century later Patri wrote in his unpublished memoir that in his years as a teacher he had taught in six schools.[58] School directories and other sources enable us to identify some of these. During the 1899–90 school year he taught in the Bronx at PS 154, an all-boys school.[59] He continued to teach while finishing his master's degree and tried to implement his new ideas, but a traditional supervisor told him to return to the standard disciplinary methods. With confidence in his convictions, Patri refused. Instead of changing his practices, he changed schools, and from 1902–1903 taught at Public School 79 at the lower end of Manhattan, with Joseph Fripp as principal. Fripp's doctrine was "I serve children."[60] Patri thrived in this positive environment, but was promoted and moved to yet another building. In 1904 Fripp wrote a recommendation for Patri: "He was eminently successful in arousing in his pupils a strong interest in their work and bringing out what was best in them. . . . I bear willing testimony to his superiority as an educator in the best sense of that word."[61]

Patri vividly described the challenges of teaching science to seventh and eighth grade boys in a school where the teachers, not the students, moved between classrooms: "The only way I could do this was to carry whatever apparatus I needed from room to room. Batteries, tubes, jars, pails, water, gas burners followed me about. As I passed down the stairs and through the halls I looked like a small moving van." After two months Patri moved yet again, this time to a senior class in PS 11 in Chelsea on the lower West Side, teaching a "miscellaneous sort of population, a mixture of races and colour. The boys lived along the docks, in the rear of factory yards where the men found employment. . . . "

Here Patri encountered hostility: "The antagonism between the school and the neighborhood was intense. Both came from mutual distrust founded on mutual misunderstanding. The children were afraid of the teachers, and the teachers were afraid of the children. . . . . The school was failing. I was failing and my whole mind was concentrated upon finding the cause and the remedy." Patri struggled, and succeeded well enough so that the principal made him responsible for school assemblies and discipline. He wrote: "I was glad. I had learned to believe in children. I had begun to analyse my own childhood more carefully. Here was an opportunity to test my knowledge in a larger way than the classroom offered.

"I began by telling the boys what a fine assembly was like in other schools. Once more I resorted to stories. They never failed. Father had done his share nobly. The big restless crowd settled down and listened." Patri established a student council which helped solve some of the school's problems. "This experience helped me wonderfully. Through it I gained increased confidence in the children, in the power of the school, in myself."[62] Patri's success was confirmed in a recommendation from the principal: "I take great pleasure in certifying to the ability of Mr. Angelo Patri as teacher and disciplinarian. He is among the few teachers who ranks "A" (Superior to Excellent) a mark accorded him both by myself and the Board of Superintendents."[63]

In 1903, while still at Teachers College completing his formal American education, and beginning an American career, Patri chose to become officially American and was naturalized as a citizen.[64] Four years later he accepted an appointment as principal of Public School 4, and celebrated with a summer trip to Norway.[65] He served as principal of PS 4 from 1907 to 1913. In this elementary school overlooking Crotona Park in the Bronx, Patri continued to experiment with humane, child-oriented, socially progressive practices until his appointment as principal of PS 45 in 1913. Patri had become American while maintaining his Italian heritage; equally important, he had become a professional educator while keeping the ability to look at life from the standpoint of a child.

Patri observing a young printer at work, PS 45
(Frank Merolla)

THREE

Schoolmaster of the Great City: The Man and the Book, 1907–1913

DURING HIS INTENSE, BUSY, CHALLENGING FIRST FOUR years in PS 45, Patri somehow made time to write *Schoolmaster of the Great City*, a lively, interesting book of 221 pages that described his early life and education, but which focused primarily on Patri's six years as principal of Public School 4.[1] Patri had previously published two books for children, but *Schoolmaster* was the first of ten books that he wrote for adults. It was widely read and reviewed, was reprinted nine times by 1925, and appeared in French, Rumanian, Russian, German, Spanish, and Chinese editions.[2] The book has since been cited and excerpted in many educational histories for its realistic yet hopeful treatment of inner-city education.

The book's popularity among educators and the liberal public may be explained partly by the timing of its publication. It appeared in 1917, the year the United States entered World War I. America's entry into the conflict was accompanied by superpatriotism and denunciation of "hyphenated Americans."[3] That same year Congress passed, over President Wilson's veto, a literacy test intended to discourage immigration from Italy and Southern Europe.[4] By contrast with such expressions of nativism, Patri's book showed that immigrants were able to successfully adapt to mainstream society and could—like Patri—contribute to its improvement.

Patri's confidence in the integrating role of the school provided some optimism to those experiencing the negative emotions generated by the war. A review in *The Nation* concluded: "In this weary time of war and ruin it is refreshing and comforting to turn to the record of Mr. Patri's life as a schoolmaster and to meditate on its subtle influence for good as it penetrates the lives of many children until who can say how far it will reach." [5]

Schoolmaster was written in a lyrical, fervent narrative style. Patri's father was a great storyteller, and Patri continued—and made public—this family tradition. He emphasized stories and morals, not details. The text includes few names and dates; for example, although Patri had three sisters to whom he was close, there is no hint in the book of their existence, and although Patri taught in six different schools between 1897 and 1907, he does not identify them.

There may have been at least two reasons for this lack of specificity and of criticism in *Schoolmaster*. First, as a former student of John Dewey, Patri very much wanted his readers to understand and accept the message that Deweyan progressive education provided solutions to urban educational and social problems, and he may have chosen to avoid distracting them with details and critiques. Second, Patri presumably wanted to avoid naming names and thus unnecessarily alienating colleagues and superiors with whom he had to work. His critique of traditional, hidebound schooling was telling, but unfocused and impersonal.

Although *Schoolmaster* has been out of print for over eighty years, it is an important part of Patri's life story, still cited by educational historians and other scholars, and worthy of analysis as one of the earliest statements by an immigrant educator of his personal and professional experiences in American schools. This chapter begins with some key events and ideas from *Schoolmaster*, explains some of the impact of the book, shows how it has been used by educational historians, and concludes with brief comparisons with several contemporary educational reformers and innovators.

Schoolmaster covers the first thirty-seven years of Patri's life until 1913, when he left PS 4 to become principal of PS 45. Patri devotes nearly 200 pages of *Schoolmaster* to his six years at PS 4, creating in the process an unusually detailed description of the life of a school. I will cite only a few incidents from the book and will use Patri's own clear prose whenever possible. (I will combine some of his short paragraphs and to minimize notes will put page numbers in parentheses.)

Patri exulted in learning of his assignment to PS 4: "Now came my appointment as principal. I stretched my arms and said, 'Free at last, my own master. I am limited only by my own vision.' I entered my new school, 'My school,' as I proudly called it. There it was, a big massive structure towering like a fortress above the elevated lines, fronting a large public park, the airy rooms full of sunshine. . . . I saw the open spaces, the sunlight, the park, and I rejoiced. These, I knew, were the teacher's best friends." The building Patri described was located at 173d Street and Fulton and Third Avenues, across from Crotona Park in the Bronx. (24–25)

Patri noted how regimented students were as they marched from room to room and sat in tightly structured classes. He "left the office and walked through the school, corridors, classrooms and playgrounds listening and watching, trying to get an idea here and there." Pupils and teachers feared the new principal. An older principal said that was good—"Take my advice if you want any peace of mind and keep them under your thumb." (26–29) Some relief came when the previous principal left with 1500 of the students to a new school. Patri could now get to know the teachers and help them with disciplinary problems. He assisted them with their most difficult children, gradually earning their trust. And in response "the children began to feel that the school was with them and for them and began to assume responsibility." (39)

As discipline became more humane and personal, Patri helped his teachers become more effective instructors. This was hard. Patri promoted new strategies in basic fields: "These subjects were so thoroughly formalised and logically arranged that no new viewpoint could be carried over through them. I began by emphasising subjects that held emotional values, drawing, composition, music, nature, literature." (45–46) Teachers tried his way, and some made it work, while others were still intimidated by test scores and superintendents' visits. But teachers were not the only sources of resistance: "Parents have been trained as have the teachers, to think of the school as a place where the children are made to obey, to memorize, made to repeat lessons." Patri saw that both teachers and parents needed to understand and accept the changes. "Only when there was a better public conception of what the schools should do would school life really change." (50-51)

Some parents objected if the school seemed to skimp on the basics or if teachers didn't assign time-consuming homework. "Because the parents want this sort of thing, the school is built to suit—a book school—one room like another, one seat like another, each child like his neighbor." (57) Patri worked to help students, teachers, and parents make needed improvements inside the school, but he had to make changes outside as well. He helped families keep their children in school longer and to keep them all in one school rather than scattering them among two or three. He heard complaints about gang activity near the school and listened to immigrant parents who were losing control of their children. "Here were children and parents living their lives apart. These children were ashamed because their parents did not speak or look like Americans. How could I help the children in my school respond to the dreams of their fathers?

How could I get the fathers to share in the work of building a school for their children?" (81)

Patri married in 1910, after living with his parents and sisters until he was thirty four years old. He and his wife Dora moved into the community, taking an apartment at 601 East 170th, across Crotona Park from his school, and lived there until his retirement in 1944. Patri saw the value of this move: "I had settled into the neighborhood to get the feel of the school in a rather intimate way. Looking out my window morning or evening I could see the school building towering over the trees. It was only a short walk through the park and all the many hours I would otherwise have spent in travel were saved for the school." Living there had clear advantages: "A neighbor could drop in any time. A teacher now and then might stop on his way home. A child or a group of them was sure to appear on a holiday. It was not so difficult to go out of an evening and meet some of the people and talk over the needs of the children." (194)

So Patri was well placed, geographically and educationally to say: "The problems of my school, therefore, loomed up as the problems of our community. . . . To save the school and the home from becoming cloistered, self centred, the culture of children would have to be a cooperative effort between the people and the teachers." (84) The children asked a real estate man for space for a school garden, and he complied. Teachers asked the park commissioner for trees to plant in the park for Arbor Day, and he gave some each year. Community meetings were held, and parents saw the good work their children were doing. Parents got one of their number appointed to the local school board. Doctors talked at parent meetings about health and diet. The parent group provided clothing for children who needed it. Patri saw the positive effects on teachers of all this community activity: "Dealing with parents in the interest of children has always seemed to me like handling a dynamic factor, one that puts power and soul into the hands of the teacher because it puts power and soul into the people. Socialising the school means humanising the teacher." (114)

Officials threatened to build an armory in the park and to use some of the land for a drill ground, but the parents resisted and saved the park for the children and the school. Two years later they defeated a plan to build a firehouse on park land. They closed down a movie theater that ignored fire codes. Patri concluded proudly: "The Parents' Association had become a power for good in the neighborhood. It had earned the confidence of the people." (121) The neighborhood was now organized enough to help establish a settlement, Bronx House, in a local mansion. It sponsored many activities, even supporting a "meat strike" against high prices. Mothers attended English classes while their babies were cared for. Ten thousand people used the facilities each month. "Music, drawing, sewing, civic clubs, athletic clubs, literary clubs, occupied all the space there was." The settlement gave Patri "hope that some day the school itself would be a bigger thing than it had ever been before." [6] (133–134)

In response to a changing school population, special classes were established for "atypical children, the anemic children, for groups of children with special defects, bad feet, bad speech, bad spines, bad eyes." (135) With the help of local physicians and two immigrant doctors from Russia, a dispensary was set up to care for needy neighbors. A woman called "Aunt Margaret" began functioning as a school visitor—an informal social worker, helping neighbors get medical care and connecting them with welfare agencies. She assisted children who were in trouble with the law and got the Board of Health to inspect bad properties. She went in the evenings to movie theaters and dance halls to find "what temptations were put before the children to attract and keep them, and then to act in accord with this information, appealing to the law, to welfare societies, and to the parents, individually and collectively. . . . The visitor's vigorous crusades always resulted in better conditions." [7] (150–151)

In all this neighborhood activity, Patri was acting on the assumption that improving the environment of families and school would strengthen the character and improve the behavior of his students. His actions and words showed that he shared Dewey's social ideas as well as his educational theories. Paul Boyer identifies Dewey as the leading thinker in the development of "positive environmentalism," noting Dewey's "insistence on the centrality of environment in shaping human behavior and his conviction . . . that the most effective social control was 'not merely physical or coercive, but moral'—not one based on the legal enforcement of rigid behavioral standards, but on 'the intelligent selection and determination of the environments in which we act.'" Clearly, Patri—like Dewey—could be counted among the "positive environmentalists" and "child-savers" of the progressive period.[8]

With progress in the neighborhood, Patri and his staff made further improvements within the school: "What we did for the special children during school time we now tried to do for the normal children, but this had to be done after school hours and in the teacher's own time."[9] They organized groups for nature study, chorus, a school newspaper, storytelling, and "festivals, athletics, dancing, embroidery classes, art classes, manual training classes." (155–156)

But literature classes continued to emphasize structure and grammar, when Patri wanted appreciation and enjoyment. A "wiry little teacher—actually Patri's wife—was a "Stevenson enthusiast," who read his poems to assemblies and selected appropriate poems for different grades.[10] "So we recited and sang and marched to Stevenson's music until his spirit permeated the school." They moved on to "Folk Tales, not scattered, but in terms of people, Russian, Irish, German, Norwegian, and Indian. These were dramatized and the songs and dances introduced. We gave the children a sympathetic appreciation of people and taught them to take home these folk stories, tell them to their parents and get the parents to tell their own folk tales. So would the children be kept close to their parents, giving and receiving values that were human." (165–66)

Such activities reflected elements of Patri's approach to Americanization. This topic is so central to *Schoolmaster* and to Patri's whole life that it deserves some background and analysis. From America's earliest days people struggled with the definition of "American" and with ways of helping or coercing newcomers to become Americans.[11] In this centuries-long dialogue Patri had the great advantage of being an immigrant and of speaking fluent Italian. Patri's first five years of life were spent in an Italian village culture, where, by comparison with his later American life, existence was simple, integrated, and poor.[12] After moving to Manhattan's "Little Italy," the family was able to maintain much of its Italian culture, but it was necessary to learn English. When Patri began attending what he called an "American school" in 1887, and when his family moved to a more "American" neighborhood, their assimilation became more rapid.

Like many young immigrants Patri went through a period of alienation from his family, as American individualization overshadowed Italian communalism: "I went to school, father went to work, mother looked after the house. When evening came, instead of sitting around the fire, talking and reliving the day, we sat, each in his own corner. . . .The demands of the school devoured me; the work exhausted my father." Home and school drifted their separate ways. "This living by myself tended to make me forget, indeed to undervalue, the worth of my people. I was ashamed sometimes because my folk did not look or talk like Americans." But then Patri visited his father at work and was reminded that, "on two-dollar-a-day wages he sent me to college. Proud of his strength I would strengthen my moral fiber and respond to his dream." (4–5)

Patri's renewed recognition of his love and respect for his parents and his original homeland helped confirm his conviction that immigrants need not abandon their heritage while becoming Americans. He became what we may now call a cosmopolitan cultural pluralist, supporting necessary adaptation to the American language, economy, and polity, the maintenance of ethnic languages and cultures, and healthy interaction among the various groups involved.[13]

Patri may have been influenced toward cultural pluralism during his immersion in pragmatism at Teachers College from 1900 to 1904, in a summer philosophy course with John Dewey in 1909, and through his ongoing reading, study, and participation in the intellectual and cultural life of New York City.[14] Louis Menand says that cultural pluralism grew out of "the pragmatism of James and Dewey . . . in response to the xenophobia induced by the turn-of-the-century waves of immigration and exacerbated by America's entry into the First World War. Three figures whose writing was seminal to this development were students of James and Dewey." Menand identifies key statements of cultural pluralism by these three: Horace Kallen, Alan Locke, and Randolph Bourne. These statements all appeared in 1915 and 1916, just before Patri published *Schoolmaster.*[15]

Whether or not Patri was directly influenced by these men and their writings, his position on Americanization was consistent with theirs. In fact, Patri echoed two key words from Bourne's 1916 essay, "Trans-National America." This was one of the earliest critiques of the "melting pot" approach to Americanization, and in it Bourne supported policies of respect and inclusion for the various groups that made up the country. He wrote: "We cannot Americanize America by sentimentalizing and moralizing history. When the best schools are expressly renouncing the questionable duty of teaching patriotism by means of history, it is not the time to force shibboleth upon the immigrant. . . . The inflections of other voices have been drowned. They must be heard." [16]

One of those voices was Patri's. Near the end of *Schoolmaster* Patri wrote: "No matter who the people are, they need the school as a humanising force, so that they may feel the common interest, revive their visions, see the fulfillment of their dreams in terms of their children so that they may be made young once more. Americanise the foreigner, nay, through the child let us fulfill our destiny and Americanise America." (219) By this he meant democratize America and make its advantages available to all in an atmosphere of mutual respect. For urban educators in particular, this presented an ethical and pragmatic imperative to actively involve parents and communities in the life of the school and the school in the life of the city. In calling on people to "Americanise America," Patri was making his contribution to the ongoing discussion of the nature of this country. Richard Gambino continued this line of reasoning in 1974, encouraging Italian Americans to "revitalize their traditions and contribute them in new forms to an enriched American culture." [17] And in a more recent example, Joseph Cosco wrote in 2003: "Ultimately, American debates over the new immigrants, particularly the Italians, and their potential and prospects for assimilation and Americanization were debates about America itself." [18]

Because issues of reform and Americanization were so critical in 1917 and were so central to the book, the first reviewers of *Schoolmaster* dealt with them extensively. A few citations from these reviews may help situate Patri's book in the broader context of American progressivism. An anonymous reviewer for *The American Review of Reviews* compared *Schoolmaster* to Jacob Riis's *How the Other Half Lives* (1890). The comparison with Riis's book is relevant, since Patri drew on it in his 1904 master's thesis at Teachers College. The reviewer wrote that, like Riis, Patri, "sees the flaws of our social and educational systems more clearly because of his foreign birth." The reviewer noted that as a student Patri "continually felt the great social gulf between the American children and the foreign-born," but that his awareness of this helped him when he became principal of PS 4 to make needed changes.[19]

Clyde Furst, secretary to the Carnegie Foundation for the Advancement of Teaching, reviewed *Schoolmaster* for Nicholas Murray Butler's authoritative *Educational Review*. Furst told how Patri helped his teachers develop their "personal interests toward special teaching in art, athletics, dancing, festivals, music, nature study and story-telling . . . Teachers made room in the curriculum for 'the folk tales of the children's ancestors.' Furst concluded his review with some of Patri's "suggestions for school betterment," including smaller classes, a curriculum related to real life, better teacher training, and "more intimate contact with the people . . . and the school cooperating with the entire neighborhood."[20]

In the influential, but often elitist, *Nation* magazine, J. L. More said that "Mr. Patri is wholeheartedly in favor of the institutional school, with its multiform activities, even to the point of despising book-learning. And, as one reads how the little children were gathered into the school out of their dreary streets and homes and were fostered and cared for, how the school reached out to the parents and brought new interests and activities into their lives, one sees this form of public education at its best." More heartily approved of what Patri was doing for immigrant children but warned that in the process the majority of students might lose "the chance of that better education which comes from a steady discipline in the thoughts and lives of the best men. And this higher discipline must come from books, the casket of men's thoughts and deeds. It is altogether probable that, under the stimulus of such a man as Mr. Patri, the usually barren vocational and nature studies become instinct with life and meaning, but given a school director of his personality so would any form of study."[21] Here More was raising issues of curriculum and methods that would recur over the decades in critiques of progressive education.[22]

An anonymous reviewer in the *New York Times Book Review* summarized Patri's early life, education, and career and concluded that: "Mr. Patri's vision of what the public school should be and should do in American life, in city and country, in rich neighborhoods and poor neighborhoods alike, is an inspiring and an aspiring vision, an ideal of a force that would be a greater power in molding and Americanizing and democratizing American life than it would be possible to find in all other agencies together."[23]

This call for "Americanizing . . . American life" was made more explicit by Randolph Bourne. His response to Patri was particularly significant since he was one of America's leading young intellectuals, an interpreter of Dewey, a writer on education for *The New Republic* and other journals, and a strong supporter of progressive education. Drawing on ideas and phrases from Thorstein Veblen, Bourne wrote in his review for *The Survey*: "Somehow the instinct of workmanship must be gotten generally into the teaching profession, this instinct which brings a disgust with routine, with verbalism, with mass-teaching, and those other evils of a congested and mechanical school system." He agreed with Patri that teaching "is a practical, even a fine, art, rather than a science. It works upon the most sensitive and complex raw material in the world, the human personality, and the educational craftsmen and artists have therefore to be of a more skillful and subtle calibre than any other craft demands." Bourne concluded with the kind of high praise that authors crave: "There is no book that will more aid such an end than this charming and intimate record of a schoolmaster's life in the teeming public schools of New York City."[24]

Going beyond *Schoolmaster*, Bourne enthusiastically described and assessed Patri's current work in his new school, PS 45, "one of the most successful results of the Gary experiment. . . ." Patri and his staff had adopted the "Platoon System" made famous by Willard Wirt in Gary, Indiana—an innovation that became the source of continuing controversy in New York. Bourne saw that Patri's earlier work at PS 4 enabled him to ease the transition to the Gary plan in PS 45, and concluded by saying that "Mr. Patri makes the technique of running a school seem like the most fascinating and complex of modern enterprises. It involves generalship, quick resourcefulness, human sympathy, a workmanlike use of material to create personality and effectiveness in the child. Schoolmasters like Mr. Patri would make teaching the most important of the professions and education the finest of the arts."[25]

These reviews were exceedingly positive about *Schoolmaster* and its author, with the *Nation*'s reviewer raising the only serious question about Patri—his apparent hostility to a bookish curriculum. It is true that Patri, never given to understatement, called for teachers who were "life-trained, instead of book-trained," but the reviewer missed the crucial point that Patri wanted to lead children from "life-training" to serious studies in literature, mathematics, history, art, and music.[26] Like Dewey, Patri wanted to begin education with the child's own interests and experiences and then integrate them with the more formal, academic world of knowledge, including bookish knowledge. Near the end of *Schoolmaster* Patri put this in perspective: "Play rooms and games, animals and plants, wood and nails must take their place side by side with books and words."[27]

Several reviewers noted Patri's critiques of administrators who failed to understand his approach to education or who, if they understood, resisted it because it undermined their authority or set a bad example for more conventional schools. But it is clear that, whatever difficulties he may have had from the bureaucracy, Patri received strong support from his immediate superior, district superintendent Joseph L. Taylor. In May 1914 Taylor wrote that he had supervised Patri for five years in PS 4 and one year in PS 45. In PS 4 Patri "organized a parents' association which is well-known throughout the city. He was directly instrumental in the establishment of the Bronx House, the efficient settlement house on Washington Avenue." Taylor cited the various special education classes Patri had initiated and went on to say that Patri had already "found time in his new situation to bring into being a very vigorous parents' organization, a savings bank, and to break up gang rule in the neighborhood."[28]

Patri was highly regarded also by community leaders outside the school system. Reverend Joseph Auhino wrote a letter in which he said: "In my work among my Catholic countrymen in New York, Angelo Patri has been one of the few co-religionists who has continually given me his effective help. He is a friend of mine and I know of the great and splendid work he has done in connection with P. S. 4, Bronx. He has been influential in awakening the neighborhood to higher civic pride and we are all proud of him. His personal sacrifices have been great and wonderful. Surely the true spirit of the deeply religious is in his heart. We could do no better than spread his influence."[29]

To put all this optimism in historical perspective it is important to recall that only seven years after Patri proposed an inclusive democratic Americanism, Congress passed the Johnson-Reed bill clearly designed to exclude, as one congressman put it, "Bolshevik Wops, Dagoes, Kikes, and Hunkies." When President Coolidge signed the bill he said "America must be kept American." That could be done by keeping out Italians, Jews, and others from southern and eastern Europe—in short, people like Patri and his family.[30]

The reviews and letters cited above presented contemporary considerations of Patri and his book *Schoolmaster.* For later perspectives we turn to assessments by various scholars who have written about Patri and *Schoolmaster.* Lawrence Cremin, in *The Transformation of the School* (1961) discussed Patri's early connection with the Progressive Education Association (PEA), noting that Patri had addressed the first meeting of the PEA and that he had been an early member of its advisory council.[31] But this connection with the PEA did not last. Cremin's student Patricia Graham wrote: "At the first meeting, representatives of progressive slum schools such as Angelo Patri of the Bronx and Persis K. Miller of a Baltimore vocational school addressed the members, but by the mid-twenties the majority of the Association paid little attention to Patri's school gardens or Miss Miller's training. The indifference was mutual. Finger painting and modern dance were not considered the most important aspects of an immigrant youngster's American education."[32]

David Tyack included a selection from *Schoolmaster* in a 1967 educational history, noting that "Patri accepted the notion that the teacher was 'responsible for what the child does out of school.' How otherwise, he asked, 'can the teacher ever know that her world counts in the life of the child?'"[33] Tyack returned to *Schoolmaster* in his influential 1975 book *The One Best System*, writing: "Docility among teachers frustrated Angelo Patri when he became a principal in New York and sought to humanize the rigid school he inherited. . . . As he passed a classroom he saw a teacher smiling at a pupil. 'I was glad and walked towards the teacher. Instantly the smile disappeared, her body grew tense, the little boy sat down and all the other little boys sat up stiff and straight and put their hands behind them.' Patri grew despondent. 'I've tried to have the teachers and children feel that I'm their friend,' he told the former principal, but instead 'they are afraid of me.' 'Afraid of you? Of course they are and they ought to be,' replied his predecessor."[34]

Paula Fass, in *Outside In: Minorities and the Transformation of American Education* (1989), quotes Patri in a statement showing his understanding of the need to make good work visible. "The school must open its doors. It must reach out to spread itself, and come into direct contact with all its people. Each day the power of the school must be felt in some corner of the school district. It must work so that everybody sees its work and daily appraises that work." Fass adds that "this idea of a community school required more than an adaptation to the perceived needs of its immigrant constituents. It required that the school respect the culture of the students and act in such a way as to produce pride in self, family, and past." But Fass cautions that "this open-door school policy was ambiguous. Like the social settlements on which it was modeled, it was at once an expression of democratic aspiration and an intrusion upon the community it was meant to serve."[35] William Bullough makes a similar point: "Gilded Age urban educators included in their definition of education the compensatory principle dogmatically applied to segments of the urban population and aspects of urban life deemed morally, socially, politically, or economically defective. In fact, many educators considered the entire urban milieu in dire need of compensatory schooling."[36] Patri felt this way quite unambiguously as he worked with Father Auhino and as he sent "Aunt Margaret" out to neighborhood theaters and dance halls to try to improve the environment for children and families.

While such intrusive acts on the part of Anglo-Saxon elitists might have encountered resistance, Patri's neighborhood crusades were apparently effective. Bullough notes that at PS 4 Patri "converted his school into a community center concerned with matters ranging from student health to parent education and neighborhood beautification." An immigrant himself, and "because he shared their experience, Patri could comprehend the problems of immigrants, win the confidence essential to effective education, and devise programs which made the school an institution relevant to working-class life."[37]

Rosetta Marantz Cohen and Samuel Scheer in 1997 included seven pages of *Schoolmaster* in *The Work of Teachers in America*. Their introduction says that Patri "describes in this account his sense of dismay at the old-fashioned methodologies and subjects that had long been a staple of urban school curriculums. Patri's emphasis on movement, discovery, and doing, his stress on individuality and his recognition of the child's 'sacred' nature are all key elements of the Progressive ideology." The editors saw that Patri expressed his progressivism both in content and method: "He organized student orchestras in his schools, allowed students to plant fruit and vegetable gardens, and generally nurtured creativity in the context of the fundamentals."[38] In reviewing this book Stephen Preskill placed Patri in a succession of progressives: "Teachers who threaten the status quo . . . find themselves again and again in jeopardy. Jonathan Kozol is just one of a long line of teachers, starting with Bronson Alcott and continuing to Angelo Patri and others, who found that innovation often engenders administrative opposition, although as in the case of Patri, enlightened educational leaders occasionally do come along who actually welcome new ideas."[39]

Preskill continued his interest in Patri in his 2001 book *Stories of Teaching: A Foundation for Educational Renewal*. He made a particular point of Patri's debt to Dewey, noting that as a new teacher he had no theory by which to guide his work. "Only after going back to the university to discover the works of John Dewey does Patri develop an underlying philosophy that makes sense to him: 'I realized then that the child must move and not sit still; that he must make mistakes and not merely repeat perfect forms; that he must be himself and not a miniature reproduction of the teacher.'"

Like other readers of *Schoolmaster*, Preskill sees that Patri places the teacher at the center of educational improvement: "Perhaps Patri's most valuable contribution to an understanding of the conditions that make education work is the emphasis he places on the intellectual and moral development of teachers. . . . In his own school he seeks to unleash teachers' strengths, to make their interests and their growth an important mission of the school."[40]

These responses and interpretations, from Patri's own time to the present, reflect in various ways some of Patri's educational experiences and essential ideas. Patri took time near the end of *Schoolmaster*, to summarize those "essential ideas." He identified and explained what he thought the schools needed in 1917. "To begin with, better school conditions must be provided for the youngest children. . . . We must spend more money on elementary education if the money we now spend on higher education is to bring forth results that are commensurate with our national needs. . . . We must keep the three R's, but they must change with the changing social needs. . . . ." After stating these ambitious imperatives Patri asked: "Have we the courage to change our class education into democratic education?" (197–202)

"The second thing to do is to train the teacher differently. . . " Patri's questions suggest what he wants: "Can the higher training include the direction of young children in club life, the participation in the work of settlements, the study of the home and street life? Should the training school period include work in the hospital for children, so that the teacher may actually learn what the physical needs of the children are, and where to go for help?" (202–206)

Continuing his critique of the bureaucracy Patri wrote: "Third, we must break the deadening influence of a too strongly centralised system; we must individualise the schools rather than mass them. . . . What the school system needs to understand is that its strength lies, not in the strength of the central organization, but in the strength of the individual school, not in making one school like another, but in making each school a distinct unit. . . . " And again connecting school and home he added: "Unless a school enters deeply into the lives of the people, that school will not enter deeply into the lives of the children or into the lives of the teachers. Unless the school is the great democratic socialising agency, it is nothing at all." (208–211)

Making essentially the same point, and continuing the proposals of his MA thesis, Patri wrote: "Fourth, we must change the notion that the school is a cloistered institution, by breaking down its walls and having it come into direct contact with people. . . . It must use the factory, the stores, the neighboring parks, the museums, not incidentally but fully and with deliberation." (211–215)

Patri's fifth point was that his idea of "Americanising America" could best be done through the children. "We must change our attitude towards the child. . . . I feel that the attitude towards the school and the child is the ultimate attitude by which America is to be judged. Indeed the distinctive contribution America is to make to the world's progress is not political, economical, religious, but educational, the child our national strength, the school as the medium through which the adult is to be remade." (215–217)

Patri extends this thought: "I have been a part of many movements to Americanise the foreigner, but I see that the child is the only one who can carry the message of democracy if it is to be carried at all. If the child fails to make the connection between the ideals of the school and the fundamental beliefs of the people there is none other to do it. The children are the chain that must bind people together." (218) In Patri's hopeful view, school reform, social change, and democratic Americanization will be promoted as people work to meet the real needs of children, their families, and their communities.

Reconsidering *Schoolmaster* in 2005, during yet another period of school reform, it is not difficult to find points of connection and comparison with contemporary educators and reformers. *Schoolmaster* shows with many examples how Patri and his staff searched out the particular talents and interests of teachers and students and created programs of study centered on those talents and interests. This approach was based on assumptions about a variety of human abilities that is similar to, though less developed than, Howard Gardner's theory of "multiple intelligences."[41]

Patri's call for distinctive inner-city schools and strong parental and community connections can be linked with Deborah Meier and her successful experiments with multiethnic students in New York City.[42] His emphasis on continual educational experimentation in each school is consistent with Tyack's and Cuban's dictum that reforms change schools but that schools also change reforms.[43] And Patri's schools, during the first years of this century, had many of the democratic characteristics of George Wood's 1993 *Schools That Work.*[44]

Laurel Tanner's 1997 book, *Dewey's Laboratory School: Lessons for Today* gives us a vivid picture of some of the approaches that Dewey used in his selective university school in Chicago from 1896–1904.[45] Patri took over PS 4 in 1907, just three years after the close of the Laboratory School, and applied in his huge school with 61 classrooms, some of Dewey's ideas that he had encountered at Teachers College between 1900 and 1904 and in his summer course with Dewey in 1909.

But the contemporary book that is perhaps most consistent with Patri's approach is Kate Rousmaniere's *City Teachers*. Rousmaniere, like Patri, asserts that teachers must be at the center of any efforts at school reform. Patri faced exceedingly difficult challenges during his ten years in the classroom and, perhaps because of those experiences, never lost sight of teachers' need for encouragement, stimulation, and protection. Rousmaniere reminds us of the importance of such support in the final words of her book: "Effective school leaders need to take into account the great variety of factors that affect teachers' work and to guide or mediate those factors for the sole purpose of improving teachers' ability to get their job done. School reform needs to be addressed to teachers' needs, respecting the legacy of their experiences at work."[46]

Patri was one of the few well-known educators of his time to apply Deweyan progressive theories successfully and consistently over an extended period in inner-city public schools. During a period of extreme nativism and narrow Americanization, he respected the language and culture of his immigrant students and prepared them to participate successfully in the culture and the economy. And, drawing on his own experience, he thought deeply about educational problems and presented realistic proposals for school reform. *Schoolmaster* showed that Patri had learned a great deal in his six years at PS 4; he would have ample opportunity to use and test his knowledge and experience for thirty-one years in his next assignment, still in the Bronx, at PS 45.

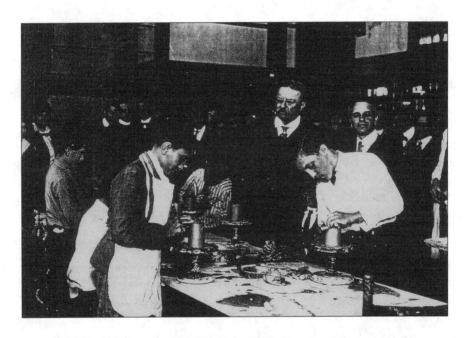

Theodore Roosevelt visits PS 45 in 1917 (Patri to Roosevelt's left)

(Frank Merolla)

FOUR

A Gary School Survives:
Public School 45, 1913–1929

PATRI'S BOOK, *SCHOOLMASTER OF THE GREAT CITY*, GIVES
clear and vivid impressions of his early life in Italy and New York, his
family and community, his schooling and early teaching career, and his
six years as principal of PS 4, from 1907 to 1913.[1] Unfortunately, Patri
never published an equivalent account of his much longer experience at
PS 45, from 1913 to 1944, but about ten years after his retirement in 1944,
he wrote a memoir of over 300 pages that summarized his earlier life and
career, and then dealt mostly with his years at PS 45. He typed the manuscript and wrote on it in longhand many corrections, apparently preparing
it for publication. It is unclear why he chose not to publish it, as he had
written or translated during his career eight books for children and ten for
adults, and knew the publishing scene well.[2] In any case, Patri wrote two
alternate conclusions to the memoir, one uncharacteristically pessimistic,
and as late as 1962, three years before his death, was struggling with how
to turn it into a publishable book.[3]

I will extract from the memoir, and occasionally comment on material of possible interest to historians, educators, students of the Italian-
American experience, and general readers. At a few points I will cite other
sources, particularly the *New York Times*, for a broader outlook on some of
the incidents Patri describes.[4] The memoir provides intriguing perspective on some recurrent educational and historical questions: What was
progressive education, and did it have any impact on schooling in general? Did progressive education succeed in settings other than elite private schools? When and why did community education and multicultural

education have their beginnings? What are the characteristics of good schools, how are such schools created, and how can they be maintained over time?

Near the beginning of their wonderfully titled *Tinkering Toward Utopia*, historians David Tyack and Larry Cuban ask several questions about educational reform, some of which are especially relevant to this inquiry: "What constitutes 'success' in school reform? Why have some successes become invisible? Why has the 'grammar of schooling'—the organizational forms that govern instruction—persisted, while challenges to it have mostly been evanescent? Why have outsiders' attempts to reinvent schooling—break-the-mold strategies—generally been short-lived shooting stars?"[5]

During much of the past century, responses to such questions have been framed in terms of traditional vs. progressive education. Often the dialogue was presented in stark dualistic terms, ignoring differences within both traditionalism and progressivism. The most widely-used divisions among progressives were Lawrence Cremin's "scientists, sentimentalists and radicals." The "scientists" were the test-givers and the efficiency promoters; the "sentimentalists" included varieties of psychologically oriented, child-centered educators; the "radicals" were those who wanted to use schools as instruments of social reform.[6] Herbert Kliebard added "humanists" to these groups, and claimed that the efficiency experts had the dominant impact in the schools.[7] In terms of these categories, Patri may be seen as a child-centered reformer.

Dogmatists in all these groups have insisted on the rightness of their educational practices, histories, and theories. Claims have been made for the success of particular schools and programs, though many of these lasted for very short periods. One of the best comparative studies of traditional and progressive approaches, conducted by the Commission on the Relation of School and College, lasted only eight years, from 1932 to 1940.[8] On the progressive side there have been numerous studies of individual schools, many of them elite private institutions.[9] Long-term studies of progressive public schools are rare, so this memoir of PS 45 may provide educational historians and reformers (these are sometimes the same people) with useful, if anecdotal, new evidence about some of the realities of reform in urban public schools.

Histories of progressive schools, including the case studies presented in Semel and Sadovnik's "*Schools of Tomorrow*," *Schools of Today*, suggest some of the reasons why independent progressive schools have received more attention than public ones: they are generally smaller and more coherent, thus facilitating focused studies; their founders have reputations to build and may have a sense of their own historical significance; private schools must continually publicize their work in fund-raising efforts, thus generating materials usable by historians; teachers in such schools often pursue advanced degrees and see their schools as worthy research topics; school records can be kept as school personnel wish—not as central office bureaucrats desire—and thus may be more accessible to historians; and finally, as overworked as they are, private school people may have more time to record and write school histories. Patri, with sometimes 4,000 students in his school had to retire before he could find the time, energy, and perspective to write about it.[10]

This chapter covers the period when PS 45 was an inclusive elementary/intermediate school, from 1913 to 1929. Chapter 6 deals with the junior high school years, from 1929 to 1944.[11] As before, I will let Patri tell much of this story in his own words, providing only enough commentary to give needed context. Patri apparently wrote most of this from memory and, as in *Schoolmaster*, provided few names or dates by which to place the events he describes. So as to interrupt his narrative as little as possible, I will minimize notes and refer to pages in Patri's text with numbers in parentheses. Patri numbered pages 1–4 in the preface and then began again with 1 in the text itself. He was an excellent writer, but had not completed editing and proofreading the memoir, so I have made minor changes in spelling, punctuation, and paragraphing.

Patri's preface summarizes his thirty one years at PS 45, notes the different names used for the school, and reveals disappointment that his reforms did not last after he retired: "Here is my story of a public school in New York City that started out in 1913 as P.S. #45 Bronx; became widely publicized as 'A Gary School'; later was officially named Paul Hoffman Junior High School . . . thereafter was popularly known as the Angelo Patri school, a combination of what Pestalozzi practiced and John Dewey preached; and after my retirement became once more P. S. #45, no matter what its present official name. The cycle was complete, the school restored to normal procedure, its place in the system re-established. All was well, save with the children, the teachers, and the parents. They did not like the change."

Patri describes the continual distance between himself and those in charge of the schools: "During my career as a principal there was always someone in authority who objected to what I was trying to do and insisted on my doing what I was told to do. The margin of difference between me and authority was at times so big even the blind could see it and sometimes it was so small it quite escaped notice. But whether it was a silent pause in the tension or a loud crackling of thunder, the feeling of a difference was

always present and resented." (Preface, page 1) Patri, a confident administrator, said that most school problems—of curriculum, methods, organization—were easy to deal with, but the challenge was in the "attitudes,
interests, desires, hopes, frustrations of the children." Patri was not only
a child-centered educator, but a teacher-centered one. "In my school the
teacher, too, was given an opportunity to teach what he liked to children
who liked the things he enjoyed and, for him, teaching became a wonderful adventure in happy living."

Patri begins the memoir itself with some of what he had described
in *Schoolmaster*: his Italian family tradition of storytelling, the American
schooling that he began at the age of eleven; the college education that enabled him to pass the examination for a teaching license; and the teaching
positions from 1897 to 1907 in which he had to learn by trial and error on
the job. Like most new teachers he had struggled with discipline: "Being a
disciplinarian had no appeal to me. I remembered a day in school in Italy
when the teacher had responded to my enthusiasm in shouting an answer
that was wrong with the lash of a whip. Was that discipline? I wanted none
of it." (6)

What did work for Patri was the storytelling he had learned from his
father. The students listened to his stories and learned from them. Patri was
promoted, and now sought guidance from Herbert Spencer, John Stuart
Mills, Horace Mann, and other authorities. He tried Herbart's five formal
steps, but "the children refused to think according to the plan." He moved
from school to school, finally finding a principal, Mr. Fripp, who said,
"'unless the children and the teachers are happy there can be no learning,
no teaching, no living, no growth, no school.' Here were Rousseau and
Mills and Pestalozzi at work before my eyes. In my nine years experience
as a classroom teacher in six schools, this was the one good school and the
one good principal." [12] (8, 10)

Patri began a master's program at Teachers College in 1900, and wrote
that in his second year there he discovered two thinkers who influenced
him greatly: "One was Frank McMurry who taught us how and why and
when and what to teach, but bringing the art of teaching out of the realm
of vague, technical, pedagogical language into the daily classroom experiences. . . . Sometimes we spent weeks discussing a single page of Dewey's
Ethical Principles. . . . It was through this teaching that John Dewey caught
my enthusiasm and helped mold my attitude. In his *School and Society* he
pointed the way to the active, thinking, doing school that should replace
the old type book school." [13] (11) Patri tolerated many "tiresome, time-
consuming" courses, but said, "thanks to Fripp, McMurry, Dewey, I

passed safely through the desert wastes of the pedagogical grind and . . . was appointed to head a school of my own." (10–12)

This was PS 4, with sixty-one classrooms from kindergarten through grade six. Patri has described in *Schoolmaster* his experience there from 1907 to 1913. What he adds in the memoir is the frustration he and his teachers felt when hide-bound administrators failed to recognize the good work being done with children and their families. When he was offered the chance to head a different school, he told a friend, "I am going to this new school. It's in the kind of a neighborhood I knew as a boy. . . .The new school was in an Italian colony, a sparsely settled corner of the Bronx. To the west was the Third Avenue elevated road, to the north Fordham University, to the east the Zoo and the park and the wide fields stretching beyond sight and to the south a neighborhood of second and third generations of Americans." (19A–20)

Patri's experience as an immigrant made him intensely aware of cultural differences: "These two groups were as far apart in language, customs and manners as if they were living on opposite sides of the world. The Italian group was self-contained, aloof, and the American group was well content to leave it so. . . . I had lived in a similar colony as a boy and I knew these people, their warm humanity, their narrow suspicion, their love of beauty, their brave struggle for a footing in this strange land to which they had come so eagerly." (20–21)

Sidney Katz vividly described Patri's welcome to PS 45: "On his very first visit he received a taste of the boisterous spirit of his future pupils. The school's roof was being repaired, and as the new principal approached, he was mercilessly pelted with pebbles dipped in fresh tar."[14] But Patri responded calmly, and Father Cafuzzi, who knew the neighborhood well, helped him deal with such obstreperous children and their puzzled parents. One angry mother started to complain about a teacher, but, Patri wrote, "I spoke to her in Italian and at the first syllable her wrath vanished. We understood each other." He asked at the end of his first day in this school: "Would the years teach what the days did not know? They must." Patri's sensitive understanding of children, parents, and community would help him to succeed in his thirty-one years at PS 45. (27, 33)

In his previous school Patri had dealt mostly with children and families who conformed to school expectations, but "in this new school #45 there was a different set of racial ways of learning and books did not, as a rule, belong with the things that held much interest." He advised an angry, frustrated teacher: "Begin with what they know and go on from there. . . . Begin at the place where the children are. . . . The children will respond." Another teacher was trying to teach Nick to spell. Patri asked what Nick was interested in, and the teacher said "horses." Patri asked, "Why not combine his love of horses with his spelling? Let him spell all the words that have to do with horses. . . . Follow Nick's way and he will learn." (35–38)

The new school had rooms for woodworking, cooking, printing, sewing, science, drawing, music, physical activity, all, as Patri wrote, "calculated to give the children a chance to do and to learn through doing." (39) But instruction in these workshops was sometimes as dull and routinized as that in the regular classrooms. Standardized district tests frightened students, but intimidated teachers even more, for their evaluations depended on their students' scores. Students skipped school and some dropped out as soon as they could. Patri saw uniformity as the problem: "The conditions I faced were insistent but not unique. They existed in most schools. . . . The same rigid course of study, the same stereotyped supervision, the same time schedule, the same group grading, the same examinations, the same teacher training, the same equipment, the same results." Patri persuaded his staff to loosen up, to be more flexible, and to make realistic demands of the students. "Slowly the children began to respond and discipline was shifted—a little—from the backs of the teachers to the backs of the children, a tiny step ahead, so tiny it hardly counted." (45–46)

Patri had written his master's thesis on "Educational Forces Outside of the Public School" and knew that some school problems had to be approached through the community: "During that first year I lived as much in the street and in the neighborhood as I did in the school. I not only wanted to know the teachers and the children, I wanted to know the people." He talked with the restaurant owner, the tailor, the doctor, and the street cleaner, and said, "I would meet the priest on his rounds, for he seemed to live more in the homes of the people than in the church and I would ask his help with some of the parents who seemed indifferent. . . . By and by everybody knew me a little and I knew them. I searched out the neighborhood leaders and discovered a goodly group of them. These I invited to school for evening meetings in my office. We talked about politics, business, neighbors, and always came back to the school and the children."[15] (47–48)

Neighborhood patriarchs wanted to maintain cultural control: "The fathers that met in my office did not want their women to be present at these evening meetings, and, too, they were resentful if any parents came from out of the narrow limits of the settlement." But occasional meetings led to useful suggestions. A violinist with the Metropolitan Opera proposed a concert at the school, persuaded twenty-five of his colleagues to participate, and arranged for singer Giovanni Martinelli to perform.

The music continued late in the evening, and "when audience and artists alike could stand no more there was handshaking and congratulations and thanks and nobody remembered where anybody else lived or what language they spoke, for everybody understood the language of music." (49, 51)

At the end of the first year in PS 45 Patri took stock: "Yes, I had something to show for a year's work in the new school, the concert which was a symbol of a neighborhood unity that was to support the life of the school through the years of my stay there. I was at home among friends." (51) Joseph L. Taylor, who had been Patri's supervisor at both PS 4 and PS 45 attested to Patri's success near the end of that year: "When new Public School 45 was ready for occupancy I asked Mr. Patri to organize it for me. . . . He has already found time in his new situation to bring into being a very vigorous parents' organization, a savings bank, and to break up gang rule in his neighborhood." [16]

. In spite of success, criticism followed Patri. At the end of that year a member of the Board of Education, Frank Wilsey, wrote to Rabbi Stephen Wise, asserting that "a candidate for any position in the New York Public Schools . . . should be a man loyal to his superiors; one who will do his duty as it is assigned to him, and not everlastingly self-seeking. . . . Mr. Patri has not in him the qualifications that go to make up the type of man that should have authority over principals, teachers, and children. . . . I do not believe that he should ever have aspired to be other than a teacher." [17] Clearly Patri was out of step with some representatives of the "One Best System" ordained by the central Board of Education, and he would be even more out of step when the Gary plan came to PS 45 the next year.[18]

For years schools had survived by just passing unprepared students along until they got discouraged and dropped out. But in 1913, the year Patri took over PS 45, the New York legislature passed a law requiring attendance until age sixteen.[19] Many students held in school by the new law resisted the dull, passive, didactic rote teaching to which they were subjected. Patri responded characteristically: "It was time, as John Dewey put it, that the active way of learning, the child's way of acquiring knowledge instead of the teacher's way of imparting information, became the basic principle, if the children were to grow in grace and power." But Patri realized that "Dewey was still miles away from the teacher's desk. The idea that each child be given the education he could take was strange. . . . The idea that the whole child went to school and that each child was different was hard to accept. . . . " (54–56)

Patri again had to go beyond the local schools for help. "In our meetings, then as now, there was persistent discussion as to what to do with the non-conforming child—how to direct, discipline, teach him. We had little faith in special classes and hardly any faith in the truant officer. We felt that segregation was not the answer. . . . Then it was that I visited the Vineland Training School for feeble-minded children. I know that 'helping the helpless often led to ways of helping those who were normal and the normal child was my business.'" Patri followed the school principal, Dr. Johnstone, around the school and saw teachers starting with whatever abilities children had and building from there. Patri concluded that "if these helpless ones could be taught to do and to serve and to think and to grow stronger each day, any child, all children could be taught." (59) Dr. Johnstone became another of Patri's educational heroes.[20] (56–59)

Patri was concerned about the flight of families to private schools: "Those who had means, and among them were a few superintendents in the city schools, continued to send their children to private schools which offered the opportunity of growth through freedom, individual instruction that would develop each child's gift, and association with children of fine social or religious circles. All the while John Dewey's ideal that the public school should be the best school that the best parent wanted for his children was preached far and wide as sacred doctrine." (62–63)

Patri became principal of PS 45 in September 1913. Just two months later an anti-Tammany reformer, John Purroy Mitchel, was elected mayor of New York on a fusion ticket, and he promptly undertook a number of reforms, concentrating particularly on the hide-bound, bureaucratic school system.[21] Patri recalled Mitchel vividly "He was young, enthusiastic, unafraid, and promptly tackled the problem of the schools. . . . He appointed a committee, not once again to investigate the city schools, for this had been done repeatedly, and recommended changes ignored, but to search for, and if possible find, somewhere in our country, a system of public schools in which common education, public school education was good, as good as the best that private schools said they were offering." They met with unusual success. "The committee set out hopefully. They returned triumphant. They had found the schools, they had found the man who had put theory into practice." The schools were in Gary [Indiana], the man was William Wirt and, they added, 'We have hired him to organize and guide our first steps in bringing about a basic change. We have tentatively selected the places where the experiment is to be tried out.'"[22] (63–64)

PS 45 was one of the schools selected, and Patri was sent to Gary to see the schools in action. He saw "playgrounds aplenty, buildings new and modern, gymnasiums, swimming pools, shops of all kinds—metal, wood, clay, sewing rooms, kitchens, art rooms, dining rooms, libraries, auditoriums big and little, music rooms, study rooms, classrooms, laboratories, museums—each school plant I saw was an answer to prayer, all that a school master could wish and more than a school principal in a large city had ever dreamed he would see and hope to get." [23] (66)

Wirt came to New York in the fall of 1914 and told Patri that his first job was to "make the school program." Patri resisted at first, wanting the program to grow out of the experiences of his staff and students. But after discussion Patri agreed to Wirt's plan, saying to him: "I hope to break the mold. We can start with your program, but, as I am assured of a free hand, it shouldn't be long before your program is considerably modified." Wirt concurred: "Once the change is made you'll be on your own." Patri asked if that was a promise, Wirt said it was, and "and so far as William Wirt was concerned, it was kept to the letter and the spirit." (67–68)

Patri had found yet another educational hero and devoted a whole chapter to Wirt, his ideas, and his schools. "I had known Fripp who ran a good old school, Dewey who promised a good new one, and now here was Wirt who had set up a school in a new city that combined the strength of the old and the promise of the new. Over and over I had heard the criticism, 'Dewey is a dreamer, forget him. His School and Society will not work—not in a public school.' But here was Dewey's idea, as I understood it, applied to a school system in a growing city on a scale sufficiently large to command respect. What could not be done was being done, and New York City was taking notice." (69) Wirt had studied under Dewey at the University of Chicago, as Patri had at Columbia, and the fact that both men were followers of Dewey may have contributed to their compatibility.[24]

Patri enthusiastically described Wirt's vision and the Gary schools that made it real. The schools were community centers drawing in parents and the public. They provided workshops in many fields appealing to the varied interests and skills of the students. But the three R's were not neglected: "Naturally the school must have its books, for through them the child acquired the culture of the race and made the discovery that he stood not alone, a more or less accidental chip tossed on the edge of time, but a distinct person, the heir of endless centuries of culture, with roots as deep as time itself and a responsibility that stretched beyond his life span. Acquisition of the basic three R's, of formal knowledge, accuracy in using the tools of learning was vitally important." (76)

Writing in 1955, eleven years after his retirement, Patri recalled: "These were the Gary schools I saw on my visit that long ago day, some forty years ago. Wirt, who, in the eyes of the committee had translated theory into practice, was the man that New York City hired to come to its aid and do what should be done to make the schools of the city the kind of schools that 'the best parent would want for his children.'[25] But it was one thing to install this program in Gary—a new city without New York's ossified practices—and quite another to transform an old school system, set deep in tradition and too often deep in politics." (78–79) Patri described the challenges of changing PS 45 into a Gary School, an effort that began in February 1915.[26] He understood the reasons for teacher traditionalism, but said, "I hoped that some of my teachers would take fire from this new venture into unknown paths and make 'a child-centered school' out of the teacher-centered school." (81)

A playground and garden were created with the assistance of various city agencies that were "willing to help because this was a school in which the Mayor and the new members of the Board of Education were interested." (84) By taking over unused land "the school had acquired a city block as a playground and half a city block as a garden." The school cellar was divided into a "wood-work shop, a print shop, a pottery shop, in one corner of which a small class in sculpture found a home. . . . Then by rearranging the classrooms it was possible to install a service kitchen, two art rooms, a sewing room, a millinery class."

Changes in the use of space brought personnel changes: "With each new activity came a new teacher. . . . In place of sixty teachers there were seventy-two. Of these the potter, the sculptor, the sewing teacher, the gardener, the printer, the milliner [and] the carpenter came directly from the trade and brought to the school the naïve attitude that they were there to teach the children to work and to enjoy the experience. . . . In the classrooms for academic studies the children were grouped into traditional grades but in shops, studios, laboratories, gym, playground, the grade groups were ignored and children were together irrespective of grades or ages, irrespective of IQs, an arrangement in which there were four periods when the familiar lock-step was broken." (85–86, 89)

The 2,500 students were divided into two schools, X and Y. The X school began the day in traditional classrooms while the Y students were in workshops, assemblies, or gardens. At midmorning the schools shifted. This new pattern attracted thousands of visitors, who responded with everything from total enthusiasm to complete negativity. Reformers hurried to extend the new system, while traditionalists resisted. Patri saw what was happening: "And soon, too soon, it was plain that the struggle between the promise of the new and the sureness of the old would center, not in what was good in either, but on who would control the school system. The haves and the have-nots were in the ring."[27] (97–98)

In April 1915, only three months after his school shifted to the Gary Plan, Patri met another of his educational heroes. He wrote, "At about that time Dr. Montessori visited PS. # 45, Bronx. She had worked with feeble-minded children and then, interpreting her experiences, had applied her new point of view towards modifying the ways of the public schools in Italy. She had bridged the gap I was trying to span. She felt that the difference between normal and abnormal was one of degree rather than kind, that the ways developed to train the weak might well be applied to the strong, who, in the nature of things, had their own weaknesses. Her emphasis was laid on sense training, on hand training, as a necessary background to understanding what the books said.

"During her visit we talked about schools in general, how rigid they were and how difficult the job of teaching. 'Your children, for the most part,' said she, 'have a heritage of people who have lived close to the soil. They won't get anything out of school until it is changed, completely changed, changed to suit their nature.' 'Quite so,' I answered, 'Dr. Johnstone, Dr. Dewey, in effect say the same thing. But when?' and my impatience was plain." Montessori, a bit older and more experienced than Patri, encouraged him to be patient and quoted a peasant adage: "Aspetta cavallo che cresce l'erba." She translated, "The horse waits till the grass grows," adding her own reminder that "the grass does grow, even though the waiting hurts." But Patri, intensely aware of the desperate needs of his students, replied: "I can't wait, the children can't wait. Waiting is waste." Patri ended his description of Montessori's visit: "In Italy she had criticized severely the rigidity of the public schools. She told me with scorn of the apparatus in the school gymnasiums that had been built especially to straighten backs curved into rigidity by sitting too long at school benches. She had rebelled against the old book school and set up new teaching techniques, established kindergartens in Rome's city housing projects and all the time proclaimed the importance of hand training for all children." (60–61)

Rita Kramer, Montessori's biographer, adds to Patri's recollections. She reports that when Montessori came to New York in 1915, she visited only two educational experiments: first, Montessori classes in a housing project and then PS 45. Kramer wrote that Montessori "talked with principal Angelo Patri, a popular education writer of the day, about the Gary system then being introduced into the public schools, praising the newly installed workshops and gardens that were part of the Gary Plan." Montessori told Patri: "You are preparing children to meet the realities of life," and later added, "The mere habit of obedience is not preparation for life in a democracy. . . . The safety of democracy depends on the intelligence and independence of the voters. Intelligence can be developed only by allowing young people to deal with actual life problems."[28]

The month after Montessori's visit, Patri participated in a conference on the Gary Plan sponsored by the Public Education Association. A
New York Times report on the meeting said of PS 45: "The Gary system,
which includes vocational training in all classes, is being tried out in the
Bronx School, and Mr. Patri gave it his enthusiastic indorsement. He
said that under the plan 'not only was it possible to provide space for all
of the children, but that the children were happier and got more enjoyment out of life, as well as a training which would be useful to them. The
parents also indorsed the system,' he said. In explanation of how the system operated, Mr. Patri said the use of playgrounds, shops, gymnasiums,
and auditoriums made it possible to accommodate many more pupils in a
school plant than at present, by alternating groups of children throughout the day so that some might always be using the school's work study,
and play facilities." Willard Wirt and others also explained the system,
and John Dewey sent a letter of support, but the identification of part of
the program as "vocational training," may have contributed to the loom-
ing conflict over the plan.[29]

Patri and his staff modified the Gary program to accommodate increased enrollments. Two hundred older students were recruited to help
younger pupils in classrooms, and teachers appreciated the assistance.
Students came to the school to work with specialists like the sculptor,
and programs were adapted for them. Patri reminisced in his lyrical
style: "After all these years I still see that host of children hastening
to their chosen work as if they had just come parched out of a desert
and suddenly found themselves facing a bubbling spring, ready to satisfy
a thirst that years of bareness had made habitual and unendurable. . . .
And the old classroom lessons were not unaffected. They too began to
take on an aliveness, a new sense of values." But Patri was still worried:
"Would the pressure of criticism that began slowly, doubtfully rise to
hurricane proportions? This I feared and I prayed in patience that the
struggle between the reformers and the stand-patters would not wreck a
promising educational venture."[30] (105–107)

Patri's anxieties were justified. "The City Superintendent, over
whose opposition the experiment had been instituted, chose to visit the
school on the day he had assigned for city-wide tests. . . . I am not sure
yet whether he came to see that I was following his orders or to see what
the new program was like, forgetting the orders he had issued. . . . When
he made a report of his findings to the Board of Education he said, 'All
I saw was children writing (making no mention that the writing was his
order), some playing outdoors, and a few digging rubbish in an empty

lot. If digging rubbish in an empty lot is this new kind of education I do not want any of it for the schools of my city." [31] (110)

The battle over the Gary program began, and Patri quoted an editorial from the *Evening Mail* that described Tammany's cynical exploitation of working-class fears: "New York is going to school. Long a truant and incorrigible, the City has finally been stirred up over the Work-Study-Play or Gary system, and isn't missing a session. Politics is the truant officer in the situation. For Tammany what's the issue? Gary is the perfect set-up. It fits like the skin to a sausage. Rockefeller, capitalistic, making workers out of the city school children. Phrases that flip well from Tammany lips." (112) The Bronx Chamber of Commerce joined the struggle, declaring: "The Gary School is an obstacle to the Americanization of our foreign pupils. To please the foundations the city officials are making cheap laborers of our children and cutting every child off from the right to become a great man and a thinker of his own." (113)

Patri reported one encounter with those who feared that the Gary schools were training such "cheap laborers." A printer official brought a group of men to PS 45, and "even before he had seen the school, announced that since we were training children for the trades, for the factory, he and his union were against it. 'You are wrong,' I explained, 'we are not teaching trades. We are giving children needed experiences that help them to a surer understanding of the world they live in. We are trying to supply in school experiences comparable to those the children of an older day shared in the home or the immediate locality.'" [32] (114–115) The printers were unpersuaded and the struggle continued.

But supporters of the plan were equally active: "As part of the propaganda the followers of Wirt, whose hopes of getting into the school system depended on the re-election of Mayor Mitchel, got Theodore Roosevelt to visit the school." (117) A *New York Times* reporter said that Roosevelt was introduced to Patri and then taken on a tour of various workshops. He visited the pottery shop, the music room where students were singing "America," a shop where a poem in his honor was being printed, and saw classes in domestic science, sewing, drawing, and regular academic subjects. Roosevelt then called for "giving the Gary system a thorough trial here. Public school pupils should also be taught to work with their hands as well as their brains. My own sons were instructed in mechanics as well as in book learning, and their mechanical education is now standing them in good stead in the war zone abroad." By connecting it with the war effort, Roosevelt made the strongest patriotic case he could for the Gary system, but he also made unhelpful comparisons between the Gary School and private schools, and the war of words continued.[33]

Patri reported the next skirmish in that war: "The United Neighborhood Parents Association appeared, and as a result of their visit announced boldly 'This kind of a school impairs discipline, diminishes the health and the efficiency of children. It is a sinister plan to prevent giving the children a full and complete education.' " (118) Some challenges also came from the high schools. Patri was upset that students who had done advanced study in his school were required to repeat the work when they moved on to high school. "Italian, as a foreign language, had been introduced into the school beginning in the seventh grade, five times a week for those who chose it. By graduation time students . . . took State Regents usually given to those taking two years of High School Italian. They passed as I was sure they would. When these graduates presented their credentials, the high school authorities refused to accept the record and insisted that the children be put with the first year Italian language group." (120–121)

A few parents, wanting only academic studies for their children, objected to having them work in the garden or shops. An artist father insisted that his son not study art, which, he knew from experience, would lead only to a lifetime of penury. But amidst such discouragement Patri took heart from the observations of visitors like philosopher Irwin Edman, Dewey's colleague at Columbia. Edman was impressed by the enthusiasm and good work of students in the gardens and shops, but noted: "When I began to worry about the three R's I was escorted to the old fashioned classrooms where this old fashioned routine was going on—lessons were heard, examples solved, maps drawn, penmanship conducted, just as well as any I did in my day. The children's education was not being cramped but expanded." (132; quoted from *Tribune* story.)

But Tammany and its allies continued their attack on the Gary system, and Patri was called before a Bronx Grand Jury to explain what his school was attempting to do. Did the school teach trades? Patri replied: "No. It is true that we have carpentry, gardening, printing, pottery, dress-making and a lot of other activities but they are not to teach trades but to enrich the child's experiences so that the things he studies are all the more significant." (134). After further questions and discussion, the session concluded, and Patri left, thinking he had been "given a fair hearing and a sympathetic understanding." But just before the mayoral election the jury's findings were published, stating that "the work-study-play school ideas were undeveloped and entirely unadapted to the requirements of a city community."[34] (135B)

Patri deeply resented the negative impact of politics on schools, children, and teachers: "There are problems that elections do not solve. Education in a big city is one of them. How could a mayor who knew little about schools, less about the way children grow, and nothing at all about good teacher leadership, be anything but what he was—a politician who, the election won, would reward his friends, push aside his opponents, and forget about the children and the schools? In my forty-seven years as a teacher this was the pattern; the only exception was Mayor Mitchel and he was beaten before he started. Patri mangled a metaphor in order to describe his experience: "Two currents moving in opposite directions had met head-on. I was in the middle of the whirlpool. Could I save the school and maintain my self-respect? Now that the pressure of opposition was on I must stand firm for what I believed, even if, like a cat, I must crawl up a tree and bide my time." (136)

The Tammany forces won the 1917 election and John Hylan became mayor. Patri summarized the next developments: "The election over, the school politicians proceeded to do the tangible, practical things they knew well to do. A new Board of Education was appointed, a new City Superintendent installed, new promotions for the faithful, word sent out to do away with the Gary experiment so that the schools might settle down into their accustomed ways."[35] Local events were overshadowed by larger ones when, in April 1917, America entered the World War and the school took part in the war effort. Patri explained the school's response and its effect: "I had acquired much goodwill during the war in which my school had naturally shared." A rally in the school playground had raised $120,000 in war bonds. The school gardener acquired forty acres of land that was used by neighbors for victory gardens. Teachers helped families with nutrition advice, with repairing clothes, with carpentry projects. The school was open from eight in the morning until ten in the evening, helping children and families deal with the problems caused by the war.

Patri described his mixed feelings: "We detested war and had no good word for those who had brought it upon us but we shared the responsibilities it imposed . . . . [W]e used the opportunities and the facilities of the Gary plan to carry a share of the load." And even in the midst of all this political and wartime furor the school quietly progressed. In 1917 the school expanded with an annex, a room for school lunches, and an indoor swimming pool, and in 1919 a ninth grade was added.[36] (136–137)

Patri and his wife lived near his school as they had when he was principal of PS 4. Although they had no children of their own, they often had the children of relatives and friends staying with them. Patri wrote: "During these years of experiment in the school and war outside it, my home had become a hive of activity." A committee met to raise scholarship funds to send Anthony Piccirilli to Europe to study sculpture. "The restaurant man might come on Friday evening and cook us an Italian dinner. Mr. Greco, another neighbor, would come on a Sunday and polish the furniture. The school neighbors were my friends and I was theirs, and through them the school and its teachers had become more important than the price of artichokes!" (140–141)

While Patri grew even closer to his community, he was alienated from many of his superiors in the school system. One supervisor, whom Patri called "Mr. Busybody," kicked a boy's books down the stairs and lied to Patri about it. He made up gossip and alienated teachers from one another and from Patri, until finally some "unknown friend" in the schools had him transferred. A member of the new Board of Education visited, obviously looking for trouble and criticized some good teaching that he didn't understand. Patri explained how he dealt with such negative experiences: "That day after school I walked home. It's a habit of mine that whenever I feel unhappy, have an unpleasant experience, to forget I try walking. I walk until the thing that's bothering me comes clear again. . . . I walked on along the avenue of elevated pillars, the cars thundering over my head, not heeding but thinking 'Yes. The Gary plan and what we are doing with it are good. It could be better if the authorities would stop nagging, forget and lend a hand, but whatever happens I hold on. The school must not be swept into the discard.'" [37] (154)

Patri and his staff did hold on and continued to make changes to benefit the pupils. Their child-centered approach to teaching made the school a good place also for teacher-education students. In 1923 New York University arranged to have PS 45 used as a summer "demonstration and observation school" for students preparing to be elementary teachers. A *New York Times* article said that the teachers enrolled would have the "advantage of noting the most modern method of handling the subject matter in relation to its acceptance by the child." [38]

In spite of success and recognition, rumors spread that administrators planned to take the tools and machines from the workshops, dismiss shop teachers, and transfer the principal. Patri wrote: "The rumors reached the few outside friends who had seen the school at work and were anxious that this one school be saved out of the wreck, and they asked the State Superintendent of schools to appoint a commission to examine the school and pass on their findings. (156–157) A committee consisting of two superintendents, a principal, and a deputy state commissioner "for two weeks lived in the building, visiting, examining, noting, asking questions of the teachers and, occasionally of the principal, and in silence departed. . . . I never saw the report they made, but no equipment, no teacher was transferred. . . . Then one day I received an anonymous telephone call to the effect that there was, on the City Superintendent's desk, an order for my transfer, which was to be made quietly and promptly at the Board meeting next day. I promptly called the City Superintendent and told him what I had heard. . . . What could he do? The transfer, if made, must be made without my knowing. But I did know and there would be a fuss, for I too had friends, so he finally said, 'That is not so. No transfer will take place.' (157–158) I accepted his word and that was the end of that. But the supervisors who came my way were given to understand that there was to be no let-up until the Gary program was abolished completely." (158)

Amidst all these changes Patri was called before a committee of the Board of Supervisors and asked why teachers and students were allowed to deviate from the city-approved curriculum. Patri patiently explained, program by program and teacher by teacher, but committee members asked: "Do you think you are running a private school? This is a public school. You are part of a great system. You are not alone." Patri saw that this was "an invitation to come back into the fold," but asked: "How could I, having always and by nature been out of it? . . . When I had to make a change, I did, but for the most part the change of a name sufficed. Dramatics as a regular activity was out but as a club activity it would pass. When some queer looking phase of the program was questioned I said it was a special program to meet the needs of the child in question." (167–168)

Writing in retirement Patri recalled intensely the conflict and struggles of this period and the hostility of his superiors. But even while they criticized Patri and his practices, district administrators supported building programs through which, between 1917 and 1920, the school grew from forty four classrooms to sixty eight. The addition of the ninth grade brought the school total to 4,000 students. It is likely that, despite administrators' disapproval of Patri's programs, they supported the school because it helped solve problems caused by tighter compulsory education laws and increased enrollments.[39]

Patri's recollections of the elementary years at PS 45 (1913–1929) were, while occasionally defensive, mostly hopeful and positive. Patri wrote in the memoir a series of persuasive success stories, and he shared with students, parents, and teachers honor for the successes. But we must look beyond Patri's memoir to place the Gary school struggle in broader educational and historical perspective. The Gary Plan was the best-known and most controversial educational innovation of this period, and was assessed favorably by John and Evelyn Dewey in *Schools of Tomorrow*, by Randolph Bourne in *The Gary Schools*, and by many other writers.[40] Diane Ravitch reported that before the Gary Plan ninety percent of the 3,000 students of PS 45 had attended only part time. She wrote that Wirt "set up a duplicate school plan, lengthened the school day, and put all the children on a full-time schedule. . . . While half the students were in regular classrooms, the other half were either in the auditorium, on the playground, on excursions, in manual-training class, or working on gardening, pottery, carpentry, sewing, cooking, or printing. Gardening classes worked on beautification projects in Bronx parks."[41]

According to the leading historians of the Gary system, Ronald Cohen and Raymond Mohl, "the principals of the schools in which the plan was first tried, Alice E.B. Ritter of P.S. 89 and Angelo Patri of P.S. 45, were . . . enthusiastic supporters. Both spoke out for the Gary schools in local neighborhoods, at parent-teacher meetings, in reports to supervisors, and in letters to newspapers."[42]

One observer wrote in 1917 that "before the Montessori method of kindergarten and primary work, which frees the child, had come to this country, and before Gary, Indiana, had put the Wirt School Plan into practical operation, Mr. Patri successfully fought with his critics and superiors, interested himself in the community, surrounded himself with efficient teachers and experimented with educational methods, until he had created a school that served the immediate needs of the children and was in fact, not in theory, a communal center."[43]

The picture of the school as "a communal center" had been confirmed in 1917 in Randolph Bourne's admiring review of *Schoolmaster*. Bourne, a leading young intellectual and progressive, wrote: "Angelo Patri came out of Little Italy. He knows from his own experience the life that is behind the children who throng the city schools. There was no one better fitted than he to know how much the congested city home needed the ministrations of the school, and how effectively the school could spread out its functions until it touches and stimulates the home. Mr. Patri's school, P.S. 45, in New York city, has been known to everyone as one of the most successful results of the Gary experiment there . . . . The Wirt idea was easy to apply because Mr. Patri had been working along the same lines. The extension of the city school is one of those fertile ideas that leaders with a love of the people and a sense of children's needs devise independently of each other. . . . The conjunction of Mr.

Wirt and Mr. Patri has produced one of the most interesting and vital-
izing city schools in the country."[44]

To get outside impressions of Patri's work after the Gary crisis we
must depend on the reports of writers like Ida Tarbell. Tarbell, who had
been one of America's leading muckraking journalists, in 1922 made an
extended visit and wrote for popular *Collier's* magazine a glowing description and evaluation of the school and its principal. In an article titled
"The Man Who Discovers Children," Tarbell described the gardens, the
shops, the academic classes, and other elements of the program, but concluded that it was the strong links with families and the neighborhood
that made the school successful. To the author this meant that "School
No. 45 has the neighborhood behind it, with it. That for the neighborhood, as for the children, it is 'Our School,' and that the neighborhood
and the children know that if it is to be kept so each must serve it, work
with it, take it as something of his own to defend, help, stand by." Tarbell
noted that Patri was consistently supportive of parents: "One of the real-
est things School No. 45 is able to do is occasionally to make children
see the value of their parents. Many of these foreign-born fathers and
mothers, handicapped by inability to speak English, to take on American
ways, to 'get on,' come to be half despised by their own children. School
No. 45 knows them. It works itself patiently into the homes, finds the
peculiar talent, skill, knowledge in father or mother, and contrives to
use it. Here is a man who, the school finds, is an experienced gardener.
He is quickly drafted. The teacher holds up his skill to his class. The
children look on with astonishment—and pride: 'Our dad is very fine
man. He know so much the school call him in.' That father has a new
authority now—the school a new ally." Tarbell described Patri's active
recruitment of parents into school activities, but reported that "it was
not until there was need of united action, of a strong front to deal with
the School Board, that those composing his slowly growing group organized, of their own volition, into a Parents' Association. . . . They were
a natural growth—school, parents, neighborhood combined to take care
of their own."[45]

The positive contemporary assessments of the school by visitors like
Bourne and Tarbell no doubt helped sustain Patri and his colleagues
through difficult times and politically inspired criticism. Their patience
and hard work paid off and the critics found other targets: "And it happened that in time eyes that had been centered on me looked elsewhere.
They had to, because once again criticism was being directed at the traditional school, their school, and they must listen and do something about
it. . . . The old school that was not good before the Gary experiment was

not good now that the experiment had been discarded." (167–168) An organizational panacea was chosen—the junior high school. Patri saw that his school had the equipment and personnel to make the new structure work. "If I might hold on to what I had, go along with the new proposal, I might build a good Junior High School. The good I knew, the good I had sweated out of the Gary experiment need not be lost." Patri hated to give up the inclusive K-9 school, but in 1929, with his usual confidence and efficiency, led the transition of PS 45 to the Paul Hoffman Junior High School, including only grades 7–9.[46] (171)

Patri's PS 45 was one exception to conclusions by various historians about the early demise of the Gary Plan in New York. Raymond Callahan's influential book, *Education and the Cult of Efficiency* said: "Two of the most interesting events in the history of the platoon school in America occurred in New York City. One was the introduction of the Gary Plan into the elementary schools, and the other was the consideration of the possibility of introducing a variation of it into the secondary schools. Both of these efforts (but especially the former) became the subject of bitter controversy and when the dust had cleared neither was retained in the schools."[47] Lawrence Cremin concurred, saying that after Gary supporters lost a critical 1917 mayoral election "New York City soon abandoned the Gary reforms." Diane Ravitch also claimed that the election "spelled political death for the Gary plan in New York schools." Raymond Mohl and Ronald Cohen were more specific, saying: "Although surviving in a few schools into the 1920s, for all practical purposes the Gary plan had come to an ignominious end in New York City."[48] In spite of this consensus among leading historians, Patri's memoir shows, on the contrary, that elements of the Gary system lasted in PS 45 through June, 1929 in the K-9 elementary/intermediate school and, as we will see in chapter 6, from September, 1929 to 1944 in the junior high school.[49] Historians may have overlooked this three-decade survival partly because Patri was wise enough to drop the discredited "Gary School" label. His emphasis on the child-centered characteristics of the Plan more than the efficiency elements may also have helped it to succeed and survive.

Some of the positive elements of the Gary program that Patri and his staff had "sweated out" in the elementary school lasted in the junior high until Patri retired in 1944, so I will defer until the end of chapter 6 the explanations for that survival. By 1927 Patri had worked in the New York Public Schools for thirty years and in the spring of that year he and his wife Dora took a trip to France, Switzerland, and Italy, participating in a conference and visiting museums and schools. Since this occurred only two years before the transition to the junior high school, I will include in the next chapter an account of that trip.

Patri talks with students in a millinery workshop

(Frank Merolla)

FIVE

The Promise of Italian Progressivism: Patri Visits Italy in 1927

by Giuseppe Pepe and James Wallace

IN MARCH 2002, I RECEIVED AN E-MAIL MESSAGE FROM *Giuseppe Pepe of Salerno, Italy, inquiring about my research on Angelo Patri; I learned from him that there was a group of Italian scholars who were studying Patri, and I began exchanging information with them. Giuseppe Pepe, Prof. Ambrogio Ietto, and others organized in 2002 and 2003 two well-attended seminars on Patri in Salerno and Piaggine. Pepe has been a teacher and principal in Salerno, and is now an Inspector of Schools, so he, like Patri, may be thought of as a "schoolmaster of the great city." Pepe was studying Patri's 1927 visit to Italy and was familiar with the areas of Italy that Patri visited, so was an appropriate person to write about Patri's trip. At my request Pepe sent me parts of this chapter, which I have edited and extended. He has been very helpful to me on my trips to Italy, and I am now pleased to join him as coauthor of this chapter. Much of this material is quoted from the writings of Giuseppe Lombardo-Radice, the director of elementary education in the Italian Ministry of Education, who was Patri's main host during this trip.[1] The combination of Patri's persistent optimism and Lombardo-Radice's florid Italian style resulted in unusually enthusiastic descriptions of the schools they visited. Sceptical American readers may wonder what the two men did not see, and whether all was as good as it was described.*

Dora Caterson Patri began teaching about 1895 and Angelo Patri in 1897. They married in 1910 while Patri was principal of PS 4, and Dora continued her teaching and administrative work in that school and others. In this two-career family both partners worked hard during the school year, but in the summers they took time for vacations at property they bought at Paradox Lake in northern New York. Patri took a brief trip to

Norway in 1907, just before assuming the principalship of PS 4, but he and Dora had never gone to Europe together until 1927. So when Patri was invited to speak at the Third International Moral Education Conference in Geneva in the spring of 1927 they decided to visit France and Italy as well and have an extended vacation and study tour. What began as a trip for professional purposes became a deeply personal pilgrimage as they journeyed near his birthplace in Piaggine.

Both Angelo and Dora were lovers of art, and they visited museums at all their stops. Giuseppe Lombardo-Radice later reported a story Patri told from their Paris visit: "One day with a group of Americans, he was visiting a museum in Paris, guided by a very cultured young Italian interpreter explaining the works of art. Patri was the only one of the group who spoke Italian and, recognizing that the interpreter was from Italy, he addressed him in his mother tongue. The interpreter pleasantly asked: 'Excuse me, but are you American?' 'Yes, I am,' answered Patri. The interpreter did not reply but continued to speak to the group in English. Patri interrupted once again in Italian. The young man stared at him and then exclaimed: 'You studied Italian with Italians or by living among them, didn't you?' 'But of course,' replied Patri. At the end Patri asked for yet another explanation in Italian. Just four or five words; his tone and gestures caused the interpreter to shout: 'I swear by God, you are Neapolitan; and don't try and tell me otherwise!' A burst of laughter from Patri, and the amazement of the bystanders to whom he explained that the youth 'had recognized him as Neapolitan by his hand movements and a few small words.' " Patri had left Italy forty-five years before, but had managed to preserve both his Italian good humor and the purity of his original dialect.[2]

Angelo and Dora traveled on to the conference in Geneva where Patri delivered to an international audience another of his impassioned pleas for schools that focused on experience, not empty words. He reminded his listeners that morality "is not learned by codes and laws and command-ments. It is learned by wholesome firsthand experiences with immutable truths and living people. The right sort of school, the school that will produce people who appreciate moral values and elect to live on ethical principles is the sort of school that will allow a child to work out his own salvation. Work it out through his hands and his tongue and senses and prove its righteousness through service to people." After thirty years of work in challenging city schools, Patri was still maintaining and com-municating his faith in the goodness of children and the ethical power of sound schooling.[3] Angelo and Dora then moved on to Italy.

Patri had followed with interest the "New Education" movement in Europe, particularly the growth of experimental schools. By 1927 the

Fascists had been in power in Italy for five years and had undertaken, under the leadership of Giovanni Gentile, Minister of Education, a program of school "reform," and Patri wanted to know how education in general, and the "new schools" in particular, fared under the new regime.[4] He was in contact with the Italy-America Society, and on February 10, 1927, Irene di Robilant, director of the Society, wrote to Giuseppe Lombardo-Radice, introducing "a famous person from the American educational world. . . . His name is Angelo Patri who, as can be seen from his name, is of Italian origin. He came here as a small boy and never returned to Italy again. He is leaving at the beginning of March with Count Russo in order to visit his father's homeland. Mr. Patri is the principal of a public school in New York which, due to his work, has become a model for this type of institution in this state." She described Patri's work as a writer and speaker, noting particularly the popularity of his newspaper column, concluding that "he is perhaps the only Italian-American who can boast nationwide fame in the States." Di Robilant noted that Patri planned a restful vacation, but that he also wanted to visit some of the new schools in Italy. She concluded: "I take the liberty of warmly recommending this writer to you as his popularity and words may prove helpful in our propaganda and also due to the fact that he is a pleasant character who is an honor to his Italian roots." She asked Lombardo-Radice for his assistance in arranging school visits.[5] Lombardo-Radice, the leading figure in progressive education in Italy, was to be an appropriate guide for Patri, who by then may have been the best-known American public school progressive.

Di Robilant's words "our propaganda" raise a disturbing question: was Patri being used by pro-Fascist groups in America? Di Robilant's language suggests an effort to do so, but I have found no evidence that Patri gave any support to the new regime. Lombardo-Radice reports no political discussions between them. Patri frequently expressed his love for Italy and his support for innovative schools, but apparently avoided the quagmire of Italian-American politics during his visit.[6]

If there was a small political cloud hovering over the plans for the trip, it was not apparent on the visit itself. Lombardo-Radice had become familiar with Patri's writings as early as 1919 and later recalled how he had welcomed Patri's coming: "When Lady Irene di Robilant announced the visit of Angelo Patri and . . . invited me to welcome him, show the Italian school reform to him, and accompany him to various schools, I was more than happy to do so. I had just finished reading the new volumes of Patri's *Child Training* and *The Problems of Childhood*, fruit of his poetic soul which had already given us that fine work entitled *A Schoolmaster of the Great City*." Students and colleagues were undertaking translations of two of Patri's books. "It was therefore a godsend that he arrived in Italy at a time when his works were creating a great amount of interest." [7]

Lombardo-Radice then wrote to his students and colleagues at the Istituto Magistero in Rome: "Angelo Patri will be spending spring here in Italy. He is coming not only to rest but also to visit the homeland of his father, a modest and intelligent Italian worker, described in such an emotional and poetic manner by his son in the book *Schoolmaster of the Great City*, a work which introduced Patri to the Americans." [8]

Segnora di Robilant wrote a second letter, to be delivered to Lombardo-Radice by Patri himself: "Following the letter I sent to you a few weeks ago, I would hereby like to introduce Mr. Angelo Patri, a teacher, writer and renowned American pedagogue. As his name implies, he is of Italian origin, but this is the first time he has visited the country he left when just a small boy. I would like to think that not only will he be able to meet you personally . . . but that he also has the possibility to visit schools and meet the teachers so that he may gather information and impressions which only he will be able to usefully divulge in America." [9]

On arriving in Italy Angelo and Dora probably went first to northern Italy, visiting Florence, Carrara, Pisa, and Pietrasanta, then to Naples and on to Patri's relatives in Rome and Paestum. [10] Lombardo-Radice wrote that in the three months of spring, 1927, together with his wife Dorothy, Patri studied elements of the Italian school system, and that while "Patri observed and meditated, his gentle companion went about collecting memories of more popular things which caught her attention. She accepted and requested pages of children's drawings, particularly from rural schools; she complemented her husband's collection with objects of artistic folklore. Every three or four days enormous packs would be sent to New York." This material was to be used by Patri to "repay his sweet debt of love to the old country of Italy." [11]

Lombardo-Radice did not go with Patri on his first visits to the Roman schools, but Patri talked with him every day, commenting on the attractive classrooms and the surrounding terraces and gardens. These, he said, are "the most beautiful things and you have them in plenty in this grand Rome, but they are nothing compared to the spirit in which the school here is built. It is everything, naturally: the old and the new, old and avant-garde pedagogy are mixed together, because no class resembles the neighboring class (which is a good thing); but everywhere there are refined and elegant methods and love of childhood and serene cooperation among those who direct the school; and beautiful smiling and brotherly faces." [12]

Lombardo-Radice later was able to join Patri on trips to some other Roman schools and to write about the visits. On one memorable expedition Patri learned that his writings were being studied seriously in progressive Italian educational circles. He "visited at length the open school directed by Miss Carmela Mungo, the greatest student of his books." Not surprisingly, Patri was particularly impressed by her new school where he "discovered there a mountain of interesting things: small tables built by the students . . . a parlour in which little ones could meet and converse . . . a song book of carols of the most lively rhythm which the school recorded for him." Lombardo-Radice experienced Patri's intense, affectionate responses: "At each discovery he embraced me as though to say: 'Look, by Jove, what beauty!' " Patri stopped taking notes, preferring to chat with "the little ones who were treating him as though he was an old acquaintance." With his strong interest in physical activity, Patri watched children in the garden working in the flower beds while others were carrying tables to the yard for "serving lunch to the whole happy community." [13]

Patri spent some time at this school and admired "the ceramic factory" so much so that he suggested that the ceramics teacher go back with him to New York and "teach this art to the teachers of his school." Lombardo explained to Patri that what he was seeing was "one of the effects of the popular school of art of the 'Master of the Walls,' the venerable Randone, from which Montessori had taken the happy idea of making ceramics in the 'House of the Little Ones.'" Here again Patri encountered the good influence of Maria Montessori, whose visit to his school in the Bronx twelve years earlier he happily recalled. [14]

Near the Colosseum was Patri's favorite among the schools he visited: the "Open School" headed by A. Baiocco, which Patri saw as "one of the most beautiful schools in the world." [15] Lombardo-Radice's description of the school make it sound much like PS 45: the pupils "become collaborators in decorating the halls of the school, and the works of the pupils, under glass, are substituted for the bare walls." Patri may have thought of his beloved workshops as he saw students ironing, washing, working in the garden, and helping in the kitchen and dining room, with older pupils assisting younger ones throughout the school. Lombardo-Radice wrote: "As for teachers, Baiocco proceeds like Patri in his old school: utilize for all the classes their specialties. . . . It is the rule that every teacher, besides running his own class, contributes work of general utility." [16]

Their most significant meetings took place in the Roman countryside. Lombardo-Radice wrote that he and Patri preferred the country to the city, because in the Campagna "it is possible to evaluate what has been accomplished in recent decades." In his reference to "decades" Lombardo-Radice was pointing out that most of the innovations they would see started long before the Fascist "reforms" that began in 1923. He explained that Giovanni Cena had influenced many progressives, including Alessandro Marcucci, who had been developing Cena's ideas since 1904. Cena was a poet and novelist who promoted Tolstoyan educational ideas. The early schools he inspired were described as "voluntary guerilla patrols in the battle against illiteracy." Connecting educational reformers in their two countries, Lombardo-Radice wrote that "it was well that the poet of youth, Angelo Patri, should meet the spirit of a poet, of Giovanni Cena." With an Italian rhetorical flourish he declared: "As from the son of a mountain shepherd in Piaggine came the works of love and art of Angelo Patri to create a new life in the modern American school, so was born as the son of a poor village in the Alps the founder of the Schools of the Roman Land which are able to serve as models of country schools everywhere in the civilized world." He contrasted the childhoods of the two educators: "But if Patri the child was saved from unhappiness by the heroic work of his emigrant father . . . Cena instead had a tragic childhood and presented always the appearance of profound pain." From these divergent childhoods in dramatically different locales, both men grew up to become promoters of innovative schools.[17]

Lombardo-Radice introduced Patri, a follower of Dewey, to Marcucci, disciple of Cena. Marcucci then took Patri to ten Cena-inspired schools in the Agro Romano and the Pontine Marshes. Patri was much impressed, saying, "I could not desire anything better in any part of the world. Anyone can come to the Roman countryside to learn."[18] Lombardo-Radice went along on some of the trips, including one to the school at Carchitti (Mezzaselva, or "Midwood"). There Patri told the children a story from his own childhood, but ascribed it to an "Uncle Nicola" rather than to his actual Papa Nicola. The third-grade boys listened carefully and quoted Patri in their diaries as saying that "Uncle Nicola, who had forgotten and left open the barn, found his donkey dead, half eaten by the wolf." Comparing their town with Piaggine, Lombardo-Radice wrote: "In such a home of wolves Carchitti grew, a hamlet of shacks of straw, which appeared to other visitors to be a hangout of brigands." But he reported that "Patri liked the modest rural buildings, perfectly in tune with their surroundings, from the artistic point of view."

Lombardo-Radice described the scene as Patri was warmly welcomed by the two teachers, Felice Socciarelli and his wife Irene Bernasconi: "When we arrived the teacher's wife . . . was directing a chorus of sixty children from the infant school, while at the same time cradling her suckling child in her arms, with her other little girl, two years of age, perhaps, holding on to her skirt, following the march and song. Her only help in looking after the sixty children was a fourteen-year-old country girl." Lombardo-Radice saw this as a model school: "In no city can one find children of a kindergarten more beautiful in order, cleanliness and educational kindheartedness." [19] Patri handed out a large pack of candy which he had brought and was soon surrounded by the group of sixty children. The scene was so vivid that Lombardo-Radice wished he had been an artist: "What a shame that I was unable to make a drawing of . . . the teacher-mamma, her choir and Patri in amongst them all like a visiting uncle, loaded with gifts, in a crowd of young ones." [20] Noting the large numbers of students the teacher had, Patri thought back to PS 45: "And we complain about forty or thirty! . . . I would like to bring my grumbling teachers here and learn from this young mamma from Ticino how to work with joy in one school! This is a miracle!" [21] After visiting the "modest little cottage" of the teachers, with its library of some five hundred books of poetry, history, and philosophy, Patri said that "his visit to Mezzaselva had been the most instructive of the visits he had made in his long career as teacher and organizer of schools." [22]

Lombardo-Radice made it clear that the good teaching Patri saw was the result of innovation that long preceded the educational policies initiated four years earlier under Giovanni Gentile: "Let us take, dear readers, Patri's praise for the new school of Italy, as an admonition, rather than a reward. Yes, we have this great beautiful and terrible responsibility not to spoil the work begun so well in our schools in the past twenty years. . . . And so, not to waste it, it is necessary to remember that educational work is by nature slow, patient, modest, and delicate. . . ." [23] Lombardo-Radice, a Socialist, "firmly and explicitly rejected the Fascist label given to the Gentile reform," saying: "I hope Italians realize that that description cannot be applied to the reform of elementary education." [24] The progressive reforms of the new education were consistent with parts of Gentile's reforms, but not with the political elements, most of which were injected later.

Given the disastrous effects of Fascism on Italy and the world, it is important to see this in context. Denis Mack Smith, a leading scholar of Italian politics, notes: "The education act of 1923 sponsored by Gentile was passed before Mussolini developed ideas of his own. . . . It stressed the value of humanist education and promoted the teaching of philosophy at every level." In spite of later misuse, "Gentile's reform contained few of the usual fascist banalities, and it helped to preserve some independence of mind in education during the dark days to come." So there was space in the system, at least at the elementary level, for the continued existence of the kind of schools that Lombardo-Radice took Patri to see.[25]

Patri told Lombardo-Radice that at Mezzaselva he had momentarily relived the magical atmosphere of his own childhood amidst the mountains of Piaggine. Knowing their plans, Lombardo-Radice started to show Angelo and Dora how to get to Piaggine through Paestum, and was surprised to learn that they had already been to Paestum. Patri explained: "I wished to see the places my father passed, driving down his flocks from the mountains of Piaggine to winter on the plain near the shore. I was moved like a child and no longer had the courage to continue my pilgrimage." Lombardo-Radice observed that Patri had "come to rest in his native countryside. Those emotions, so strong, did not help. The physician had recommended absolute mental rest."[26]

Patri had earlier confessed to Lombardo-Radice his intense personal reasons for the trip to Italy. "Never will I be able to pay sufficiently my debt to the country of my birth. . . . I have two fatherlands. I love the new, very, very much, and I can call myself completely American. So it is. But Italy continues to be my land, and I have come to visit it, to retrieve the vague uncertain visions of my early childhood; to look at Italy with the eyes of my father who will not see it again. And then his eyes lighted up with tears, or so it seemed to me."[27] Lombardo-Radice later commented: "They both loved the great historical memorials and much of their time was dedicated to monuments of our great antiquity, to viewing the works of art, medieval, modern, contemporary. . . . But they were really looking for something else, and not schools alone, besides the works of art and the ruins of ancient Rome. This trip was a pilgrimage."[28] One day as they looked at a Roman aqueduct Patri said, "See, Lombardo . . . we Italians know well how to care for and conserve every ruin. Because history is never dead, and memories are the most alive things of a people who are taking part in its actual development. . . . It is easy for you to remain a great people in the new history, because none of the past is lost."

Lombardo-Radice believed that Patri was looking for "the Italian life of the common people in order to find there the *proof* of his faith in the old Italian of Piaggine, son of Nicola the digger, the wall-builder; of Nicola the player of the flute to the stars, the teller of the tales of the knights, the singer of the mountain dirges . . . of Nicola, finally, Italian, coming down through the centuries, traveling the centuries with tranquil, serene security."[29] Patri's guide felt that in looking for "the son of Nicola" Patri was searching for himself—for that part of himself that was deeply and permanently Italian.

Later some men who had met Patri told Lombardo-Radice that "a gentleman staying at Paestum talked with them, asking about Piaggine and the Conte family. At a certain point he was moved to weep like a baby, hearing that they were neighbors of the Conte family, and thus were relatives." Patri had already gone to see his Conte cousins, on his mother's side of the family, who had moved to the district of Eboli, not far from Paestum.[30] Patri had always kept in touch by writing to Rosa Conte and other relatives in Italy. Rosa gave further details about Patri's visit as well as an account of the feelings and generous actions of her American cousin. She said that Patri decided not to go on to Piaggine partly due to transportation difficulties.[31] The plains of Paestum were linked to Salerno by the railway, but Piaggine was reached only by bad mountain roads. Piaggine is over 2,000 feet above sea level, and Patri, who suffered from pleurisy, would have had difficulty getting there. People in Piaggine had been looking forward to Patri's visit, and Lombardo-Radice wrote that "Piaggine waited in vain, but let Patri know that his own people would never be resigned to not seeing him personally. It is a son whom they await, and the old shepherds welcomed him as a son. He is a teacher whom the good and industrious teachers of Piaggine wanted to receive into their school which is . . . also his, spiritually."[32]

Despite various invitations, Angelo and Dora never had another chance to return to Italy. The death of Lombardo-Radice in 1938 deprived Patri of his friend and guide. But Patri kept in touch with other friends including Biagio Bruno, a Piaggine schoolmaster, until the last few years of his long life.[33] Today, in the small community of Piaggine, one of his generous acts is still fondly remembered. Biagio Bruno wrote about it in 1961 in a newspaper article describing Patri's trip to Italy: "Some years ago he returned to Italy to visit our schools. He was met in Rome by the Prof. Lombardo-Radice who introduced him to the teachers of Piaggine by means of a flattering letter. Before leaving for America, he left a sum of money for a foundation bearing the name of his mother and father 'Nicola and Carmela Patri' and the proceeds of this sum are awarded each year to the best student from his native village. In this way Angelo Patri, through this noble gesture of the foundation, typical of his Italian nature, wished to embed in the hearts of so many children, whether young or old, near or far, the thoughts of an Italian and American Educator who lives with the name of his Homeland engraved on his heart."[34]

There is no record of Dora and Angelo ever returning to Italy or traveling outside the United States. But in 1950, as was recorded in *Biondino*, the schoolmaster in Piaggine asked Patri's permission to name a school after him. It may well have been that request that inspired Patri to write *Biondino*. While the published versions of *Biondino* were addressed "To My Readers," a typescript of *Biondino* in the Library of Congress is addressed "To the Youth of the Elementary School of Pruno." Pruno was the part of Piaggine where the Patri family had its small farm, and it was the Pruno elementary school that was named after Patri. So, although Patri did not get to Piaggine in 1927, memories of him were kept alive there in the name of the Angelo Patri School. (Incidentally, there are now Angelo Patri Schools in Salerno, the Bronx in New York City, and Tacna, Peru.)[35]

Disappointed that they had not been able to get to Piaggine, Angelo and Dora returned to New York, where Patri completed two more years in the PS 45 elementary school and where in 1928 he wrote *Pinocchio in America*. It seems more than likely that Patri's trip to Italy and his return to America inspired him to write this book, with its hints of autobiography. It begins as Pinocchio swims to New York to avoid school in Italy, but ends up in school in America. As I read this charming book I could see "the great building set in a beautiful park" as Patri's school, and I imagined Patri as "the polite gentleman" who met Pinocchio at the school door. A bit later a Patri-like doctor appears "dressed in spotless white," who gives Pinocchio a new coat of paint and advises him: "This is the place to learn. Work hard. Do your very best." This is difficult for the errant Pinocchio, but he struggles, survives, and decides to return to Italy. As his ship pulls out of New York harbor the Statue of Liberty says to Pinocchio: "We are all alike and all different. . . . If you want to be happy, you keep on asking questions of whatever, whomever you meet without ever taking the answers as the last word. Always go ahead to the next one with the next question. In that way you sometimes get new answers and that makes you very happy. You ought to be very happy. Goodbye and good luck to you."

He immediately applied her lesson: "And what," thought Pinocchio, "what do you suppose is behind that?" Patri had enlisted this great American symbol, "Lady Liberty," to communicate this pragmatic, skeptical message to Pinocchio, the classic resistant learner. As for Patri himself, with a strenuous trip behind him and one of his better books published, he would be prepared two years later to work with his faculty and community to help develop PS 45 into a successful junior high school. He had seen the promise of progressivism in several Italian schools and was ready to fulfill a similar promise in his own transformed school with a new population of students.[36]

Patri admiring a student's needlework, PS 45

(Patri Papers)

SIX

Preserving Progressivism in a Junior High School: PS 45, 1929–1944

THE 1929 SCHOOL YEAR BEGAN IN SEPTEMBER, JUST weeks before the great crash that initiated the depression of the 1930s. The general economic depression led to an educational depression as well. Diane Ravitch described what happened in New York: "The Depression's first impact on the schools was crippling, because of a general curtailment of funds: teaching positions were eliminated, programs were cut back or killed altogether; all school employees took salary cuts; class sizes were increased; evening schools, summer schools, athletic centers, and vacation playgrounds lost funds." [1] And, of course, the impact of the depression on children and families was devastating. Families lost income, heat, and housing, and suffered from cold, homelessness, and hunger. Various measures were taken in response, including a School Relief Fund that provided lunch to thousands of children. School personnel, observing daily the plight of their students, gave more than $2 million to the fund. In 1932 *New York Times* reporter Diane Rice interviewed Angelo Patri, who acknowledged the depth of the crisis, but said: "Not in my experience have I seen a more splendid piece of work than the care given the pupils by the teachers during this crisis." Patri thought that most families were coping well, but worried about those most directly affected: "I know of one family where the parents go without necessary food in order to give it to the children." There was increasing theft and truancy, and Patri worried about the future: "If times get worse conditions will get worse and naturally standards will be affected." [2]

Amidst these troubled times Patri and his staff managed to transform Patri's beloved K-9 school into a full-fledged junior high school for students in grades 7 through 9, enrolled in sixty-one classrooms. This was part of an increasing move during the 1920s to establish junior high schools in New York City and throughout the country.[3] In his memoir, written a quarter of a century later, Patri wrote in a resigned spirit: "The break between the Gary School idea and the Junior High School must be accepted. I felt sad about it. I had liked the idea of a school from Kindergarten through the ninth grade. There had been much good that the younger children got from watching and seeing what the older ones did, in the playground, the garden, the mending and repair work, the decorations of the classroom. And there had been much good to the older ones from their contact with the younger group. This attitude had improved not only the classroom work but the all-around behavior. A marked degree of family pride had crept into the daily conversation. . . . The talk at home and in the neighborhood revolved around the doings of the school. With the transfer of the children below grade seven there was a definite loss of strength. But there was no other way of holding some of the major gains that had come out of the Gary experiment." (172) [As before, to minimize notes I will put page numbers from the memoir in parentheses, continue to use Patri's words whenever possible, and make a few corrections.]

"The superintendent with whom I must cast my lot had much skill with a scissors and a glue pot. Nothing wrong about that, but the obligation to understand and carry out in practice the implications of the ideas he had assembled should not be forgotten." (172–173) Patri refers here to William O'Shea, superintendent from 1924 to 1934. Diane Ravitch writes of him: "Even a conservative official like Dr. William O'Shea . . . found it useful to adorn the system's policies in progressive trappings. O'Shea and the progressives in the PEA [Progressive Education Association] shared nothing more than mutual revulsion, yet under O'Shea certain policies were instituted which had progressive roots. Vocational education was expanded; junior high schools were increased, in part to relieve high school congestion, but also to provide a place for the vast numbers of over-age elementary school children."[4] O'Shea might be classified as one of David Tyack's "administrative progressives," but like many such, he was far more administrative than progressive.[5]

Tyack has made a useful distinction between "pedagogical progressives," responsive to the needs of children and communities, and "administrative progressives," who focused on standards, statistics, and efficiency. These categories parallel Lawrence Cremin's "sentimental-ists" (child-centered) and "scientific" progressives. His memoir, like *Schoolmaster*, confirms Patri's role as a child-centered pedagogical pro-gressive who continually critiqued administrative progressives. Patri encountered persistent resistance to his actions: "During my career as a principal there was always someone in authority who objected to what I was trying to do and insisted on my doing what I was told to do." His unconventional approaches were "questioned, criticized, suspected, and disapproved by the school authorities." (1, 17) Patri could not have survived in New York's rigid bureaucracy without the strong parental and community support that he cultivated.[6]

The transformation to the junior high school followed the usual educational pattern: "Many conferences followed, and as the shape of things to come took form we knew that the words were mere window dressing. With each conference the fluid school, the child-centered school vanished in a fog of confused ideas and rigid plans." School lead-ers proposed ability grouping as the panacea. "We were told to classify the children according to their intelligence, as if that were the cure-all instead of the curse it turned out to be." (175) The administration proposed sorting the students into four levels, each with a different curriculum and a different vocational destiny. Detailed courses were developed for each level but the tracking was wrong psychologically and socially: "This thing that we were instructed and ordered to do ig-nored both the nature of the child and the needs of society. It burdened the children with a program that was an affront to them and it embar-rassed society by training its children to fit into a groove which might be nonexistent by the time the child was ready to follow it. . . . Was this class stratification and narrow education anything but a lopsided train-ing for lopsided living?" (177)

Appearance was more important than reality: "The plans piled feet high but the promised new equipment failed to arrive and prop-erly equipped teachers were scarcer than hen's teeth. . . . How did I meet this juggernaut that threatened to plow me under? Here was my way of seeming to conform. I adjusted the monthly reports to show that the Gary plan was out and Junior High School #45 had taken its place. How? By the simple device of renaming the classes already estab-lished. . . . I asked for more teachers and more equipment, and that was a definite sign of acceptance of the order. To my surprise both teachers and equipment were granted without question and the school which had been liberally provided for during the Gary days was the first to get added teachers and equipment." (178–179)

An administrator offered a bookbinding shop and teacher, and Patri eagerly accepted them. The administrator then asked if he wanted "an art weaving class that's coming out of another Gary school that's going back to normal? . . . As there were no funds in the budget for carting the machines involved in the transfer, my school fund furnished it. That was a very concrete sign of my readiness to go along with the system and now there was little need of putting me in my place." So Patri got the equipment and teachers, and "in a short time there were added to a school already rather well equipped, more art rooms, more science laboratories, a library and a librarian, a teacher of dramatics, an additional sewing class, a typewriter room, a guidance teacher transferred from a trade school to help advise the children as to the courses they were to choose." Patri made this counselor's role more child-centered: "With me she would adjust children's programs by fitting the school with its wealth of activities to the needs of the child, instead of fitting children into fixed courses." (180–181) By 1933 there were twenty-four different activities to which she could send students. Among them was the study of Italian, which enrolled 1,124 students—41 percent of the total student body of 2,749. Such enrollments were possible because in 1922 Italian had been recognized as part of the curriculum in New York City, equivalent to other foreign languages.[7]

Patri discovered the advantages of being a sometimes obscure part of a large bureaucracy: "And now there was equipment adequate to meet the needs of the three thousand adolescents that made up the school and that need would not be confined to the prescribed course of study. In a huge system I could count on being overlooked. . . . The 'circumlocution' office was a long way off and could not know, and never did know, what I was doing." Patri described the adolescents of his school, varying in age, interests, and abilities, and affirmed that "the work-study-play program, the Gary program, was made to order for the children under my guidance. Once more, as in the Gary program, the big school was divided into two units and the program was exactly the same as that of the Gary program—namely—five periods of academic work, two periods in a shop, a science or an art room, one period of auditorium and one period of physical training—a school day six hours long." (181–182)

Within that structure, programs were adjusted to fit children's needs and interests. "In a large school variety is possible far more than in a small one. Soon I found that in this school of three thousand adolescents there were not many problem children, many rebels, not more than could be reasonably helped, because once a child found a satisfying routine he was anxious to hold on to it and through it he set in him-self useful habits, developed skill, and was lifted to a place of dignified self-approval." (185–186)

Patri continued to assert that successful schools were teacher cen-tered as well as child centered, and described how he and his teach-ers learned, by working with individual students, to find or create the programs they needed. "It was plain that in trying to meet the prob-lems of the adolescents, teachers were learning fully as much as they were teaching, and that included the principal. The Junior High School working on the Gary plan was becoming not only a good school for the children but for the teachers as well." (201)

Patri, the inveterate story teller, related anecdotes with a recur-rent theme—adjust the school to the child's needs—and occasionally stopped to point out a moral: "To each his chance in the way he was able and ready to take it, and this in a public school of three thousand adolescents, this in a large rigid school system. Why need one despair of public schools, of education? What one teacher can do, what one school can do, others can and in time will. . . ." (208) But ever the real-ist, Patri rarely missed an opportunity to remind teachers not to give children free rein: "The fluid school is not a 'go as you please' school, but a school conscious of the child's needs and eager to find a cure. . . . Dewey's notion that the curriculum was an expression of one's self had meaning, more than a teacher might know—unless experience taught him." (208–209) Patri expressed this same idea in a 1938 letter: "Courses of study . . . are merely the incidents with which we work at times, for the course of study is the organized experiences of the child."[8]

As they visited various workshops Patri and an Australian visitor saw the enthusiasm of teachers and students, but noted that it was a focused enthusiasm that channeled energy into serious, meaningful study. The visitor asked, "How much carryover into academic subjects is there?" Patri answered by explaining changes in the teaching of writing: "In my day, as in yours, learning to write was, for most children, a dreary business. The teacher assigned a topic, a letter, a description, a sto-ry. . . . In my mind's eye all I see as I look back are sheets of paper full of writing and interlaced with red marks to indicate the mistakes." But writing should arise out of student interest: "Of course writing cannot be a matter of set exercises; it is something intimate, personal. Feelings, words, ideas merge, and take form. The corrections, the changes, the formal elements of spelling, punctuation, penmanship must wait until the greater need is satisfied. . . . The teacher guides each child to write a story, to illustrate it and to bind it into a book." (Patri's thoughts on writing are consistent with current literacy research, as Ruth Shagoury shows in chapter 12, below.)[9]

Patri and his guest examined some of the books that students produced, noting how personal interest promoted good writing, careful editing, and imaginative illustration. They read Alex's story of growing up in the province of Basilicata in Italy, and of having at age eight to join the Ballili, the Fascist youth organization. Alex was able to get to America, attend school, and write a small book about his experiences. Another boy, Philip, wrote his book about his main interest, his pigeons. Others wrote about what intrigued them: "Three thousand children each writing a book that he could call his own, keeping it among his precious possessions, is no slight achievement." (218–223)

Given this focus on student interests, it should be no surprise that Patri disliked most tests: "I had little patience with speed tests where the teacher stands over a child, watch in hand, 'Now everybody ready, when I say "go" you start and work as fast as you can.'. . . These tests are not arithmetic. They do not teach, they exhaust children. . . . Arithmetic is an exact and an exacting tool, a most important and perfect tool; it need not be an instrument for torturing children." (230–231).

Responding to conservative misunderstandings of active education, Patri occasionally clarified his position: "I have no quarrel with the book, but with the idea that the book is the beginning and the end of a child's struggle to get learning. . . . The beginning may be a book, or the teacher's lectures, or an experiment or an experience, but the end must be an enthusiastic acceptance of man's attempts to organize the knowledge he has painfully discovered into serviceable form." (242) Patri's hero, John Dewey was more specific about the origins of student inquiry but took it in a similar direction: "The positive principle is maintained when the young begin with active occupations having a social origin and use, and proceed to a scientific insight into the materials and laws involved, through assimilating into their more direct experience the ideas and facts communicated by others who have had a larger experience." [10]

Patri told "how large a part music played in arousing enthusiasm and made so many people—children, parents, teachers, visitors, supervisors—happy." (243) He devoted five impassioned pages to describing, explaining, and defending music as an essential part of good education. He showed how a school orchestra is organized, noting that "it is not the demands of a musical selection that dominates the instruction but what the children are eager to do." And, starting with actual student interests and skills, "gradually the periods of practice lengthen, the daily drill takes root. In a couple of years the school and the parents discover they have an orchestra that plays in tune most of the time, that gets and gives a lot of pleasure to everyone concerned." (244–245) Patri strongly supported school programs in the arts: "The orchestra—the Glee Club which with us numbered some four hundred selected voices, the dancing group, the dramatics—all were part of this thrilling harmony of effort and achievement. The chosen sang, danced, played, acted, and the rest of us were drawn into the charmed atmosphere and breathed deeply and shared happily in this enthusiasm where music was supreme." (248–249)

Patri repeated his call for schools that are both child centered and teacher centered: "The school that captures and encourages the enthusiasm of children, also lifts the teachers out of a drudgery that is oppressive, to a job that is satisfying, and they come to school with eager feet, with a smile instead of a scowl, with hope instead of emptiness, with courage instead of fear, with interest instead of indifference." (249) But Patri knew that, even with student and teacher support, school reform was a long and difficult process. He stood back from his years of experience and saw that "life in P. S. 45 had passed through three stages: One: A more or less routine marked by over-emphasis on discipline as such—where the teacher did the telling and the child the obeying. . . . Routine discipline or routine teaching always had a place in my school, even though it is subordinated and, in time, limited only to what was necessary."

With routine discipline established the school moved to the next stage, the "experimental period. That was long but not too long; a time of many mistakes, of many adjustments, of many heartaches, of some laughter, of full steam ahead and precipitate retreats. But out of it comes an awareness of the unexpected, and courage to take advantage of every opportunity that flashes its signal."

Learning important lessons from the experimental stage, the school moved on to a "stage of relative sureness, where self-control guided effort and measured achievement. It's wonderful to discover that what you want to do can be and is done. This did not mean that as the years rolled on there were fewer problems, in fact there were more, for the world was more unstable and difficulties had piled up. . . . We had learned to move slowly and doubt held promise, for it walked on the feet of hope and experience." (250–251)

Patri described the life of the school in this third stage, when the key was openness. His office was always open and the school at large was open to parents and other visitors. "Teachers in groups from colleges, from near-by school systems, from far countries came as if on pilgrimages. Usually they too stopped to rest, to look around, to ask questions of the white haired principal. . . . Students from fashionable schools dropped in, and they too asked questions and their questions resembled Dr. Dewey's—'Yes—I see fine work here. How do you do it?' Only the children's questions had a personal angle—'Why can't we do these things?' " In the ensuing dialogue a key difference emerged: the visiting students had art, science, or orchestra only once a week. Patri's students had such activities every day for an hour and a half. (252–253)

Visiting teachers described confusion in their own classes after being required by faddish administrators to adopt half-understood activity programs. "Such an interpretation of the activity program, of progressive education, is gross ignorance, and ends, as one teacher put it, in 'Chaos, chaos, Mr. Patri.' . . . Even changes made with good intentions may throw out the good with the bad, confuse the sure ways of learning, overlook the experience of trained teachers, ignore the natural laws of child growth." Patri claimed that by contrast, his faculty was realistic about the needs of children and of society: "In this junior high school that I had come to call ours, progressive education, activity program meant what it said, a satisfying way of learning, growing, living. . . . Education, we felt, must prepare the child so that he is equipped to meet adequately the conditions that life imposes. . . ." (255–256)

The visiting teachers who complained about pseudoprogressive activities were responding to new programs implemented by O'Shea's successor as superintendent, Harold Campbell. In June 1934, six months after becoming superintendent, Campbell appointed a committee "to determine what may be done better to adapt our elementary schools to the varying needs of the children." A long, detailed, first-page article in the *New York Times* described the proposed study in progressive terms, and gave some background for the committee's work: "Under the so-called progressive school system the pupil, rather than the curriculum, is made the centre of activity and close attention paid by his teachers to the pupil's particular aptitude." The article singled out two progressive leaders: "Angelo Patri, principal of Public School 45, the Bronx, for several years has been devoting his energies to the capabilities of his pupils, especially with reference to those with artistic leanings. . . . Professor John Dewey advanced the progressive school idea many years ago in a pamphlet called, 'The Child and the Curriculum.'" [11]

The year 1935 marked the beginning, in sixty-nine schools, of the "activity program" about which Patri's quoted teacher complained. As Larry Cuban reports, it had some successes, but one evaluation showed that even after six years of implementation, "36 percent of teachers in the activity schools preferred the regular program; in regular schools, unsurprisingly, 93 percent favored the regular program. . . . In comparing the supposed benefits of the Activity Program, these teachers remained convinced of the rationality, if not effectiveness, of conventional instruction."[12]

Patri, in his memoir, ignored most of these broader developments, preferring to describe what he and his staff were discovering in years of work at PS 45: "The school with the open door had, through years of trial and error, learned some important things about schools and children. First things should come first. The hand too needs training for the hand is a basic tool. . . . In setting our educational house in order, the development of the thinking hand became important." Patri recounted fifty years of demands that "school be set in a different mold, not the scholar's school for the child, but the work school, a school that is not only a place of books, words, lessons, but a place of shops, laboratories, studios." Thinking back to the heady days of the Gary program, Patri affirmed that Willard Wirt had been "wise in bringing in the cobbler, the tailor, the cook, the gardener, the laborer who used the simple tools to make what was needed. . . ." Patri's "work school" is in the same line of thought as that presented in Theodore Sizer's proposed school forty years later: "The governing metaphor for the school would be student as worker. To learn is to work, sometimes drudgingly, sometimes joyfully."[13] (256–258) Patri understood the need of children to acquire and practice adult skills: "Let the child enjoy the venture of feeling grown up. So set the stage that he not only learns to write, but he is, for a time, a writer, an actor, a dancer, a mathematician, a scientist, an historian, a carpenter, a potter, a sculptor, an orator, a teacher, and this in an atmosphere of reality, the stern master that marks the slow steps in character growth. When we talk of the activity program, the child-centered school, the doing school, we are trying to make clear that the hand must be given an important place in teaching children—all children. That was the idea on which Junior High School #45 based its practices." (259)

Patri recognized the value of voluntary groups and clubs organized for children, but in most schools they met only once a week for a few hours. "How can a once a week meeting compare with the daily program of play, of hobbies, of studies, of moral teaching? An hour or two each week for the few is not what the children of the many need. It is the daily job that counts." Patri was quite willing to expand the role of the school: "With a longer day, shorter vacations and these social welfare activities and organizations as part and parcel of the school program, the public schools of the country would go far towards directing the hungers of children into healthy living." (262)

Patri knew that his approach was suspect among traditionalists, so again clarified his position: "In emphasizing the hand am I forgetting the humanities, the books, the three R's? Far from it. The school of action must see to it that the child knows the standard books, that he drink deep of their wisdom, their beauty, for in these is the very life blood that feeds the aspirations of mankind." Integration of physical and mental was the key: "This seeming over-emphasis on hand training does not imply a subordination of the three R's, the necessary tools to understanding. Every child needs to read and read with care. He needs to write clearly, accurately. He needs to learn about numbers and their use in practice and in theory. . . . Hand and brain. It is both together. . . . ." (263–264)

Ever the realist, Patri defended humane discipline: "It is right that sometimes a child must be under strict regulations if he is to live in peace with himself and others. He must do what he is told, when he is told, and how he is told, and this until habits are set . . . and he goes his way content because he learned the basic things thoroughly enough to lean on them and feel secure in them. . . . The laws of habit formation, imitation, repetition, reviewing, each step right, making sure errors are not set, concentration, hard work, may be old but they are true, and progressive education does not, cannot repeal them. It can and it must appropriate and make use of them." (265–267)

In spite of recognized success and many honors, ten years after his retirement Patri still smarted from the critiques of PS 45 during the 1917 Gary struggle, and still took pride in his graduates: "The judges who presided at the grand jury before whom I was summoned wanted to know 'what became of the children of my school after graduation?' There are doctors, teachers, lawyers, politicians, policemen, scientists, musicians, business men, artists, workers. Dr. Mitchell carries on a school for the handicapped. Victor d'Amico is in charge of the children's department of the City's Museum of Modern Art, George Hassler is in charge of the Children's Museum at Fort Worth, Remo follows a radio career, Mollie teaches in a school in India, Fred teaches astronomy in a mid-west college, Joy writes, Tony is a sculptor and a craftsman at the height of his profession. Frank is with a newspaper chain. One heads a bank, another a department store. One is in the diplomatic service. There are priests, ministers, rabbis. There are artists and artisans. There are Pulitzer Prize winners and the one who

won the Prix de Rome in sculpture. . . . " And, Patri sadly acknowledged, "There are the failures. Once I visited a reform school and the
first greeting came from an inmate, 'Hello, Mr. Patri.' . . . To be sure
I speak more of success than of failure. Why not? But I haven't forgotten the lost ones. The thought that I was not wise enough to help still
plagues me." (275–276)

Patri consistently asserted that he was leading a teacher-centered as
well as a child-centered school, and, appropriately enough, devoted an
entire chapter of his memoir to teachers. He wrote that in the hands
of the teacher "a discarded old book may open the doors of wisdom,
a stable become a temple of learning, a stone by the wayside a pulpit,
a log with a pupil at one end, a teacher at the other, a university." He
began, as usual, with a story, this one about Mrs. Rosen, who called on
Patri to be sure that her three boys, Abe, Max, and Meyer, would get
good musical instruction. The Philharmonic sent a harp teacher for
two hours a week—enough to inspire the three boys to practice until
all graduated and received scholarships, Patri exulted when, "one day,
years later, the three boys came to school and gave their old teachers a
concert. The three harpists! It was one of the rare moments that glad-
den a teacher's life. The Right Teacher! . . . The right teacher and the
right pupil, a merging of two souls and life is good!" (277–281)

Another pupil, another story. Marie, the drawing teacher, was
looking for something to interest Fred, a new student. She sent him
to Mr. Frey, the printing teacher, to get some linoleum blocks. As she
had hoped, Fred was intrigued by what he saw in the print shop and
soon discovered a talent for the work. Mr. Frey took Fred along when
he went to printing plants and to the New York Public Library and
Fred was inspired to do a series of eight prints proudly labeled "Bible
Stories by Fred Slavin, age thirteen." People commented favorably on
the prints and Fred said, "Before I came here nobody paid any attention
to me. Now I am encouraged to express myself and when I do everybody smiles at me, even my mother." Patri concluded more briefly than
usual: "Find the teacher and the child is safe." (281–287)

Patri moved on from stories to describe the "good-old-time teacher" who was indeed effective "for those who could take what he had to
give. . . . But for the children who could not take what he had to give—
what of them? No cheers, no friendliness, no pride, only rejection."
That kind of teacher was too limited for the new inclusive school: "The
modern teacher is a somewhat different person. He must teach each
and every child . . . and if he cannot teach his charge he asks for help,
goes to a teacher who knows more than he does, to a doctor, to anyone

who has more skill and greater understanding of the child's difficulties—for no child must be abandoned until he is safely on his way." [14] Patri described the different challenges facing the primary teacher, the teacher of the "in-between grades," the teacher of adolescents. "The modern teacher is a far different person than the old. . . . The modern teacher must know all that the old teacher knew and a great deal that the old one never even dreamed of." (292–294)

But how do we get such paragons? "It is no longer good to leave the selection of this modern teacher to a system of examinations. The sorting must be done early and with more discretion. The teacher is an artist and he must start young to learn his craft. . . . In his eyes not a single child can be tossed out on the waste heap of life. "Patri described a group of recalcitrant, resistant students who were famous throughout the school as "the forty thieves." A young substitute art teacher told Patri of his difficulties with the group. Patri asked, "What are you interested in most? What can you do best?" The teacher loved working with puppets, so Patri equipped a shop for him, helped him get materials, and arranged for him to have the forty students ten at a time for an hour and a half each day. The teacher's enthusiasm captured the interest of the students, who settled down to work and learn, put on a successful public puppet show, and carried their workshop success over into other subjects. (295–300)

Never given to understatement, Patri wrote: "Training children to sanity in a world gone mad is a task for giants." Given the immensity of this challenge, Patri proposed asking these questions about a prospective teacher: "Is he in sound health? . . . Does he like children? . . . Has he an ideal to serve in serving children? . . . Can he work with other people? . . . Has he knowledge? . . . Is he socially fit? . . . Can he be kindly in opposition and graceful in authority?" The demands were high, but so were the rewards: "If he is something like this admixture of leader and follower, scholar and student, full grown man and eager child, he is ready for election to a full, colorful, interesting life, of undemanding love and unflinching loyalty, of a living honestly earned, honorably achieved, and of friends who walk beside him all his days." (301–305)

Patri clearly believed that in his school he had gathered and trained teachers capable of this "task for giants." In spite of his preference for the old K-9 school, Patri's assessments of his Junior High School were characteristically positive, so it is helpful to get other perceptions. Alice Bell, from the William Fox School in Richmond, Virginia, in 1939 spent a day in PS 45 and published a glowing, effusive account of her visit. The school at that time had 2,300 students, eighty teachers, and about twenty workshops. It had expanded to fill the whole block, and had no playgrounds, but compensated with four gymnasiums. Bell described the pupils and their principal: "The children are mostly underprivileged, and crime is prevalent in the area in which they live, but the faces of the children radiate with happiness. Angelo Patri lives the school and the children live Angelo Patri." Bell explained "Patri's belief that everyone has a feeling for one of the arts and that this feeling is necessary to his well-being. . . . That is why these workshops are set up. The child has the privilege of selecting any one shop, but art is compulsory for the first ten weeks of school." After students select a workshop they spend ninety minutes a day there and the rest of their time "with one teacher in the academic studies."

Bell spoke of Patri in exalted terms: "The children look upon Patri as a god. He loves them, they love him. He understands them. They understand him. . . . The school radiates with children's work. Mr. Patri's office is an exhibit in itself. There are oil paintings, water colors, batiks, potteries, rugs, tapestries, stained glass effect windows, portraits, illuminated books, and furniture all made by the children." After describing the happy children smiling and singing in the halls, Bell noted the importance of community involvement: "The school is also used by adults and parents in the evenings. There are classes in English, art, music, etc. conducted for them. They are a definite part of the school. They have donated most of the equipment and supplies used in the shops. The parents live school with the children."

One might assume that the success of the school depended on Patri's ability to choose his own teachers, but Bell said that he could not do that: "Mr. Patri has no power in the selection of his teachers. . . . He contends that with a group of teachers as large as he has, all are not in accord with what he is doing, but 'when you have some of the strong character and the genuine feeling for children, you have your school.'" [15] (It is worth noting here that although Patri could not select his teachers, it is possible that, within bureaucratic constraints, they could select the school. PS 45 was well known, and teachers sympathetic to Patri's approach would have been likely to apply to teach there.)

Testimony from a better-known observer was positive, but somewhat more subdued. Popular novelist Dorothy Canfield Fisher spent some time in Patri's school in 1940 and published an article about it in the *Reader's Digest*. "When I stepped inside the building I had a surprise. Against the usual drab background of public schools was color everywhere, bold splashing paintings, posters, tapestries, above all window paintings—transparencies through which the reds and blues and yellows fell richly on the ugly brown walls and floors." Fisher noted that Patri and his teachers looked for children's particular talents in sculpture, printing, painting, music, book-binding, athletics, or other fields, and used those talents in helping them learn other required skills and knowledge. She wrote about one boy with a low-tested IQ and a history of school failure. The librarian noted that he had a passionate interest in rabbits: "In order to learn more about rabbits he learned to read. In order to show his system of making hutches, he learned to draw to scale. In order to make clear statements about food and marketing, he learned to figure—enough to allow him to function in his small way in the modern world. Are you saying that all this is familiar stuff in 'progressive schools'? But remember that this took place in public school, not as a matter of educational theory but as a practical way to open a door to life to a future citizen, apparently sealed shut in black disheartenment."

Fisher concluded: "This Italian-American teacher felt, as we all do, that the old stability of the home is gone. With his artist instinct he has steered his charges toward a surer immaterial stability, the stability of coherent, long-continued, self-directed creative effort." Fisher, who had been a teacher herself, understood and appreciated what Patri and his colleagues were doing in the challenging environment of PS 45.[16]

Regarding Fisher's casual dismissal of educational theory, it is clear that Patri had in fact constructed a theory, based on his studies at Teachers College, his reading of Dewey, and his own lifetime of experience in his home, the streets, and in schools. The theory, in short, was: Begin with a deep knowledge of children based on careful observation; identify student interests and build educational program from there; develop individual skill and knowledge within a healthy social environment; involve the parents and the broader community; and use the school to coordinate the efforts of other agencies to form children and reform society.

Patri had another significant visitor to his school that same year. On April 16, 1940 Dewey wrote to his future wife, Roberta Grant, that "Angelo Patri phoned me & invited me to his school in the Bronx & for lunch, saying he would send his car. . . ." The absent-minded Dewey had also made an appointment with Roberta, but was unable to reach her, so had gone ahead with his visit to Patri's school on April 15. A biographer deeply interested in both men can't help picturing the sixty-four year old Patri greeting the eighty-one year old Dewey and showing him about the school. Which workshops did they observe? Did Dewey compare them with the "shop-work" in his Laboratory School? [17] Over lunch did they discuss PS 45 as a later, larger, and public version of Dewey's Laboratory School? We can only indulge in such brief fantasies and then record Patri's invitation primarily as an example of his desire to maintain his connection with Dewey.

He renewed the connection four years later in 1944 on the occasion of Dewey's eighty-fifth birthday, when he sent Dewey this note: "The notice of your birthday in the Times delighted me. Your photograph showed you in good shape for which, like the rest of your thousands of friends, I am deeply thankful. I hope you live to keep your work glowing through this generation. You are needed now more than ever. Long life and good health to you for years to come." [18]

When Patri retired that same year, *Newsweek* ran an article titled "Good-by Mr. Chips-Patri," which began: "After 46 consecutive years in New York City schools the American Mr. Chips is retiring. Angelo Patri, principal of the famous Bronx P.S. 45 (Hoffman Junior High School), writer of the syndicated column, 'Our Children,' with an estimated circulation of between 7,000,000 and 8,000,000, and one of America's outstanding practicing progressive educators, will give up active school work this fall to write. Thus ended one phase of a remarkable career to which Dorothy Canfield Fisher once paid this tribute: 'Angelo Patri has made one of the finest contributions to civilized life in our nation.'" The *Newsweek* article described Patri's successful school programs and asserted that "Patri went down the line for the John Dewey school of progressivism. . . . Urged by his friend Mayor Fiorello H. La Guardia, to take a post on the New York Board of Education . . . Patri declined. Politics, he avers, is not for him." Instead, he planned to write and "lead the quieter life of a 'Consulting Educator.'" [19]

Given Patri's preference for his K-9 elementary school, it is interesting that, because of his success with Paul Hoffman Junior High School, he was identified as a leader of the new junior high movement. When the Conant Report, *Recommendations for Education in the Junior High School Years* was published in 1960, a *New York Times* article said: "Angelo Patri, whose own contribution to the growth and development of junior high schools is now history, puts the ideal of the junior high school this way: 'Through it life in all its phases must flow to nourish the changing, searching child. Crafts, the arts and sciences, books, all that the race can offer, go to make the school a center of pulsing life where each child can find the one right way of life for him.'" [20]

If ever an institution was the "lengthened shadow of a man," it was PS 45, often called "the Patri School." Here Patri had persevered on his progressive course through the challenges presented by complex times and events inside and outside of the schools: New York's fight over the Gary system, World War I, the conservative 1920s, the junior high movement, the Depression, New Deal, and World War II. Through all this Patri and his staff adapted progressivism to dramatically different situations and conditions. During those thirty-one years at PS 45 he and his faculty managed also to respond creatively to the changing politics and practices of the rule-bound New York City school bureaucracy.

David Tyack has written that an "important—and often neglected—job in educational politics and policy is to conserve what works in schools. . . . Good schools are hard to create and nurture, for they require healthy relationships of trust, challenge, and respect, qualities that take time to develop. These values become embedded in institutions as part of the common ground that unites the members of the schools. When teachers, students, parents, and administrators create such schools, it's important to preserve what makes them work, to sabotage ignorant efforts to fix what ain't broke, and to share knowledge about how to create more good schools." [21]

Against determined and powerful critics, Patri and his staff had developed a common ground that sustained PS 45 and preserved in it the more child-centered and reformist elements of the Gary experiment, while the other New York Gary schools reverted to their traditional status.[22] How did he manage this, when other Gary principals did not? There are a number of possible reasons, some of which may be relevant to current efforts to create and sustain good schools.

Patri remained a realistic pragmatist and worked from successful models. An important factor in PS 45's survival was the fact that Patri had already led one progressive school and was convinced that such schools were better for children, teachers, families, and communities. This conviction, combined with Patri's confidence and willpower, energized him to resist conservative administrative intervention. Patri had been impressed by the Gary schools when he visited them, believed that they could be adapted to the older New York system, and felt that he and his staff successfully made that adaptation. In this he had crucial assistance from Willard Wirt, and he never lost faith in him or his recommendations. Wirt continued to support and encourage Patri long after the other New York platoon schools had folded.[23] The examples of Wirt and his other heroes—McMurry, Dewey, Fripp, and Montessori—no doubt strengthened Patri in his efforts.

Drawing on recent research on the principalship, Harold Wenglinsky recently wrote: "Principals who are leading teachers in schools with diverse populations need to understand the richness of the sociocultural environment, and draw upon it as a school's strength rather than a weakness." With this understanding the principal can choose to "embed himself or herself in the school community rather than the bureaucratic organization of the school system."[24] Patri did not have much research to draw on, but he knew from his own experience the importance of understanding and becoming part of the school's environment. The fact that Patri was Italian-American, spoke fluent Italian, and lived in the community no doubt helped him and his teachers use the resources of the neighborhood to increase the power of the school. Much of the opposition to the Gary program in New York came from immigrant families who feared that the schools would steer their children into lower-class trades and crafts rather than help them gain further education and higher status.[25] Patri made sure that the basics were well taught along with the more experimental parts of the program. He reminded parents that their children were motivated to stay in school partly because of the interesting workshop activities, but he consistently assured them that the children were getting solid academic preparation as well. Patri built strong community support and enlisted the help of priests, businessmen, shopkeepers, musicians, and others to make the school succeed and thus be worth supporting.[26]

This neighborhood backing encouraged support by those administrators who worked most closely with him. Patri in turn made nominal program changes sufficient to satisfy some of their concerns. During his first three years at PS 45 Joseph L. Taylor provided critical support. He had supervised Patri at PS 4, and at the end of Patri's first year at PS 45 wrote a glowing recommendation, concluding: "Mr. Patri's influence upon children is remarkable. He can mold them to his will, without force or bluster, by quiet suggestion and the stimulation of their better impulses. In like manner, teachers respond to his treatment with cheerful alacrity."[27] Patri received equally strong support from 1927 to 1935 from district superintendent Anthony Pugliese, one of his closest friends. At a higher level, his friendship with Fiorello LaGuardia, mayor from 1933 to 1945, may also have shielded him from unfriendly administrative actions.[28]

By the time Patri retired he had written nine books for parents and seven for children and had published thousands of columns in newspapers and magazines. He had had many speaking engagements throughout the country as well as various nationally broadcast radio programs. In 1923 Tufts College in Medford, Massachusetts, awarded Patri an honorary degree as a Doctor of Humane Letters. Although he did not sign himself "Dr. Patri," he was thereafter often labeled that way by newspapers and magazines. The doctorate may have led to his incorrect identification as a "child psychologist" by various writers. Although Patri was a careful student of child psychology, he did not have a degree in that field and did not call himself a psychologist.[29] All this contributed to Patri's reputation as a writer and speaker that may have provided some protection from heavy-handed administrative maneuvers. Blatant interference with his school work might have brought unwelcome publicity to the district.

By choosing both his allies and his battles carefully, Patri avoided getting caught in the squabbles between progressive and traditionalist educators.[30] In fact, he rarely described himself publicly as a progressive, claiming only that he was a child-centered, teacher-centered reformer, interested in running what Larry Cuban later called simply a "good" school.[31] Somewhat ironically, avoiding the label "progressive" helped Patri to maintain a truly progressive school.[32]

Patri's private life sustained his public career. Patri had a strong, loving marriage with Dora Caterson, who was also a school administrator and thus well understood the challenges of his work. He maintained an active and supportive family life and did such simple things as take walks to reduce tension and maintain physical and mental health. In the late 1920s he and Dora bought a summer place in Paradox, New York, where he relaxed with friends and family, and in the mid-1930s he bought a beautiful, secluded country home in Patterson, New York, where they spent weekends and vacations and where they eventually retired. Patri's satisfying family life, his vacation homes, and his healthy activities and habits no doubt helped him sustain the patience and equanimity required to outlast his critics.[33]

Whatever the actual mix of explanations, Patri was able to maintain the essential progressive elements of his school for three decades. As contemporary educators struggle in this new millennium to preserve hard-won gains in a variety of schools and alternative programs, they may gain some insight and perspective from the experience of Angelo Patri, who came to this country at the age of five, acquired a good education in tax-supported institutions, and then repaid his adopted country many times over by serving for forty-six years as a progressive, humane, and sensitive teacher and principal in free public schools.

In 1917 Patri had shown in *Schoolmaster* that as a young man he could teach, lead, and write effectively; his memoir of PS 45 and the testimony of others demonstrated that the mature Patri could continue to do all this and more during three difficult decades. In the next chapter, "The Last Day," Patri recalled his thoughts and feelings as he cleared out his office after all those years in the New York schools.

Patri in a mathematics class, PS 45

(Frank Merolla)

SEVEN

The Last Day and the Last Years: Reflections by Angelo Patri and PS 45 Students

*I*N MAY 1943, MAYOR FIORELLO LA GUARDIA ANNOUNCED
*that he was trying to persuade Angelo Patri to accept appointment to the New
York City Board of Education, saying, "I am hopeful of getting Dr. Patri to
retire and become a member of the board. He's a real educator and knows and
understands children." He had tried once before, in 1935, to get Patri to serve on
the Board, but in both cases Patri refused the appointment, considering himself a
teacher, not a politician.[1]*

    *Patri did, however, retire the following year, and during the summer of 1944
he cleared out his office and turned his beloved PS 45 over to his friend, assistant
principal Harry Krail.[2] The* New York Times *editorial said that Patri's retirement was "sad news for his hundreds of pupils and tens of thousands of alumni.
Beloved by his students and teachers, admired by the parents of his community,
Dr. Patri has carved a unique niche for himself in the educational world. Through
his writings his school philosophy has traveled far beyond this city, reaching all
sections of the country. At 67 he may retire for a well-deserved rest, but his ideas
and his warm sprit will continue to be felt for many years to come." Out of his
own immigrant background Patri had "developed a sympathetic understanding
of the child in need of help, of the underprivileged pupil, of the 'average' youngster. He has achieved a reputation for fairness, for honesty, and for professional
integrity. He has ruled, not by force, but by shining example. His retirement is a
loss to the city school system. His record can serve as an inspiration for educators
everywhere."[3]*

    *Two months later Patri wrote a letter addressed "Fellow Teachers," saying:
"It has been plain to me for some time that I would have to retire, but I carried*

on against the advice of wiser heads than mine. Now I say good-bye to you, my friends. I am grateful for your smiles, your words of encouragement. From now on I shall lean on my memories of you. Working and living together we have come to understand many things that seem mysterious to others, but to us are an open book, for we know that the teacher is the school."

This letter was part of a flyer prepared for a testimonial luncheon held for Patri in November 1944, and attended by about 150 of his teachers and friends. This event brought to a ceremonial end Patri's long and distinguished career in the New York schools. As "The Last Day," showed, Patri had strong emotions about leaving his students, staff, and teachers, but he went through the necessary stages of separating and grieving and settled quickly into his retirement routine.[4]

In the preceding chapters I have quoted extensively from Patri; here, because it tells so much about Patri and his school, I begin with most of a chapter from his unpublished memoir. Patri expressed his thoughts and emotions as he cleared out his office, preparing to retire after forty-six years of work in the New York City schools. There is an immediacy about this material that suggests that Patri may have written it shortly after he retired, and then later included it in his memoir.[5] Following Patri's heartfelt essay I include selected recollections of some students who attended PS 45 during or soon after Patri's tenure as principal.

"The Last Day," by Angelo Patri

I sat at my desk for the last time, sorting papers, some to be taken along with me, but most for the waste basket, for my desk must be made ready for my successor. In a few days school would open for the fall term and I would not be there. Alone in an empty school house, not believing what I knew to be true, I continued sorting papers. Among them was a letter from Margaret. It had come years before from Mexico, after she had just been married to the one man in the world for her. It was a lovely letter, brimming over with joy which she wanted to share with her old teacher friends. She thanked the school for what it had done for her. It had understood the vagaries and the longings of her unformed spirit and given them free play and now she wanted us to know how happy she was. That was Margaret, always wanting to share what she had with someone else.

Margaret was a plump, competent young person. I shut my eyes and looked back and saw her in the pottery shop busy and happy, making vases, waiting patiently for the baking, getting Mr. Jarvis, her teacher, to help with the right glaze and then again waiting anxiously to see what would come out of the kiln, as expectant and excited as Cellini was over his precious Perseus. If she was pleased with the result, and she would look at her work critically, she would come with it to my office.

"What do you think of it? A nice blue isn't it?"

"Great."

"Would you like it for your office?"

Whether I would or not depended on the longing desire in Margaret's eyes. If there was in them the wistful pride of a mother for her offspring, I would say, "No, not this time. Take it home. You keep that one. I'll have the next one."

Margaret loved the old potter and the two were great friends. Jarvis had come from that group of English potteries where potters are artists as well as artisans. The thing was in his blood. He was forever trying out new designs, new glazes, always on week-ends and vacations going on long walks, to catch, if he could, some delicate color shade, some hint to give fresh vigor to his pottery. He loved his work and thought of little else. He was frail, so thin the soul of him seemed to shine right through his body. Jarvis was old when he first came to us; by the time Margaret met him he was older and so tired that at times he would fall asleep in his chair. "I don't know what's the matter with Mr. Jarvis," said Margaret. "He seems sick. Is there anything we can do?"

"Yes, there is. You go up to the kitchen and get him an eggnog in the middle of the morning. That may help him." Margaret did that. She tended him like a daughter would a father whom she dearly loved, and a deep sense of fellowship pervaded that pottery room. Margaret graduated soon after and Jarvis was so tired that his fellow teachers sent him at their expense on a vacation, but he never returned. He died in his sleep dreaming of his pots, his flowers, his walks, his children. It all came back as I sat and reread her letter. "I don't know what it was that I got out of school," she said, "but it's something precious. Whenever I do something a little better than anybody else does it I think of the old school."

Bless you, Margaret. The school got something out of your spirit that helped the lockstep to go out and humanity to come in. Margaret didn't know at the time what it was that she was getting out of her school experiences. She did not stop to analyze. It was enough for her that she lived fully each day as it came. But as the years ripened and took on meaning she was able to interpret her school life and to understand that the daily experiences had given her a heightened comprehension of the good, the true, the beautiful. Margaret's letter would go home with me and I would cherish it as something warm and comforting.

There was a letter from Joe, John's friend. "When I left New York I did not stop at towns long until I came to the little town of Empire, in the Rocky Mountains. There I decided to rest for a while and for several months I roamed the surrounding hills exploring deserted cabins and mines, hunting and fishing, sketching to my heart's content, resting under the tall pine trees, reading with a rushing stream by my side, and for several months I chopped wood, helped to build cabins, took care of babies on Saturday nights while mama and papa attended the movies at Idaho Springs, ten miles away, painted and fixed chairs and tables and even painted two houses, thereby earning my room and board and free haircuts from the barber mayor of Empire, Len Sharpe. I always make friends especially with mayors, sheriffs and teachers.

"I have a two-room studio in Denver and a cast of sixteen puppets. I perform at various public schools and private parties and run a school of puppetry on Saturday mornings; there are five pupils. A young chap, eighteen years of age, who is quite clever, a graduate of Mrs. Herrick's School of Dramatics, also in Denver, travels with my puppets and may come back to New York with me. Do write and tell me lots of news. Busy as I am I'm lonesome. Vagabond Joe." That letter, too, would go with me as a memento of a lovely friendship—Joe and John, the one who died before the promise could be fulfilled and the one who reached the heights of his career and then he too died, crucified by life.

And here was a letter from a Chinese boy who had to leave the school a few months after he had come. "Since I had my land to leave and entered C. class, I accepted the extraordinary attention from my dear teacher, Miss Capadiferro and you and all the class; so I was very pleasant with the school and did not think that I have to depart it so soon. But I knew it well; I must have an independence with my living. Of course I rather not miss my lovely school to receive the hardships of war. I promised to accept a certificate from you and I also promised my music teacher to play solo in the Auditorium; and the last picture of my drawing is still not finished yet. And now all these things will impossibly be enclosed. I feel regretful for them. This war. I fight for my China. I come when the war go away. As I have an opportunity I write you. Please give me instruction by letter. Your pupil, Hom Hay."

And Ida's letter would be added to the stack at my right hand. "Before coming to #45 I attended a newly built school, with wide shining corridors and airy spotless rooms. Then I was thrust into #45, it was terrible. The dingy, narrow halls, the dismal stairs and the battered desks. The queer smell of its back entrance, the perpetual scrubbing of the inside yard, which was cleaned and cleaned and never seemed to look any cleaner. I was sure that I could never get used to it, let alone like it.

"The next term I joined the orchestra. The last week before the holidays was spent in the joyful confusion of rehearsals for the Christmas program and the final editing of the school magazine. One day we were given an especially long lunch period in which to recuperate. A group of us visited Poe's cottage, near the school. We didn't realize how late it was until someone mentioned it. 'Let's hurry,' I said, 'or we'll never get home on time.' Everyone laughed at me for calling #45 home, but I knew then it was more than a slip of the tongue. It was my opinion of the school and it still is."

To bolster my conceit I must keep William's letter. William is a naturalist, follows the wild things wherever they are, and takes with him the children of the museum he happens to be connected with. "It is always a pleasure to think back over my school days at #45. There was something so human, so quietly impressive about school that it left a mark on one's mind and character which was very deep but hard to describe. I enjoyed the shop periods more than almost anything else at the time and have profited by that experience in many ways and on many occasions since. In my fourteen years at the American Museum, the machine shop and carpentry shop practice came in handy. My ability to work with my hands undoubtedly helped a lot but my experiences in the shops at #45 have been of paramount importance to me in my Museum work, in the field and in photographic work."

I thumb the visitors' book.[6] There is Annie's signature and her husband's. I didn't know her when, after twenty years, she came into my office with her husband. The school was issuing sugar rationing books and I thought these two came for their allotment. "You want books for sugar?" I asked. "You don't know me. I am an old pupil of yours. This is my husband. We are on our way to Washington from South Africa on war business. We had two days in New York so I thought I'd come up and show the school off to my husband. Can I take him to the apartment where I learned to cook?" Then I remembered what twelve-year-old Annie had said to the visitor who had watched her at work and asked—"Why are you so interested in cooking?" and Annie's answer, "So that when I get married my husband will say 'What a fine wife I've got,'" and I remembered that as the two stood before me I had said, "Yes, go ahead, you know the way, and I am sure your husband says 'What a fine wife I've got.'" Annie had smiled warmly, "Yes, you do remember me. I am so glad."

I turn the pages in this visitor's book and I stop to glance at a list of names of Japanese teachers who had come to visit the school some twenty-five years before. "We come to your school", said the Japanese spokesman, "we want to see the school, see everything. You show us."

"I will gladly show you what we have. Is there anything special you are interested in?"

"Yes, everything. We see everything. We stay today and we come back tomorrow. We want to know what you do."

"I'll do the best I can to answer your questions. Let's begin in the Auditorium. That's on the ground floor." So we walked down from the office to the yard and in through the rear door of the Auditorium. The place was in darkness. Somebody was showing pictures and talking about them. Quietly we filed in. What was on the screen? A street in Tokyo! There it was, shops, flags, advertising signs, people, cars. A child's voice came to us out of the darkness. "And this is the main shopping district of Tokyo. This is where you buy anything you need, dresses, groceries, everything."

I was astounded. I turned to the visitors. They stood rooted to the floor, their eyes wide open, their cheeks paled as if by shock, their silence so deep that the whole auditorium of four hundred children felt it. The voice of the speaker, plump, bright-eyed, twelve-year-old Fanny, unknowing of the drama going on in the rear of the room, flowed smoothly. "Japan is a very important nation. Her people are fast learning the ways of the Western people." In wonder and awe we filed out. The next day I asked, "How did it all happen?" "Not so mysterious as it seems," said the teacher. "We let the children talk every chance we can get. Fanny knows about Japan because her father is a silk merchant and he makes many trips to China and. Japan. He has a collection of pictures. Some he has put on slides to entertain his friends. Fanny knows these slides like a book. Today she told her schoolmates what she had learned from her father." "But to pick the day the Japanese visited!" "No, the Japanese picked the day that Fanny talked. And they'll never forget this school to their dying day. To them it must be sort of a miracle, something to talk about to their children's children. . . ."

The Visitor's Book is put with the letters. Still I sit in the office that has been mine for more than thirty years and look about me. On the wall hangs the tapestry of the Hunchback of Notre Dame and a Knight and His Lady. It's a lovely thing. Theresa wove that. I see her as she was when she began work on the tapestry, a boy-crazy adolescent, high heels, abbreviated skirts, rouged lips and the devil-may-care look in her eyes.

And there's Charlie's copy of Sargent's Battle of the Crusaders. I like the picture. It's full of action and color, and somehow Charlie has caught the spirit of the artist and his copy is not a slavish thing but rather an interpretive appreciation. Charlie is a doctor now. He had wanted to be an artist but his father said "No! Artists suffer too much, earn too little. Charlie must acquire a profession he can rely on." Recently Dr. Charlie and I had dinner together. We talked of old times, his friends, his teachers. I talked about his art. "Well, I still paint," said he. "Yes, at night when I am through with the hospital routine, and it's time to go to bed, I take my brushes and my canvas and go down into the morgue and paint the faces of the dead."

There's Tony's Lincoln. It presides over my office as a guardian angel. Under the head of Lincoln is a chair where visitors sat as they waited their turn.[7] But as I look at Lincoln and see that chair I see, too, an old man with close-cropped hair, the smell of age about him, sitting there waiting his turn. I do not know him at first and then I recognize that he is another of my old pupils, older than I am, once my lemon man, once a member of my night school class for foreigners, in the first year I taught. More than forty years had gone by but he had come to visit his old teacher once more. I remembered him well for he was one whom I never succeeded in teaching to read, never got him any further than the primer on which he began. "My hat. Is this my hat? Yes, this is my hat." Each night he would sit in the seat beside my desk. Each night he would read the same lesson at approximately the same time. The routine was fixed. At the end of that school year I had resigned my job as a night school teacher, gone my way and forgotten my friend Telemachus Minervini, but not for long.

A year or so later as I came home from school, my mother said, pointing to a pile of lemons, "A man was here—a lemon vendor. He says you were his teacher. Everywhere he went selling lemons he inquired for his teacher. Now he has found you. He left these lemons for lemonade. Sunday he will pay you a visit. Sunday he came, a bag of lemons in his hand. "Are you well? Lemons are good for health. Please ask your mother to make lemonade for you." "Thank you. Lemonade for us, Mother," I requested.

"I find you. I am happy. See I have the reader you gave me. I practice every night. Will you hear my lesson?" "Surely, I'll be glad to." Deliberately he reached into his pocket and out came the battered old first reader. "My hat. Is this my hat? Yes, this is my hat." He smiles, closes the book and back it goes into his pocket. We chat awhile, we drink lemonade and he bids me goodbye and promises to visit me again. The family moves but before long I am found again. The story is repeated. The family moves to a better house, for now I am a principal of a school. When the lemon man finds me he sees lines of worry on my face and wants to know how come? I marry and move again. Thirty years go by. I have forgotten my lemon man. And one day when I come back from lunch, there he is, gray, ill-kempt, poor, but his eyes still bright. On my desk he has put an old paper bag, lemons for lemonade, a tribute to his old teacher. We chat. There is no book, no story of "My hat." As he is about to leave he says, "I have followed your career. Today I came to see, to see if my little professor was the same, or if, like all the others, he too is spoiled."

Puzzled and a little dazed, my heart aches, for this is my last day. I take one more look at the paintings that hang on the office walls. There is a series of twenty odd Norwegian Tales. The children had been reading these tales out of a beautifully illustrated book, and the drawing teacher decided to have the children copy them in a size suitable for framing. When framed the pictures made a lovely panel. Ranged along the upper part of the wall of my office they had been for many years a pleasant reminder, not only of a job well done, but of Mr. Jack's first attempts to break away from the set course of study in drawing. And once again I see Mr. Jack fuming because the work laid down by the course of study was uninteresting. I see him edging away from the set routine and the supervisor looking on protesting, complaining, until the head of the drawing department swooped down upon us and told us he would not tolerate such disobedience. We were to do as we were told. But we couldn't and didn't.

The janitor has helped me pack and carry out the few precious things I am to take with me. He looks at me now as I stand up ready to go my way, his eyes fill with tears and he mumbles "I can't take it" and stumbles out the door. Neither can I. But we do. I am alone as I take Valentino's portrait of himself under my arm. Valentino was always a fine boy, but his looks, his moods, his poverty were all set against him. His face was pale and pimply, his clothes were ragged, he was plainly under-nourished and he was oppressed by it all and his resentment was deep. The result was unsatisfactory work and from his teacher's point of view complete lack of effort. At promotion time he was left back. I met him on the way to the art room the morning he had been told there was no chance of promotion. He looked thoroughly beaten. I stopped to ask him what was the trouble. He told me and ended up with—"I don't blame the teacher. Look at me. What can you expect? But they don't know me. They see the outside of me. Leaving me back won't do any good. But it will crush the inside of me, the part of me they do not know. Wait, I'll go home and show you something." In a half hour he was back, under his arm a canvas, a portrait of himself, painted in the way of the old Masters, dressed in a rich and colorful costume, haughty, bold, clear-eyed, clear-skinned. He handed it to me saying "That's me, the me my teachers of Math and English cannot see."

"Fine, fine piece of work. I am proud of you, Valentino. You have earned your promotion. Congratulations." That portrait hangs in my dining room. Recently I heard that Valentino was in Rome, using his G.I. rights to study portrait painting in the halls where the great Masters still live and teach the elect.

Slowly I walk out of that open door, Valentino's portrait under my arm. Slowly, I leave a host of parents, teachers, children, and visitors who have gone in and out of my school. They had come for all sorts of reasons, but I fancy that no matter what the reason, they were always a little happier when they left than when they entered. As for me, the school had given me peace and happiness and moments when my soul had touched the hem of the Infinite.

For the last time I raise my eyes to Tony's Lincoln, the bust he made that was to look like Lincoln and feel like Christ. I glance at the empty chair, see the ghost of my lemon man sitting there with that strange question in his eyes—"Had I made good?" Well, time never measures up to the dreams of men; enough if it moves in their direction.

———————

Patri had heartening memories of his school and of many of his former pupils. They, of course, remembered him and his school as well, so for further perspective on Patri I have gathered here some recollections by students from their time in PS 45. I am often as interested in how writers create their stories as in the stories themselves, so I will describe here how I gradually learned the stories of some of Patri's former students.

The Last Years: Reflections by Students of PS 45

Child-oriented Patri would not have been satisfied with his own positive judgments of his work and those of other adults, if his students themselves were not happy. All the medals, honors, awards, and testimonials to Patri's work would have been meaningless unless students were content with the educational experiences offered by his school. Sixty years after Patri retired, searching from used bookstores to the Internet, I was able to find testimonials that PS 45 was indeed a good school, at least for those students who left records of their years there.

A statement by Ralph Waldo Emerson gives historical perspective for the kind of approach that Patri used and that students remembered. Emerson explained how good parents and teachers should respond to children's interests: "If a child happens to show that he knows any fact about astronomy, or plants, or birds, or rocks, or history, that interests him and you, hush all the classes and encourage him to tell it so all may hear. Then you have made your school-room like the world."[8] In a similar pattern, Patri and his faculty made a point of noting and encouraging students' interests and skills and connecting them with the larger world outside.

Stories by some of Patri's former pupils show how this encouragement worked. It is appropriate to begin with the best-known story about Patri— how in 1926 he rescued Julius Garfinkle from what promised to be a life of frustration and anger and helped him to find himself, study drama, and to go on to a successful career as a popular movie actor under the name of John Garfield. This story was familiar to many at the time because Garfield was well known and because for several years he made visits to PS 45 to acknowledge his debt to Patri. Among many versions of the story, one of the most personal was in Larry Swindell's lively 1975 book *Body and Soul: The Story of John Garfield*. Swindell, a cultural historian, tells the story in the dramatic prose of a film biography. He writes that "on a fall day in 1926, Angelo Patri made his first acquaintance with a fairly new student who had been ordered to see the principal as a disciplinary measure. Playing in the outfield during a recess softball game, the boy had scaled a chain fence to retrieve a ball that had been socked into the street, and in his leap he had trampled some Patri-planted dahlias.

"The boy Patri regarded had a Jewish name but a fair-skinned, dark-haired handsomeness that could as easily have been Italian. . . . Patri sensed the boy's uncertainty and embarrassed guilt, but also detected a tendency to pose. Julius Garfinkle, Patri reasoned, had a compulsion to show off; and he could find nothing wrong with such a tendency.

"And Julie was confronted by a striking picture of a man, with comical overtones. At fifty, stocky Angelo Patri had a large, square head with a thick wavy mane gone white in the best Italian tradition. And he wore a bright green suit, an individual trademark since having first bought one to impress some of his Irish students on St. Patrick's Day."

Patri recalled his impression of Julius: "He seemed full of antagonism, as if he believed everybody—all grown people—were against him. But there was really nothing wrong with Julie, and I liked him. He had a nice embarrassed smile, and because he lacked confidence, he had that bad stammer. . . . " Patri had a gift for matching students and teachers, and sent Julie to Margaret O'Ryan, "a stout, agreeable young woman who had an easy way with boys. . . . She was the first teacher he ever *liked*, and it amounted to a schoolboy crush." She began having Julie recite aloud to develop his confidence and then included him in plays presented in school assemblies. Julie spent less time in boxing—another interest and talent—and more in drama. Patri recalled that "Julie found himself the moment he began acting for Mrs. O'Ryan. He could be convincing in any part, the king or the beggar."

While Patri and Mrs. O'Ryan encouraged Julie to consider an acting career, his father, David, was skeptical. "Patri, who regularly became involved in the lives of his most diversely promising students, got to know David Garfinkle and they became friends, although the principal's ideas made no sense to Julie's father." Julie was staying with an uncle so he could be in the PS 45 district, and Patri visited the house, finding that Julie slept in a pile of coats in a hallway. "The next day Patri had sheets, blankets, mattress, and a spring bed delivered for Julie, whom he came to regard as an investment." Patri invited the parents to see Julie in a play, and they were pleased and surprised at his talent. Then Patri helped Julie enter and win student debate competitions.

Julie completed his studies at PS 45, and Patri arranged for him to attend Roosevelt High School and then to get a dramatic scholarship from the Heckscher Foundation. Julie appeared in performances of *A Midsummer's Night's Dream*, and Patri took noted actor Jacob Ben-Ami to see him. Ben-Ami was sufficiently impressed so that he recommended Julie as a student with the American Laboratory Theatre. Julie dropped out of high school, but Patri gave him five dollars a week to help pay for his study of drama. This continued until 1930, when Julie was making a living in New York theater. He moved on to Hollywood, adopted John Garfield as his stage name, and eventually made thirty-one films.

In 1938 Julie made a well-publicized return visit to New York. "Up in the Bronx, Julie's father was a minor celebrity and Angelo Patri was almost a major one. All of his teaching theories had been realized in John Garfield. Patri joyously contacted Julie with a request that he address the PS 45 graduating class. Julie said he would do it. Afterward he would try to make a visit with his old principal an annual event, but always accompanied by photographers."

After completing his fifth film Garfield returned again in 1939 and told the graduates that "but for the influence of P.S. 45 he could have ended up dead or in jail, as so many of his early friends were." At he end of the talk, as the students applauded, "Angelo Patri appeared on the stage, dressed as always in bright green, and presented Julie with a leather case. 'Here's something you forfeited seven or eight years ago. We feel it's coming to you now.' Tears came into Garfield's eyes as he accepted the principal's gift."

Garfield on another occasion said: "For a lost boy to be found, someone must do the finding. Dr. Patri found me, and for reaching into the garbage pail and pulling me out, I owe him everything. The good things that came my way would not have been possible but for that sweet, funny man."[9]

When Garfield died of a heart attack in 1952, a reporter for the *New York Post* interviewed the seventy five-year-old Patri, who remembered Garfield "with deep affection." He said that "As a child John had an unholy hatred of grownups. He had been shoved from one member of the family to another and when he came to my school he was living with an uncle in a hall bedroom." Patri recounted the story of Garfield trampling the flowers, his talks with Garfield, and the boy's eventual enrollment in an acting class. "All through the years the school never let go of him. He often recalled his teacher in that dramatic class, Mrs. Margaret O'Ryan, and John said that she was the best dramatic coach he had ever had, even after he went to Hollywood." The childless Patri concluded the interview with the significant statement that "I suppose you might even say we were like father and son." [10]

I learned about another student in 1997 when Frank Merolla, Patri's grandnephew, took me to the Bronx to visit the Angelo Patri School—a large multicultural intermediate school where Patri would have felt quite at home. After our visit the principal, Rose F. Clunie, sent me a Teacher Corps document that included an article about Patri by his former student Anthony Vilhotti. Vilhotti had known about Patri from his parents and siblings even before he attended PS 45 himself in the early 1940s. He knew the John Garfield story and told another concerning a student named Steve Mauriello. Steve was a promising young boxer who was hit by a truck, smashing his leg so badly that there was talk of amputation. Patri persuaded a surgeon to operate, the leg was saved, and Steve continued his boxing career.

Vilhotti recalled Patri's neighborhood involvement: "He purposely built a relationship between the school and our parents by starting after-school activities for us and getting our parents interested. He held assemblies in the evening where folk tales and plays were acted and where pupils sang and danced." Vilhotti described an event when a truck killed a boy on a street next to the school. A crowd gathered, blocked off the street, and threatened other truck drivers. "A delegation of parents . . . went to see Dr. Patri to stop the violence. Dr. Patri went into the street with the parents and asked each group to come to a meeting to be held that evening in the auditorium. . . . A delegation was selected to visit Mayor La Guardia with Dr. Patri the following morning . . . . Exactly four days after the accident, on the day the boy was buried, each cross street on 189th street had a new stop sign."

Vilhotti continued his recollections more personally: "A polio condition in early childhood had left me with a limp in my left leg and an overly sensitive reaction to the jibes of my classmates." He fought with them and verbally threatened a teacher who broke up one fight. "Threatening a teacher with physical abuse was the one infraction that required mandatory referral to Dr. Patri." In the office Patri asked, "Anthony, do you have any pain in your leg now?" They discussed Anthony's family, his polio, his truancy, and his other troubles. "I don't remember how long we talked. I do remember that we were not interrupted once. The office seemed very quiet. I was sitting very close to his desk in order to hear the questions he asked me . . . nothing I said angered him. At some point in the talk, the sense of shame I had felt was no longer there; I was strangely relieved." They had two more talks in the office, and sometimes would meet elsewhere in the school. "When he had the time he would stop me, cup my chin in his hand, question me about my work, and insist I come to see him, if he could help in any way."

For years Vilhotti thought about returning to the school to thank Patri for his help, but he first wanted to achieve something worthy of Patri's approval. "By the time I had earned the doctoral degree, Dr. Patri had long since been dead. Along with my sense of loss there was always the regret that I had not let him know the results of his efforts for me and the debt I owed him." When he began to work with the Teacher Corps in a new school and was told that it was to be named the Angelo Patri School, he wrote, "my regrets disappeared. My debt to the man can now be repaid in my commitment to the school that bears his name." [11]

In San Francisco in 1999 I discussed Patri at a meeting of the American Italian Historical Association and was delighted at the end of my talk when a charming elderly man stood up and declared with pride, "I am Joe Dongarra and I was one of Patri's students." I talked with Dongarra after the meeting, and he invited me to send him questions about Patri. I did so and learned that Joe had skipped two grades and had been admitted at age nine to Patri's junior high school. He attended the school for four years and remembered it with great pleasure. I'll quote his responses at some length, because he gives such vivid impressions of Patri and his school.

He began with happy memories of the school and its principal: "The reminiscing that your questions about Angelo Patri and P. S. 45 inspire, I am delighted to notice, is both full of cheer and full of mirth. I would go back to that place and time in a flash, if I could. And that would plant me smack in the middle of the Great Depression, a time full of economic and other kinds of woes. . . . ."

Dongarra remembered most clearly the workshops that were a central part of the school program: "I recall doing 'printing,' 'blue-printing,' 'cabinet-making,' 'art,' and, of course, 'library.' My 'art' teacher was, I believe, a Miss Bauer, a wiry, lively grey-haired muse who got me to enter some efforts of mine in a couple of local contests. (I won!)" But it was the work in the print shop that connected young Joe directly to the principal. Something he wrote had brought him "to Patri's amused attention and to his office. . . . I do believe it was a small piece that I had type-set, a 'fait-divers' from the Daily News of a singularly comical (to my mind) act of delinquency. What Patri had to say about that I can't remember, but I do remember his natty, nubby light grey sports jacket, his purple tie, his beautifully combed hair. And us laughing a lot."

The workshops that Dongarra remembered were central to Patri's approach, as they had been in Dewey's Laboratory School decades before. Louis Menand in *The Metaphysical Club* recently wrote that at the Laboratory School "children were involved in workshop-type projects in which learning was accomplished in a manner that simulated the way Dewey thought it was accomplished in real life: through group activity." [12] In Patri's much larger public school such workshops provided variety, motivation, and hands-on discovery learning for students from a wide range of backgrounds.

Dongarra recalled with pleasure the diversity of the school and the opportunity to continue to study Italian: "As for the ethnic composition of the student body, it was to my unwary eye, thoroughly unremarkable: Italian-Americans, Irish, Jewish, and other European nationalities. There must have been an African-American or two, for there were, to my intense delight, at summer camps I went to . . . . I did take classes in the Italian language at P. S. 45. But by the time I got to take them, I was already proficient in the Sicilian version of Italian (my mother tongue) and in the Tuscan version. . . . Now you already know that I am a retired (1985) professor emeritus of Romance Languages (Patri must get some of the blame for that)." [13]

My contact with Joe Dongarra led to correspondence with his older sister, Catherine Dongarra Strobel, who attended PS 45 in the 1930s. She recalled Patri as "a kind and gentle man. He never raised his voice, and was well-liked." She also had warm memories of the school, particularly the workshops. "I belonged to the clay workshop run by Mr. Robinson . . . . I also participated in culinary arts, which was very enjoyable. . . . . Our classes included English, Math, and Biology, and also the study of Italian. Mr. Caruso was our instructor—he was an excellent teacher—he loved opera and often regaled the class with opera renditions, especially 'Che Gelida Manina' from 'La Boheme.' All in all I enjoyed being a student at PS 45." [14]

My search for surviving students took me to the e-mail site for the American Italian Historical Association. I sent a message inviting responses from anyone who had information about Patri and had a prompt reply from Teresa Cerasuola, who referred me to some oral history she had written about the neighborhood around Patri's school. In the article reporting her interviews she said: "The influence of Angelo Patri, child psychologist and first Italian-American principal of a Junior High School in New York City, was strongly felt by attendees of P.S. 45 on Hoffman St." Among her interviewees was eighty four-year-old Marie Bevona, who said, "Patri really knew children; he created an innovative curriculum, initiating a scholarship program whereby graduating students were encouraged to attend high school. As one of the recipients of this grant, I graduated from a commercial course in Evander Childs High School in 1920, and secured a job in a Wall Street insurance firm, an almost impossible feat for an Italian American woman in those days." [15]

Teresa Cerasuola also connected me with Rocco D'Erasmo, who has assembled two lively, personal books about the Fordham neighborhood in the Bronx: *Fordham Was a Town* (1978), and *Memories of Fordham* (1987). *Memories* has photographs of Patri and a reprint of an old "Principal's Message," to his students, that ends with Patri at his most optimistic and sentimental. "You, my young friends, are the world as it should be. You are the beginning of progress. You drive the world on. . . . You achieve, you reform. . . . Because of you I too have become strong. You have made me free. . . . What a place for dreams is this moving, singing, restless thing we call school." [16]

D'Erasmo, who attended PS 45 from 1941 to 1945, had a clear understanding of Patri's approach to Americanization: "Mr. Patri, small in stature, but big in heart, encouraged all of us to try to succeed in any venture we undertook. Most of all he stressed the understanding, love, and respect for our parents. He made us understand the need to study the language of our parents' heritage. Mr. Patri believed that in studying Italian, the students of Italian descent would have the opportunity to understand the contribution of their ancestors to the civilization of the world. We were taken on field trips to art centers and even toured the Italian liners when they came into New York harbor. Patri's political connections helped his students personalize the value of integrating their old and new heritages: "This was also the start of Americanization—learning American history and geography, but not forgetting the good and noble traditions of our forebears. My greatest thrill occurred one semester when the school gave a party that was attended by the mayor of New York City, Fiorello

LaGuardia. Meeting the mayor through Mr. Patri was the highlight of the party. . . . "

D'Erasmo recalled two particular teachers who connected students with their Italian roots: "Mr. Calitri and Mrs. DiDiodato helped make the Italian classes more interesting by relating experiences of their travels to Italy. During the summer months on their holiday through Italy, they would pick up souvenirs to bring back for display in our classes. . . . There were maps of Italy which helped us identify the little towns our parents came from." [17]

In several letters D'Erasmo added further thoughts about Patri, calling him "one of the finest persons I ever knew. . . . I remember him as a quiet, reserved gentleman but forceful in dealing with the so-called tough guys. I knew quite a few of them—but he had his way of dealing with them. . . . Patri wasn't tough with the toughies, they were aware of his very high esteem in the school system and knew that he didn't hesitate to sit down with the students' parents to try to resolve any problems. . . . The police and local priests worked with the school system. When a boy was picked up for petty thievery, the police turned him over to the school or local priest who worked with the parents in getting him to see the problems he was posing to the parents, school, and church. This was done so the boy would not wind up with a record that would follow him thru-out the years." One of these priests was Father Cafuzzi, who had helped Patri know the neighborhood when he became principal in 1913. Father Cafuzzi was the cofounder of the Church of Our Lady of Mt. Carmel, which, along with PS 45, was one of the centers of this Italian colony. [18]

Teresa Cerasuola, continuing her practice of oral history, interviewed her husband and sister, who had entered PS 45 in September 1944, three months after Patri retired. Teresa's husband, Frank Cerasuola, remembered "the excellent craft courses offered, where he learned the art of bookbinding and cardboard furniture making." Her sister, Julie DeAngelo, recalled that "a large portrait of Patri, with white hair, hung in the main hall of the school. . . . Home Ec for girls was stressed, where they learned to cook and clean and use the wringer washer in a three room model apartment. . . . Her music teacher, who apparently had leftist leanings, taught the Russian revolutionary song, which I think was called the Meadowlands. There were two swimming pools, outdoor athletic programs, and after school hours co-ed dances. . . . Julie feels that there was a heavier stress on the trades/crafts than on the academics." However, Frank's friend Ciro Marino claimed "that the school was more than adequate in its academic programs and prepared him well for his career, later, as a pharmacist. He studied Italian with Miss Costanzo and remembers the drama teacher who also mentored John Garfield. . . . Ciro especially enjoyed his printing courses, but not the horticulture classes conducted in the outdoor gardens and greenhouses," which may have been World War II victory gardens.[19]

As I gathered these memories I was intensely aware that I was hearing from only a tiny sample of the thousands of students who attended Patri's schools. It would have been challenging indeed to search out more students until I found the failures, the drop-outs, those whom Patri and his colleagues had not rescued. But Patri had found some of them for us. He consistently acknowledged the existence of these students and expressed his concern for them. For his twenty fifth graduation announcement in 1938 Patri wrote a message to his students addressed with significant capital letters:

"To ALL the children of P.S. 45, the Bronx:

To ALL those who are present, and those who are absent;

To those who were graduated and to those who were not;

To those who have achieved distinction and to those who serve the day among the crowd, un-noticed, but beloved;

To those who have followed the straight hard way, and to those who have strayed from it;

To those who have succeeded in their life's ambition and to those who have yet to realize it,

The School that has mothered them gives affectionate greeting.[20]

Patri freely confessed his own failures with some of these students. Near the end of his memoir he wrote: "Once I struck a big boy because I saw him tripping the little ones who were marching out to the playground and as each one fell on his face the big foot shot out and tripped the next helpless victim. It was no gentle slap that I administered in my anger. Then I discovered I had struck a boy who was drunk and the bitterness of my offense is, after fifty years, still with me. There was no justification for it and no comfort in the memory of it." [21]

The fact that Patri had no children of his own may have enabled him to spread his care and affection more widely among all who crossed his path. Patri's contact with students diminished drastically when he retired in 1944, but—resilient man that he was—he found many ways to enjoy his retirement and to continue to be useful to the country to which his family had brought him six decades earlier and which had changed so drastically during those decades.

Patri's vacation and retirement home, Haviland Hollow
(J. Wallace)

EIGHT

Country Gentleman:
Patri in Retirement, 1944–1965

PATRI BEGAN TEACHING IN 1897, BECAME PRINCIPAL OF PS 4 in 1907, and principal of PS 45 in 1913, so when he retired in 1944, he had worked for the New York City school system for forty-seven years. For the last thirty-one of those years he had, during the school terms, gone each morning to the same office in the same building and returned each evening to his nearby apartment. The only variations in routine occurred when he attended meetings, had speaking engagements, or talked on the radio. With his decades of work in schools, one might expect some difficulty in adjusting to retirement, but that was not the case. Patri and family seem to have moved smoothly into a new and welcome pattern. They gave up their apartment in the brownstone building on 170th Street where they had lived for over three decades and moved to the country.[1]

The apparent ease of the transition can be explained partly by the continuities in Patri's life. The first of these was that since the mid-1930s, during his last decade of school work, Patri and his family had spent weekends, vacations, and summers at their country home in Haviland Hollow in Patterson, Putnam County, New York, about fifty miles north of the Bronx.[2] The extended family included Patri, his wife Dora, her sister, Anna Morrison, and a man named John Dacey Blonk, who lived with the family in the city. Patri's cooks and housekeepers, Alice and Josephine Mohrs, helped form what Patri called "a family by mutual consent."[3] Patri's grandnephew, Frank Merolla, Jr., later wrote of the Mohrs: "They had all the knowledge and skill to care for the entire estate. In addition, their strength and stamina were equal to the long days necessary for the job. . . . Jo and Alice, through their love and loyalty, made it possible for the family to live out their lives in the place they loved."[4] Their work was eased by the efforts, at various times of maids, a gardener, and a chauffeur. Now Patri and family had more time to read, relax, and enjoy the gardens and sculptures, some of them carved by Patri's former pupil, Antonio di Filippo.

Josephine Pugliese, Angelo's oldest living sister, visited often, sometimes accompanied by her five children and five grandchildren. (Josephine's husband Carmine had died in 1945.) After Josephine's death in 1961 their closest family contacts were with the Pugliese's second daughter Anita, her husband, Frank Merolla, Sr., and their son, Frank Merolla, Jr. The Merollas had lived near them in the Bronx, and until 1943 had a vacation home about a mile away from the Patri's place in Haviland Hollow.[5] The families were close enough so that Patri made Frank, Sr., the executor of his estate. There were less frequent visits from Jennie, his other surviving sister, and from relatives who lived farther away.

A second continuity was Patri's writing his weekly column, "Our Children," assembling books from the columns, writing articles for magazines, and preparing and delivering speeches and radio addresses, occasionally in Italian.[6] Patri continued to receive hundreds of letters from parents, teachers, and others, and he responded to them in his columns, in his radio program, and in his occasional public lectures. Sometimes he dealt with local requests in person, inviting parents to his home to discuss their problems. Richard Renoff wrote about one such situation. He had a retarded brother, and his parents were looking for ways to help him. A relative arranged for the Renoff family to meet with Patri at Haviland Hollow. Half a century later Richard recalled two things from the meeting: that Patri's advice was simply to keep the brother active and that he did not charge a fee for the consultation.[7]

Patri's habit of regular, moderate physical activity was a third continuity in his retirement. In the city he had taken walks for exercise, to clear his mind, and to deal with stress. In Haviland Hollow he walked, gardened, and occasionally played golf, sometimes with the Merollas and occasionally with neighbors like radio commentator Lowell Thomas.[8] Richard Renoff had another connection with Patri: he caddied for him in the 1950s at the Ridgewood Country Club in Danbury, Connecticut, just across the state line. Richard recalled that Patri was "very elderly and only played nine holes. The caddy fee was seventy-five cents for nine holes, and Dr. Patri would give a fifty cent tip in addition. (Very generous.) He did not hit the ball far but hit it straight. Therefore the guys liked working for him."[9] Patri sounds like a caddy's ideal golfer, walking slowly around a restful nine holes, not driving the caddy into the rough for lost balls, and tipping generously at the end. Richard's memories of Patri are consistent with those of others who knew him; he was as considerate of his young caddies as he was of his golf partners.

A fourth continuity was financial. Through his and Dora's pensions, supplemented by substantial royalties and fees for speeches and radio talks, Patri and his family maintained a prosperous, comfortable, and pleasant existence. Unlike many retirees who had only their pensions to live on, Patri and family could enjoy their comfortable country home and 170 acres knowing that their lifestyle need not decline. Thus the continuities and pleasures of family, home, work, and financial security carried Patri through the sadness that he felt on leaving his school, city community, students, and colleagues.

Just a year after his retirement Patri wrote lyrically about his country home: "The farm is bounded on the north by the old mountain covered with a blanket of pine and hemlock and a scattering of hardwoods. On the south by the meadows rising gently toward the hills. On the east by the rolling hills of Connecticut and on the west by little hills that fold themselves into the lovely Harlem Valley. Overhead is the infinite sky, the gorgeous sunrise and sunset, the starlight and mystic moonlight and the glorious high day, all with a beauty so beautiful it beggars my pen."

Patri appreciated the resident animals as well as the plants: "When the lawyers handed us the deed signed and sealed with such ceremony, we thought we owned this place but we were mistaken. We were loaned it, to share it with a group of inhabitants whose ancestors had lived upon it for years unnumbered. We found this out when we set the orchard and the garden." The gardener was the first to notice: "Felice was beaming with the gardener's pride upon his rows of hatted beans. 'Very good, nice beans,' he said with the love all Italians have in their voices when they speak of beans." But the woodchucks ate the beans, and Patri described the struggle with them and with the rabbits, chipmunks, skunks, crows, and deer that had been there first. They solved the problem with good fences and by planting extra berries for the birds and extra trees for the deer. And, rarely to tell a story without a moral, Patri proposed that the newly forming United Nations adopt similar practices in dealing with new and old populations on land around the globe. [10]

Valentina Pugliese Perrone was the daughter of Patri's life-long friend, Anthony J. Pugliese, and Patri was her godfather. She was born in 1906, so knew Patri for nearly sixty years, until his death in 1965. She had warm memories of Patri and Dora both before and during their retirement and in a paper she wrote after Patri's death recalled visits to Haviland Hollow:

"The house was situated on a rise back from the road overlooking the brook which ran under it and into their meadows beyond. A high hill, a mountain, really, rose precipitously behind it where they planted the orchard. . . ."

Valentina told of one special gift the Patris received: "One summer, poet Louis Untermeyer went to Europe and in his travels acquired a pair of tiny Sardinian donkeys. The female did not survive the journey and Louis began to wonder if he hadn't been a bit impulsive. Would Angelo and Dora rescue the other? They would, and for many years the donkey lorded it over all and sundry, showing good will only when he was treated to a cigarette butt. They named him 'Don Quixote.' " This donkey may have served as a long-delayed replacement for Patri's childhood pet donkey, which was killed by a wolf high in the mountains above Piaggine.[11]

Frank Merolla, Jr., was born in 1941, so knew Angelo and Dora for over twenty years. He recently wrote this note, giving his recollections of Patri and family. "A visit to 'The Hollow,' as Uncle Angelo's home was called, was always a special treat. When I was told we were to visit, the joyous anticipation began. That was true from my earliest recollection to my last visit before he died. The visits to that home since his death have rekindled such warm, loving memories that the sadness of his death is pushed to the background."

Merolla described the drive past New York City reservoirs to the Patri home when, as they got closer, "the rolling terrain turns to low hills then small mountains at Haviland Hollow Road. Our arrival was announced by the crunch of the tires on the gravel driveway which ends between the house and the barn. The white farm house, its front aproned by a covered porch, sits on a small plateau on the side of a mountain. . . . Across the driveway were gardens of flowers, vegetables, berries and boxwood. Orchards of apple, pear and peach were to the east."

On his many visits to Haviland Hollow young Frank was impressed by the house itself. The "original construction of the main buildings probably occurred in the late 1700s. The foundations were of thick stone, the beams great hand-hewn oak. . . . High ceilings made the rooms cool in summer. The plaster walls were textured and wavy. Ten-inch wide planks with wood dowels made up the floors. Their love of their home was in part an appreciation of the craftsmanship that had gone into its construction. . . ."

The house could be seen in part as a museum for Patri's school: "Scattered through the house were gifts from the children of PS 45. In the library one would find books assembled in the book-binding shop. On the walls were water colors of varying sizes and topics done by children of varying ages and talents. . . . On the mantel over the fireplace were Don Quixote and his servant, Sancho Panza, sculpted by Attilio Piccirilli. . . . On a coffee table rested a large book of photographs of some of the finest pieces of art created in his school. A great glass cabinet sat proudest of all in the hallway between the dining room and living room. It contained wood carvings and breakable pieces of porcelain and clay the children had given him." Patri gave away freely his own amateur carvings and other objects, but could not bear to part with art by his students: "Visitors were treated generously with a piece he had carved and painted, or books from the library, but even in his great generosity the creations the children of his school had given him were never bestowed as gifts. That is how greatly he treasured them." [12]

Visitors were greeted in the living room, which had a large fireplace. "In the winter a roaring fire blazed and spread its warmth to everyone present. . . . Nearby was a low, soft, welcoming easy chair in which Uncle sat. The space in between was home to a child-size rocking chair, my favorite place. What could be better than sitting in a comfortable chair my size between a roaring fire and the great storyteller?" Later as an adult Merolla was familiar with Patri's *Schoolmaster of the Great City* and recalled from that book "Uncle Angelo's father, my great grandfather, sitting by a fire telling stories by the hour. Did Uncle learn that skill or was it an inborn gift?"

During the visits Patri first wanted recent news of his sisters and their families. Frank recalled that during the discussion, "Uncle was as good a listener as he was a storyteller, especially with me. In your mind's eye picture one seven-year-old with two older generations, sitting, listening and enjoying himself for an afternoon. Uncle made sure that I was part of the conversation and that my words were important." After getting caught up on family matters, Patri wanted to talk about recent news, including movie star gossip, politics, sports, "and of course, children and the schools. These and other topics were all discussed, his insight apparent, his opinions expressed but not dictated."

The high point of the visit for Frank was when Patri would tell a story: "Oh what a joy that was! His voice was soft and even, and his delivery spellbinding. There was no hint of the country of Angelo's birth in his speech. Aunt Dora listened, occasionally adding a tidbit with a gentle, 'Leo did you forget about . . . ?' As I look back over the decades I realize how in tune they were." The stories could be the retelling of a classic like *Don Quixote* or a true account of "a deer that had been injured on the mountain behind the house and protected as it healed, or a child growing up to be an artist. An hour had passed and no one had moved. The adults were as enraptured as I. The warmth of the storytelling would last all the way home and for days after—and now fifty years."

Frank recalled that leaving was as pleasant as arriving, for Patri always had a gift for him. "I would be taken for a trip across the foyer to the library to pick out a book or two. With a little guidance and a gentle suggestion I always left with a book I'd be able to read and enjoy." There were gifts from the garden as well: "The cellar had canned fruits, vegetables, and jellies—quince was my favorite. The root cellar up the lane was full of apples, pears, peaches, zucchini and the like. If it was summer the choices would include figs or a basket of tomatoes, corn, lettuce, carrots which we picked ourselves." They would walk through the gardens accompanied by Dora's beloved dog, Shawn. Frank, like Patri's students, acknowledged Patri's influence: "I learned lessons without knowing I was learning. His lessons made you forget all else. A warm good-bye with a smile and a gentle hand on the shoulder topped off the day. I felt important."

Frank, who was twenty-four when Patri died, recalled how their talks had evolved: "My inclusion in the conversations moved over the years from my current teacher to what I thought about my summer job, my specific academic interests and that special young lady—now my wife for thirty-eight years." Frank ended this brief memoir with warm appreciation for his Uncle Angelo: "He retired from the New York City school system but not from writing for another fifteen years. He never retired from life. Uncle's mind remained active, inquisitive, current, and retrospective. He was truly an incredible man." [13]

In another memoir Merolla describes Patri as "not a tall man, probably 5'3", and of slight build. His posture was erect, not stooped by age or his many surgeries.[14] As he walked there was a bounce to his step. Any hand gestures were welcoming ones. He had a twinkle in his eye like a mischievous teenager and a hint of a smile that easily broke out. The friendly face was topped by a full shock of pure white hair." Like other observers Merolla was impressed by Patri's natty wardrobe: "His dress was impeccable—usually in summer suits of white linen, and in the winter heavy woolen Irish tweeds. An accompanying tie was a bright solid color, green, or orange or yellow. Aunt Dora's loving hand had produced the wool argyle socks he wore. If there was a hat on his head, it was worn at a jaunty angle. In spite of the warm glow of friendship that he emitted, you could tell people were in awe of him." [15]

In the summer of 1955, Frank, then fourteen years old, spent several weeks with the Patri family. He recently recalled what a typical day with them was like: "Mornings were his work time. The bundle of letters that were referred to him weekly by the newspaper had been prescreened for appropriateness. Uncle and Aunt Dora would spend time reviewing them again and selecting topics that were current and might have broader appeal. 'At what age should a child be given tasks around the home? How much homework is appropriate for a fourth grader?' . . . A column would be written and prepared for the newspaper. Often a personal letter would be sent to an individual whose situation was unique. Aunt Dora played a major role in this effort, helping to review the letters, serving as a sounding board, aiding in a rewrite and typing. . . ."

Having completed the day's writing Angelo and Dora relaxed. "In good weather Aunt Dora would spend the afternoons in the flower or boxwood gardens. An exception would be to can or freeze something that had just ripened in the garden. Uncle might hit practice golf balls back and forth in one of the pastures. Occasionally he would be driven to Danbury to the Ridgewood Golf Club to play nine holes. . . ."

Patri, a lover of art, tried his hand at simple sculptures. "In later years, after Aunt Dora died and the newspaper articles were a thing of the past, carving took a larger and larger part of the day. . . . The bulk of his subjects were from the outdoors; flowers, bears, dogs, butterflies, birds and an eagle." [16] When he wasn't carving he was likely to be reading: "The monthly publications of the Junior Literary Guild were sent for his critique. . . He had become a voracious reader early in life and his interest in literature never waned. More serious reading and re-reading books from years before entertained him also. . . . Another part of reading every day was the *New York Times*. He was always current. . . ."

The day began to wind down with an early dinner, at which "the family and staff shared the meal and conversation seated together at one large table. Evening conversation included what chores had been completed that day. Depending on the weather forecast, the next day's chores were planned. The early evening was spent around a radio listening to relaxing music and doing light reading." These visits and the weeks spent with Patri made a deep and lasting impression on Frank, who wrote near the end of his account: "Throughout my life when I've had a big decision, he comes to mind. Almost forty years after his death he is part of my conscience." [17]

In this rich and beautiful environment, Patri entertained visitors, including the occasional interviewer. In November 1946, Virginia Irwin, a reporter for the *St. Louis Post-Dispatch*, called on Patri in his home and wrote: "On a small farm just an hour's train ride out of New York lives a man who will probably go down in history as America's best-loved school teacher. His name is Angelo Patri, and now in the quiet years of his life he does little but read, tend his flowers, and watch his fig tree grow in his greenhouse, and pour into a syndicated newspaper column all the wisdom he amassed during the 30 years that he was principal of New York's Public School No. 45." Irwin described Patri as "the idol of some 90,000 children who benefited from his guidance in those 30 years."

Irwin described the community surrounding PS 45 and wrote: "Next week Patri will be 70 years old and the people of that neighborhood where he lavished affection, attention, and personal guidance upon their children will dedicate a community center to him. Master of ceremonies will be the movie and stage star, John Garfield, a product of Angelo Patri's public school." As they walked about the grounds Patri showed Irwin a garden sculpture by another former pupil, Antonio di Filippo, and then in the house various gifts from pupils, all made in school workshops: rugs, batiks, paintings, pottery, and sculptures. Patri said, "I think I am the most fortunate person in the world. Besides my memories, I have all these treasures bequeathed to me by my children." [18]

Long after his 1927 visit to Italy, Patri corresponded with relatives there. In 1953 he replied in a reflective mood to a letter from Rosa Conte, his mother's cousin: "I am grateful to you for a very beautiful and moving letter. You are to be congratulated. There is nothing more rewarding than fine children—an experience that has been denied me and my wife. But I have had much honor and happiness in teaching the children of the schools to which in my forty-four years as a school master I had been assigned. My life has been blessed with the love and affection showered upon me by parents and children alike. Now in my declining years they still find their way to my door and smile upon me. Life has been good and still is." [19]

Early in his retirement Patri was busy with his speeches, newspaper columns, and magazine articles. In 1948 he published his most substantial book for parents, *How to Help Your Child Grow Up*. Then he wrote for young adult readers the autobiographical *Biondino*, published in Italy in 1950 and in the United States in 1951. [20] Continuing the autobiographical theme, about 1950 he began his most extended retirement project, writing his story of PS 45. He was disappointed by the school's return to traditional practices and no doubt wanted the story of the school under his leadership recorded for posterity.

Patri wrote a draft of 327 pages, ending with an idealistic two-page chapter titled "The School," and an alternative final chapter of eighteen pages. This chapter, apparently written in 1954, sometime after the others, is different in tone from most of the memoir. It begins with invidious contrasts between the schools during Patri's time and the current schools into which they had devolved. Patri gives examples of general school decline reported by parents, a visiting teacher, a classroom teacher, and his former student Tony di Filippo, and then reports unwelcome changes in his own beloved PS 45. A man who lives two blocks from the school tells him: "The principal's door is shut. No chats in the office of a Monday morning. No parents play in the school orchestra. There is no sharing. We are treated as strangers." Patri says of one of his former teachers that "the nagging confusion of many supervisors, of too many things that do not count, too much unrest, too much talk, have her down." She told Patri, "It wasn't so in the old days. We did our work and enjoyed it. Now the thrill of getting something done no longer counts."[21] (IV, 2)

Patri moves on from his own school to a depressing national picture of rampant juvenile delinquency and gang activity and the negative impact of war on educational reform. He admits that these problems are not new, and cites examples of them from his own experience and from the newspapers. He proposes solutions, but ends uncharacteristically with worries about the future of school and society. Patri may have drafted this second version of the last chapter to give the memoir more contemporary relevance, but writing it could well have been so depressing that it caused him to set the manuscript aside. Or perhaps one of his recurrent bouts with pleurisy may have hindered publishing plans.[22] I have seen no evidence that Patri ever tried to publish this memoir. He made many handwritten corrections and additions to previous chapters but almost none in the two alternate final chapters. This memoir was a substantial work, and must have occupied him for many months, so it may have been one of the few disappointments of his retirement for Patri to leave it unpublished.[23]

Dr. Benjamin Fine, a veteran education writer for the *New York Times*, visited Haviland Hollow in May 1962, and wrote a glowing report that may have comforted Patri somewhat as he gave up his popular newspaper columns: "After 65 years of teaching and writing about education, Dr. Angelo Patri, one of the master teachers of this century, has decided to retire. This month he is putting 'finis' on his school columns, which for nearly half a century have appeared in many of the nation's major newspapers."

Fine had known Patri for years, and recalled that he was distinctive right from the beginning of his career: "Dr. Patri brought a breath of fresh air into the teaching profession when he became a teacher in 1897. His philosophy was simply expressed: children are the most important aspect of their school system. Their needs, desires, dreams, and imaginations must not be trampled underfoot." Fine was pleased to see that the eighty six-year-old educator was "still vigorous, eager and alert. His enthusiasm for children has not abated. For more than six decades he has combined actual classroom teaching with school administration. As principal of Junior

High School 45 in the Bronx, Dr. Patri set the educational world on its heels with his unorthodox approach to learning."

Fine was not surprised that, in spite of old age, Patri maintained his strong opinions on educational developments: "Dr. Patri, now white haired, slight looking, but with keen, flashing eyes, and an eagerness that belied his age, called for more 'heart and soul' in education and less mechanization." Patri always had a story to illustrate his theories, and he told Fine about Jacob, who "refused to be promoted. He wanted to remain with his teacher. 'So I promoted his teacher!' the educational patriarch explained. 'You must respond to the child's needs if you expect the youngster to do his best.' "

As in his memoir, Patri observed decline in the schools: "Our children have become statistics. Our teachers are technicians. Mass education has destroyed the warm relationship between pupil and instructor." Asked what was needed in schools currently, Patri replied: "We want teachers who have courage, who aren't afraid to be themselves. We want teachers who are enthusiastic, who want to help young minds grow and develop, even as buds open up in the springtime." [24]

On October 21, 1961, Patri's beloved wife Dora, age eighty seven, died after a marriage of fifty one years. Valentina Perrone had visited them two years earlier, and later reminisced: "On one of our last visits, Dora and I were talking in the kitchen. She, at the time, was 85 and she said: 'Death is a beneficent angel and I do not fear him. I hope Providence will privilege me to live longer than Angelo. I want to care for him all of his life.' Her wish was denied, and she was the first to go." Valentina wrote Angelo a note of sympathy to which he responded: "Thank you, my children. God called and Dora answered his command. In a world gone mad, He might have need of her. I grieve and you grieve with me for her share in a long and happy life was precious. May yours be as long and happy." [25]

The following January 1 Patri, eighty six years old, began keeping a diary which ran through September 30 of the same year. [26] Without Dora to talk with he needed an outlet for his feelings and thoughts. At the beginning he wrote in the diary every day unless he was ill; toward the end there were long intervals between entries. Usually he began with lyrical descriptions of the weather and the woods and fields around the farm. He recorded the activities of his household, visits from the Merolla family and others, observations on the news, schools and school politics, dreams, his writing and woodcarving, baseball games, and memories from the past. Occasionally he would report on a book that he was reviewing for the

Junior Literary Guild. In most of the entries we find the Angelo Patri we are familiar with—engaged, optimistic, energetic, eager for the joys and challenges of life. But, with his wife gone and his health worsening, we occasionally find other emotions in these notes: sadness, loneliness, bitterness over past slights, guilt over a few regretted decisions, fierce anger at politicians and the Russians. Patri had suffered from pleurisy for many years, and this and other ailments made it difficult for him to sustain his usually positive outlook.

A very private man, Patri apparently expressed these negative emotions only in the diary. During this time Frank Merolla, Jr., frequently drove Patri back and forth to family gatherings, an hour each way, and during their long conversations heard "no hint of depression" even after Dora's death. Merolla recalled: "Our talks were never anything but positive, uplifting, and current."[27]

A few selections from Patri's seventy-four page diary reflect the tone and content of the whole. I will comment as appropriate.

January 2: "The chapter I was working on is still waiting." (The memoir of PS 45 that he had begun in 1953.)

January 9: "Harry showed moving pictures of Dora in the garden, the greenhouse, the kitchen. . . . The look at her as she was gave me a sense of ease that has been absent since her departure into the unknown."[28] (Patri refers here to Harry Krail, his successor as principal.)

January 27: "This valley was settled by Friends (Quakers). I still like to feel that their spirit persists. . . . I am sure that Dora—a friend to all the world if there ever was one—strengthens the tradition. . . ."

January 30: "'Good morning Miss Dove,' bought by Dora to read to Joe and Alice has been a nightly recreation. The three of us sit and read, usually half an hour. . . . As a good night parting it is a pleasure."

February 1: "Frank, Anita, and son Frank, home for a few days, came in. All looked well, especially the young man. He is taking hold."

February 13: "Am trying to get the plan and the reason for the book [the memoir] into an understandable shape. The battle of what to choose and how to organize is about as demanding as can be."

February 17: "Anna got from the doctor that Dora died of a blood clot. Her heart just stopped—her heart that was so strong had had too much. Her heart that spread its love, its warmth, its affection to all that came her way. . . . Her heart that had carried the responsibility of the family, the weight of my work, would go no more and she must rest . . . ." (Anna, Dora's sister, lived with the Patris for many years until her death in 1964.)

February 18: "This morning I felt so lonesome as if I had been deserted by all my friends—all successes save me." He listed members of the CCNY class of 1897 who had been promoted to high positions in school central offices, and added: "Only one not promoted, not recognized by his official superiors. Only one with all my friends that in the eyes of the system was not deemed worthy of promotion." (It is significant that Patri felt this way. He was far more famous, influential, and prosperous than most of his classmates, but clearly resented the failure of the New York Public Schools to acknowledge his good work with offers of promotion.)[29]

February 22: "Can it be that my worries have to do with a shrinking income and an increasing expenditure? . . . Surely I have enough set aside to carry me safely to the end."

March 8: "I am doing penance for my great sin—when I compelled my wife to sign her maiden name on the paper that the Cardinal demanded. Dora felt that I had divorced her, abandoned her. She died of a broken heart—Mea culpa—and so too shall I, God helping me." (This is a puzzling entry. I can only speculate that Patri and his wife had a secular marriage in 1910. Perhaps near the end of his life he wanted the blessing of the church on their marriage, and the Cardinal insisted on Dora's signing the document with her maiden name to indicate that theirs had not been a true marriage, that is, one blessed by the church. Frank Merolla, Jr., suggests that whatever occurred, his uncle's "reaction was more severe than Aunt Dora's.")[30]

March 25: "A chapter needs a couple of lines about report cards that take apart a child, tabulate him and find somewhere the sting that the search for perfection in statistics always brings."

March 25: "Harry went home after dinner with a preface to the book to type, a half bushel of apples, and a promise to be back soon." (The book Patri refers to was a *Graded Course of Study Correlated with the Book of Knowledge*, for which Patri wrote the introduction and Harry Krail the science section. Patri's preface was included from about 1941 to 1964.)

March 30: "Bad news—the syndicate job is over. It was expected, for the past five years it has been dragging. No complaint if that is possible without a pang." (The syndicate was the North American Newspaper Alliance, which had carried Patri's column, "Our Children," for many years.)

April 2: "Did over a story. It looks better, but wait until tomorrow. It's how it reads the next day that counts."

April 4: "After 18 years of retirement from the school system I have lost the touch of immediacy which is the heart and soul of daily writing. The schools somehow have run away from me."

April 7: "Got a postal card from a pupil in P.S. 4, the school where I first served as principal. Jack Fruengloss remembers that I married Miss Caterson. He wondered whether the man who writes the children's Daily Column is the same as his old principal, a son perhaps, for his estimate of my age is over 90. Not that far along yet. But it was a guess considering that Jack was about eight years old at the time. So they come, the unexpected, out of the day, of time. To be remembered is a measure of worth."[31]

April 9: "How I miss my partner. The spring was always the high point of the year. She planned the garden, helped to raise seeds, discarded and replanted to her heart's content. How happy she was. . . . A span of fifty years, and every year a garden to look forward to, plan, admire, and put to sleep. . . . She radiated strength and joy to all who were about her."

May 29: "Been feeling that the president [Kennedy] has some basic make up that is troublesome—a combination of ambition that even the presidency cannot satisfy, a fear that demands the support of his brother the attorney general, a boastfulness that strides ahead and a caution that is cowardly."

June 5: "The world is a mess—a monument to political hypocrisy—greed—dissatisfaction—utter selfishness, sheer despair—the smart wise writers are telling the truth—and the politicians hate them. What's true to a mind that's chained?"

June 28: "Evenings after supper before the girls [Alice and Josephine Mohrs] go home from the day's work, we sit down in my room next to the kitchen and I read to them and for my own comfort some bit I have found pleasant. Our goodnight parting means just what it says—friendship, service, pleasant living, healthy thoughts. . . ."

July 4: "The first national anniversary that I have spent alone, since 1910 when Dora and I were married. . . . Her words were comforting, her smile a benediction, never a soul so brave, so unselfish, so rich in kindly thoughts, so sure in good deeds."

July 5: Patri read Irving Stones' *The Agony and the Ecstasy*, about Michelangelo, and wrote: "I have read the story, leisurely, slowly and with each chapter my interest grew. I stopped long to review my visits to Florence, to Carrera, to Pisa, Pietra Santa, the white marble that the sculptor carved with such deep appreciation."

July 11: The space flights inspired Patri's contrasts of industrialists and politicians in a rare burst of angry and ungrammatical eloquence: "So does industry marvel on. It's the adventures of these industrial leaders that make the nation achieve. . . while the politicians, maggots who take all and give nothing—the show-offs—the planners for self-aggrandizement, selfish pride, the men who take all and give only trouble—the world's troubles would come to an end if we could just get rid of the politicians—that would free the world of graft—murder—deceit—lies—wickedness—the major disease of modern civilization and for that matter all the civilizations of history—these are the gangsters gone berserk. There is no good in them."

July 16: "Mt. Carmel Day—one the family—my father's family celebrated each year. . . . I remember mother telling me, when I first went to college, that her family were the *Contes*—and in the days of Dante, in the days of the Guelphs, Ghibellines, her family were driven out of Florence and migrated south to Rome, to Naples, to Salerno and over the hills to live while the Bourbons ruled. . . . All the time I read Stones' story of Rome I saw my father who traced his family back to the days of Scipione Africanus."[32]

July 20: "Got a letter from a classmate, Aaron Salant, the valedictorian of the class (CCNY, 1897). He too lost his wife. He complains of being tired. Well, tiredness after 85 is as natural as the tirelessness of childhood. . . . Lucky he who leaves good deeds when the curtain falls."

July 24: "Measuring time by doses of medicine. Sleep, eternal sleep would be preferable. To be and then not to be—what a blessed relief. This today leads to tomorrow. Dull monotony—what could be worse!"

September 30, 1962: "Shawn, Dora's dog, died of grief. Her constant companion during her sick year died eleven months later. The dog never forgot. The dog lies with Alice's and Joe's dog in the backyard. . . . The days are not easy, the going is rougher." Patri had lost one more connection with his beloved Dora and could bear to write no more diary entries.

The next notes in the diary were dated August 1963, addressed to Dr. Frank Merolla, and included statements of bequests to family, employees, and others. Each bequest is on a separate page, and each has been initialed by family members to indicate acceptance. Patri left to Alice and Josephine Mohrs, who had worked for the family for thirty years, shares in the estate equal to those received by family members. He also left them the dog Contessima and the cat Mikey and a painting of the house. He left to Jane Kroll, his only surviving sister, a silver tea set "on condition that the set stay under the tapestry woven by the pupils of P. S. 45 in Miss O'Brien's class." To friends he left a sculpture by Piccirilli, and he encouraged the Merollas and the Puglieses to take anything they wanted from the house. He left his many wood carvings to Dr. Merolla to dispose of.

A final note, written on August 16, 1965, says: "I have come to the conclusion that my funeral service take place in the St. John's church in Pawling now in charge of Father Storm. This is a change. I had wanted the service to be in the old church at 187 St. New York but changed. Alice

Mohr in charge." This new locale for his funeral suggests that Patri's connections with his country place, where he had spent twenty-one retirement years with his beloved Dora, were now stronger than those to the city where he had worked for so many decades. He died less than a month later. Valentina Perrone wrote of his four years without Dora: "He busied himself with his writing, reading, and wood-carving. . . . But it was never the same. The light was dimmed, and he followed her in September, 1965."

Angelo and Dora enjoying their garden
(Frank Merolla)

NINE

The Childless Patriarch: Patri's Family Life

THE PROCESS OF RESEARCHING PATRI'S FAMILY LIFE, primarily through interviews, has been as intriguing to me as the information I learned from that process. My search for Patri began logically enough with the *Dictionary of American Biography*, which had much useful information, but which noted that as of 1965 "no collection of correspondence has been located." However, through a friend's computer search I found that in 1966 Dr. Frank Merolla, who had married one of Patri's nieces, and who was executor of the Patri estate, had contributed ninety boxes of Patri's papers to the Library of Congress. Dr. Merolla had died in the meantime, but I was able to locate his son, Dr. Frank Merolla, Jr., in Valhalla, New York.[1] I corresponded with the younger Dr. Merolla and he gave me information about some of Patri's nephews and nieces who were still living.

During the summer of 1997 I flew to Denver, Orlando, and New York City, and interviewed some of the few remaining relatives who had clear memories of their "Uncle Angelo." These interviews follow sequentially as a modest case study in how families preserve their sometimes conflicting memories and how we construct our understandings of other people's lives. To clarify some confusing matters I will occasionally interject additional material in brackets. Throughout these interviews I felt as Daniel Boorstin may have when he wrote: "We see how we have come from seeking meaning to finding meaning in the seeking."

A review of some Patri family history may help in understanding the interviews which follow. Patri was born in 1876 to Carmela Conte Petraglia and Nicola Petraglia di Angelo in Piaggine in southern Italy. In 1881, at age five, he came to New York City with his mother Carmela Petraglia, her brother, Gaetano Conte, and younger sister Maria, to join Patri's father, who had preceded them to America. Maria died soon after they arrived in America, but the family went on to have three more daughters: Josephine, born in 1882, Rose, in 1889, and Joanna Isabella, in 1891. Josephine grew up and married Carmine Pugliese; they had two sons and three daughters, one of whom, Anita, married Frank Merolla. His son, Frank Merolla, Jr., Patri's grandnephew, became my chief informant and connection to the rest of the family. Frank gave me the names and addresses of other relatives, and I arranged to visit those who knew Patri best.

My first interview was with Jeanne Greco and her son Donald Greco in Denver, Colorado. Jeanne, born in 1917, is the only daughter of Angelo's youngest sister, Joanna Patri, and her first husband, James Reilly. When Jeanne was born Patri had been principal of PS 45 for only four years. Jeanne knew her Uncle Angelo for forty eight years, from 1917 until his death in 1965. Jeanne had four children, including Don, who was born in 1943, and thus knew Patri for twenty two years.

Early in our talk, Jeanne told me that her mother's name was Joanna Isabella Patri, which she "promptly changed to Jane as soon as she knew that Joanna Isabella smacked of foreignness."[2] Jeanne's most vivid memories of Patri centered on his country home, Haviland Hollow, in Pawling, New York, which he probably purchased in the mid-1930s. Jeanne had six cousins, two of whom, Bob Pugliese and Dick Bause, were several years younger than she. She said that when they visited their uncle "we were sent outside to play in the back yard, or we were in the kitchen, if it was too cold to go outside. We had to eat in the kitchen while the family had dinner around the dining table. . . . On occasion they let us sit under the dining table and listen to them, but we got rambunctious sometimes and we got hauled out."

Jeanne said that Uncle Angelo gave her away at her wedding "because he was the older brother. I had no Reilly relatives—that was my father's name . . . so my mother said to ask Uncle Angelo to give me away. . . . Uncle Angelo and the three girls were a little like their mother, my grandmother Patri. They were small in stature, and what they lacked in stature, they made up for in personality. They were very strong personalities." She described Patri as "soft-spoken, and unflappable. I never saw him show an excess of emotion other than kindliness—you know, a pat on the head and 'aren't you a nice girl' kind of thing. You can see I wasn't very close to him." I asked if Patri had an Italian accent, and Jeanne and Don agreed that he did not.

Don had clear memories of Patri and family. "Aunt Dora was his wife and Aunt Anna was her sister and she lived with them. At the time I knew them they had very mannish haircuts . . . and they always wore trousers. For the time it was amazing." [However, all photographs that I have seen show them in dresses.] I asked about Aunt Dora, and was told that her name was Dorothy Caterson and that her background was Scotch-Irish Protestant. At this point Jeanne put her nose in the air, and I asked if Aunt Dora's nose was in the air. Jeanne said no, that Patri's sisters' noses were in the air, suggesting "What's he doing running around with some . . . ? She wasn't demonstrative. She didn't hug and kiss like my Italian aunts."

I asked if marrying out of the Catholic faith had been a problem. Jeanne: "Definitely. In those days it was not looked upon as easily as it is today. I asked if Patri continued to attend church and practice his faith. Jeanne: "No, because I can remember my mother talking about the fact that he probably went as a young man or when he was married and now he didn't go to church and they were very distressed about that." Jeanne described family gatherings at the oldest sister's home: "We were always by Aunt Jo's. I was an only child and Dick Bause was an only child. My Aunt Jo had five children and my grandmother lived with her, my Grandma Patri. So any events we had at Aunt Jo's house, like Thanksgiving and Christmas. . . . And Uncle Angelo would show up—not the whole time. . . . He would come and see us all on those days. . . . On very few occasions do I recall going to his house until I grew up, until I was in college and came to find out who this man was."

Jeanne and Don showed me some letters to Patri from Romania and said that Patri had served as an adviser on education to the Romanian government. We discussed Patri's reputation, and Don said: "I named my son after him, hoping that something would go off. My son Alex's middle name is Patri." Jeanne said, "When I was a child everyone was in awe of him, the children particularly." Don added, "When I was young it was the same sort of thing. When I was in college or high school we would go to visit him and it was rather a big occasion. . . . He was very much the patriarch of the family."

Jeanne described the neighborhood of PS 45 in the Bronx: "Those sections were divided by country. The Germans lived here and in the next block were the English and the next block were the French and the next block were the Italians . . . and they only mixed if there wasn't a great rivalry between them." I asked about Patri's politics, and Don said: "I think he was quite liberal in his politics, because I saw him a number of times in the very early '60s. . . . I was in school then and I would go to New York quite often to visit my grandmother [Joanna], and we would go see

Angelo, and that was rather a turbulent beginning of a turbulent time. And I remember having a few conversations with him about, I think principally civil rights . . . and he was quite liberal, certainly thinking that what was going on was right and should have been going on forever." Jeanne added, "I know that when he opened his school it was for poor, underprivileged, non-English speaking Italians for the most part. He devoted his life to constructing some form of education for immigrants. You know this was many, many years ago for a first generation, and one thing he insisted upon was that everybody learn English and speak English."

Our discussion returned to Patri's personality and both described Patri as warm and kind. Don said, "Aunt Dora and Aunt Anna were very sweet and kind to me too." Jeanne described a different response: "Well, they weren't sweet and kind to me. I was so in awe of them. I was so frightened of them I didn't even dare say 'boo.' Well, first of all they would look at me this way [nose in air], because my mother dressed me in frilly socks and short skirts, short dresses. I was the only little girl and I was like a little doll and . . . they were not very friendly." I said that from her descriptions Patri seemed warm and his wife cool. Jeanne said, "That's my impression; this is what I felt."

Jeanne and Don talked about Patri's country home, Haviland Hollow, and recalled that Lowell Thomas lived nearby, that he and Patri were friends, and that they did some radio programs together. This led to further speculation on Patri's politics and Don said: "I have no idea whether he would be Democrat or Republican, but I think he was a liberal, in whatever field he was in or camp he chose to be in. He seemed to me that he would be somebody above petty politics. . . . And he was very cognizant of things till the time he died. Certainly the last time I saw him he was in his late '80s. He was clear as a bell." We discussed how Patri dressed. Jeanne said, "I never saw either my uncle or my aunt in anything casual except when they were working in the garden. Don added, "They were very dapper people. They had great style, but evidently that whole family did." Jeanne noted at the end of our talk, "I left New York City in 1943 and that was the end of any close relations that I had with any members of the family and Dick's family went down south in 1979." (Jeanne is referring here to Dick Bause, her first cousin, whom I was to interview next.) Jeanne's recollections are her first childhood memories from about 1920 to the year before Patri retired in 1944, while Don's continued until just before Patri's death in 1965.

My two hours with Jeanne and Don extended my picture of Patri substantially. I had previously assumed that he lived the typical modest middle-class urban life of a New York school principal and was surprised to learn that by the 1920s he had a substantial income and an extensive country home. I discovered that, although he was childless, he was seen as the patriarch of his family. I found that family members and others were proud of him and his successes, but that his marrying out of the faith and nonattendance at church may have been tender issues for his sisters. In my next interview, I would get additional perspectives on Patri both before and after his retirement.

After my talk with the Grecos I flew to Orlando, Florida, and interviewed Dick and Marjorie Bause. Dick was born in 1925, the son of Patri's second surviving sister Rose, and her husband, Herman Bause. He was the youngest of Patri's nephews and nieces and knew Patri for forty years. Dick, seven years younger than Jeanne, was able to tell me more about Patri during the last years of his career as a principal and throughout his retirement. Our conversation began with Dick's description of Patri's first summer home in Paradox, New York, in the Adirondacks between Schroon Lake and Ticonderoga. Dick said: "He must have bought it in the late 1920s. There were three houses there that I remember. . . . The farm house was there and then he had built a big house on the hill." I commented that Patri must have been fairly prosperous from his speaking and writing and Dick said: "He used to speak a lot. I don't think he was really wealthy; they didn't spend a lot of money. . . .This was in the early '30s. My mother and I would go to one house and the Pugliese's mother, the other sister, Josephine, had the older farm and Uncle would be up there, and Aunt Dora. . . . I think he owned the lake and we had boats and a little miniature golf course there. . . . He played golf a lot, even into his eighties. I used to play golf with him when I was six or seven. He'd come down the hill in his Packard with the chauffeur, and we'd go down to Ticonderoga and we'd play golf."

I asked if Patri was relaxed. "Yes, he was. He was a great storyteller and there was a Junior Literary Guild and he was on the selection committee, and he always had books around. He would give me books." I mentioned Patri's translation of Pinocchio in Africa, and Dick said: "I was in his office in the school . . . down in the Bronx. He had a Pinocchio puppet in there, a big puppet. . . . I was only there once and I only remember being in his apartment a couple of times."

Dick listed the previous generation in order: "Angelo, then Josephine . . . and then my mother Rose, and then Jeanne's mother Jane (Joanna). There was another sister—I don't know how old she was—but she died as an infant or a very young child. . . They talked about her red hair." We discussed Patri's school and students and Dick said, "I do remember that if the kids would draw or paint then he encouraged them. John Garfield was one of his students. . . . At one time I think he wanted to make a picture about Uncle, a movie, sort of like Mr. Chips."

We returned to Dick's memories of Paradox: "He had a lot of people come to see him. I think Eleanor Roosevelt was up there once. [This is correct. There is a photograph of tall Eleanor and short Angelo in the garden.][3] I used to wander up there to his house a lot and I would stay for supper and they would telephone down the hill or ring the dinner bell to let my mother know I'm staying there for supper. And Aunt Dora was great. She worked in the gardens and she did a lot of canning, putting up preserves, jellies and jams . . . and I only did see her dressed up once. She would wear dresses, not overalls like they do now, but the long dresses. When Jeanne was married, Uncle gave her away. Aunt Dora showed up and . . . she was all dressed up with a hat and nobody recognized her. . . . She was very quiet and she had a good sense of humor and she was always nice to me."

Dick showed me a videotape, made from home movies taken at various times and commented as we watched. "She [Dora] was always poking around in the flowers. They had a lot of statuary. . . .The cousins always said that I looked like Uncle. . . . When he had Paradox, sometime in the early '30s, he bought this farm in Pawling, New York. It was called Haviland Hollow. . . . He bought it because it was closer to New York and . . . that's where he eventually retired. It was right over the hill from Lowell Thomas's. . . ."

"That's me on the donkey. . . . He always wanted a donkey. . . . There's pictures of Uncle riding the donkey. . . ." I commented that Patri seemed to be pretty cheerful on the donkey, and Dick confirmed that he was generally in good spirits and that he had never seen Patri angry or unhappy.

"This is 'Uncle Jack.' I don't know who he was. He was kind of a character. . . . He wasn't a relative. . . . There's Uncle's car. He had the big Packard and Willy the chauffeur." We returned to our discussion of Aunt Dora and I asked about her background. Dick said, "I think she was 'black Irish'—no, she wasn't a Catholic." I asked if that was a problem and Dick said, "I don't think it was to any of the family; he was never ostracized. Of course all the sisters looked up to him; he was the big brother." We discussed Patri's religious life and Dick said: "I don't think he went to church, because when we were in Paradox we used to drive in every Sunday to Ticonderoga or Schroon Lake to Mass and he never came along. Although in Paradox, Tony, my cousin . . . built a chapel up there that looked like a kiosk, and he built it up on a hill, and there was a pool there and lots of flowers. And I remember that somebody came to bless this place. There were nuns there." [Tony would have been Anthony Pugliese.]

I asked if Patri spent all summer at Paradox, and Dick said, "Most of the summer. One thing about him, he always used to wear white suits or very light tan suits. And his neckties—he'd have a solid color. Orange tie, bright orange, and bright green. He liked bright colors." I asked if Patri ever got down and played with the children. Dick: "No, he never played with us. I remember once we were talking about I always wanted to go to Canada. He said we would take a hike to Canada and I guess Aunt Dora made up sandwiches and we had a knapsack and we went off in the woods and probably walked about half a mile and that was Canada. Then we had lunch."

Dick noted that several family members worked in the schools. He recalled that Uncle Carmine Pugliese, Josephine's husband, was a truant officer and added: "My mother—he had her teach school too. . . . She taught up in the Bronx. She used to teach what they called ungraded students. I expect that they could read, but there was a lot of making hooked rugs and carpentry. . . . Jeanne's mother used to work in the office over at the DeWitt Clinton High School." [Joanna Reilly.] Aunt Anna, Dora's sister, was also a teacher. She was a widow who lived with the Patris at Haviland Hollow. [Anna was actually a divorcee.]⁴

Since Jeanne hadn't had much contact with the family after 1943, my interview with Dick and Marjorie further extended my impressions of Patri. I saw that, although Patri led a busy and active professional life, he spent much time, particularly in the summer, with his mother and sisters and their families. I noted that he shared his prosperity generously with his relatives. Jeanne's impressions of Patri as a warm, friendly, kind, decent human being were confirmed. Dick, perhaps because he was a boy, and younger than Jeanne, didn't hear any of Patri's sisters' possibly critical early responses to Dora that Jeanne reported.

I then flew to New York where I gained further insights into Patri's life and relationships in my talks with Frank and Mary Beth Merolla. Frank, Jr., born in 1941, is two years older than Don Greco, and, like him, a member of the next generation. His grandmother was Josephine, Patri's oldest surviving sister. Her daughter, Anita, married Frank Merolla, and Frank, Jr., is their only son. The Merollas lived near Patri during his retirement, so, although Frank and Mary Beth are from the next generation, they knew Patri very well during his last years. They have inherited family photographs, some of Patri's sculptures, Patri's diary, and the visitor's book from PS 45. I interviewed them just as they were about to move out of their family home in Valhalla, New York.

We began with a discussion of Aunt Dora, and Mary Beth said that she was considered rather judgmental. "I don't mean judgmental in a bad way, but she made decisions quickly about whether she liked you, and if she liked you, you were in. But if she didn't like you, you were probably distanced." Frank added: "She was very quiet. She was always in the background in public, and he did most of the talking. . . . But she was nobody's fool. She was very smart and very warm. I don't know that she was as warm as he was, but she had warmth."

Mary Beth asked, "Did you hear the story about Dora as assistant principal? Aunt Dora was the assistant principal and expected to get the position of principal. When Uncle Angelo was appointed principal in 1907 she was really very unhappy and she intended to quit because she thought that he had been appointed because he was a male, or for whatever reason. And she was very annoyed about the whole thing and they ended up getting married." Frank added, "She was certainly an assistant principal in his building, and whether she was there before he got there . . . I don't know." [Dora apparently was assistant principal at PS 4 when Patri was appointed principal in 1907. They were married three years later in 1910.]

The next day Frank drove me to Patri's former home in Haviland Hollow, a handsome country estate with beautiful flower and vegetable gardens. Nobody was home, so we took the liberty of exploring the yard. The house was large, and Frank recalled that it had a library, guest rooms, and space enough for Dora's sister Anna and the friend of the family named Jack Blonk. [The "Uncle Jack" whom Dick Bause had mentioned.] There was a gatehouse called "Toad Hall," and a service house that included a country kitchen, an apartment for the gardener, Felicci, and butler and maid quarters. There was a greenhouse, barn, boxwood garden, orchard, root cellar, sunken garden, brook with a bridge, and much statuary. The Patris loved animals and had a dog, cats, and a donkey.

Frank said: "Uncle was very interested in politics, very up to date on current events, and he had very well-informed opinions based on a lot of information. Basically very wise feelings . . . philosophical in a sense, but also practical. . . . He talked politics a good bit. . . but he refused being a superintendent many times because of the politics involved in that. I think his local politics were different from his national politics. . . . I think he was fairly conservative nationally." Thomas Dewey was one of Patri's neighbors, and Frank said, "My recollection is that when Dewey was not elected Uncle was happy for the neighborhood because of the confusion it would cause, but he was not generally happy for the country." We discussed Patri's attitude toward religion, and Frank said, "I do think he was a religious person . . . the outward manifestations are not something he participated in throughout his life. But I don't think it mattered at all as far as how he lived his life. Some of us are better because we don't hear someone preaching to us. And in his case it didn't matter."

Frank recalled that Dora's sister, Anna Morrison, "lived with them forever, as far as I know. . . . She was left with a son, Ted . . . and so they took her in with the child and she lived with them for I don't know how many years. It could have been fifty years. She was a young woman with a child alone and they took them in and they supported them and I don't know that she ever worked." [Anna lived with the Patris as early as 1920, and died in 1964, so was with them for at least forty four years.][5]

Frank recalled vacation activities: "The summers were family peak times. In the earlier years . . . they traveled a good bit in the summer and he would lecture along with the traveling." We discussed the trip that Patri and Dora took to Italy in 1927, and Frank said: "He was certainly very interested in his Italian heritage. His interest in art and music was very Italian. His dress was very Irish: white linen suit, the wool tie in the winter, tweeds, heavy, heavy woolen tweeds. Three piece suits, usually . . . I never saw him in a suit that wasn't tailor made."

Mary Beth recalled: "Uncle was always interested in the crafts, and said that children . . . sometimes needed time out, so he had needlework. It didn't matter if you were a boy or a girl; you did some kind of needlework. And if you needed a break from academics, that's what you did. You just went and did needlepoint for a while." Frank: "He surrounded his home with the works of his students. Some of them were the works right out of the 7th and 8th grade and some of them were people who had made careers of it. Those things were all around his home; at least something out in the garden."

Mary Beth said that when she and Frank were married, his parents were not pleased because they were young, and Frank was still in dental school. But at Thanksgiving dinner, after the engagement was announced, Uncle Angelo read this inscription on a serving spoon that he had given to Frank when he was christened: "Fear God and take your own part." Frank and Mary Beth understood that Uncle was blessing their marriage and welcoming her to the family. Frank attested to his Uncle's benign influence: "Well, my parents were never happy about it, but it's true that after that it was easier."

The Merollas showed me various photographs, art objects, and awards. Among them was a presentation from Columbus Day, 1951 which read: "Columbian Civic Award to Angelo Patri, whose intellect and wisdom have produced masterpieces of literature and whose deep understanding of his people has led the way in molding our systems of education so that the energy and creative talent of youth is awakened, guided, and developed for the future enrichment of every field of human endeavor." Frank noted the ethnic connection: "When they say 'his people' it's obvious—an Italian-American organization in the community that was predominant then."

The next day Frank and I drove to the Pawling Rural Cemetery and visited the Patri family plot. There is a large headstone topped with a statue of a nude woman carved by the well-known sculptor Attilio Piccirilli.[6] We read the dates of birth and death on various gravestones, and Frank explained who each person was. He noted that Aunt Anna Caterson Morrison, Dora's sister, was four years younger than Dora but outlived her sister by three years. She lived in Haviland Hollow until her death in 1964. John Dacey Blonk, known as "Uncle Jack," lived from 1874 to 1941 and was the first to be buried in the family plot, so it must have been purchased in 1941 or before. Nobody in the family seems to know who Jack Blonk was or how he came to be part of the household. [Marilyn Shea later determined that Blonk was a boarder with the Catersons before Dora and Angelo married in 1910. He then lived with Angelo and Dora until his death.][7]

As we stood there in the cemetery, Frank talked about life at Haviland Hollow. "Aunt Dora was a very good story teller . . . I wouldn't say that she was his equal, but she was an excellent story teller and she always seemed to defer to him. Certainly in public situations I remember her deferring to him and being in the background, and being happy to be in the background but being proud of the adulation . . . and the respect that he was receiving. I remember the time I spent there when my mother had some surgery, the fact that I participated in what was going on through the day. . . . I do remember quiet times . . . when Aunt Dora or Uncle would be sitting with me and would tell a story, particularly in the evenings.

"I remember stories that she told about Shawn, their dog, and things along that line—the types of stories that a seven-year-old would find intriguing. Very, very relaxing, gentle, loving-type stories, and told in a very calm, loving way. . . . I do remember when we would visit, I would be high school or college age, and they would play Canasta. Aunt Anna and Uncle and my mother and father and I, the five of us would rotate through playing Canasta. Aunt Dora would sit on a loveseat nearby and knit wool argyle socks for Angelo, and sweaters. . . . She would observe the kibitzing . . . and laugh at the little fussy arguments that you have over cards and be part of whatever conversation was going on."

We had earlier discussed how much Italian was spoken in the family, and Frank returned to that topic: "My grandmother Josephine, Uncle's sister, spoke Italian. Aunt Jane (the youngest sister) understood Italian but I never heard her speak Italian, and I don't know that she understood as much as my grandmother . . . but she could get by in a conversation as far as listening is concerned. My grandmother could speak Italian, could understand Italian, but as the years went on she used it less and less. I know it got rusty. My father's family spoke Italian. My grandparents on my father's side spoke Italian, particularly when they didn't want us to know what was going on. My father was able to handle Italian very well. He had a knack of mimicking dialects that I remember hearing about. Very rarely, he would speak Italian to my maternal grandmother [Josephine, Patri's sister]. . . . I remember my mother being able to understand Italian. . . . When my parents traveled to Italy, she was able to understand what was going on from her recollection of Italian around the home. . . . I would think Aunt Dolly probably understood some because she was older and exposed to more in the home as a child. She traveled a great deal, too, mostly Europe, among other places." [Dolly was the nickname for Josephine, Frank, Jr.'s, aunt, named after her mother Josephine, Patri's sister.]

Frank talked about the various people who worked for the Patris at the Hollow, including a pair of sisters, Alice and Josephine Mohr, "who they thought very highly of and who they left something to in the will equal to what they left to family members." Frank said: "I think I knew Uncle best from the mid-fifties. . . . In roughly 1940 my parents owned a house on Haviland Hollow Road, so there was a connection there between my parents and Uncle, Aunt Dora, and Aunt Anna that strengthened then. In the 1950s we would visit quite regularly. . . . I would say they probably visited once a month or once every six weeks. . . . When Aunt Dora died . . . Aunt Anna and Uncle came to White Plains [the Merolla's home at the time] regularly for holidays—Thanksgiving, Christmas, and Easter. . . . As I was older, eighteen or twenty, I would be the assigned driver. I would go and pick them up and take them to Mass; Aunt Anna went to Mass and participated even though she was not a Catholic."

Frank discussed Jeanne's responses to Dora and Anna: "There may have been a little bit of a rub there because Aunt Jane [Jeanne's mother] really . . . tried to Americanize herself. You know, she dropped her baptized names and Americanized them." Jeanne had recalled feeling criticized by Dora and Anna, and Frank speculated: "I think some of the scowling that she remembers was probably a form of discipline because Jeanne was a lively child . . . she was certainly very outgoing. I think maybe the combination produced an atmosphere or aura about her that was not the homebody or career type that may have been acceptable in those times. I don't think there was a dislike. I think it was an attempt at the 'schoolteacher look' to create a little bit more decorum."

We discussed Jeanne's perception that Patri's three sisters may not have approved of his marrying an Irish Protestant. Frank dealt with the possible issues sequentially: "The Irish thing certainly shouldn't matter because Aunt Jane (Jeanne's mother) married Jim Reilly. The non-Italian thing shouldn't matter because Herman Bause was French-German. . . . The non-Catholic thing, I really don't know, but looking back at Uncle's life as a practicing Catholic, there may have been something to that. . . . I think he lived a rather religious life, but I don't think . . . falling into a groove with a specific denomination was something that happened. Nor for her . . . when they were married. But when she died, he did go back to the church and receive the sacraments. It didn't happen as a deathbed illness kind of thing. It happened early on. In fact to some degree it was happening when she was still alive because there would be regular visits from the parish priest, Father Storm."

But some of the differences encountered in the next generation were problematic: "It is true that when my grandmother's middle child, Anthony Pugliese, married a Jewish girl, Julia Jones, there was upheaval in the family and from Uncle also. Uncle really helped . . . my grandmother's children with their education, certainly with encouragement, and I think probably to some degree financially. When my Uncle Tony decided he was going to be an artist, that was fine, but . . . studying art in Paris in the thirties and the late twenties I think disturbed him. . . . When Uncle Anthony returned from Paris and married a Jewish girl and had what the family called socialistic ideas, I think that was a little hard to swallow. . . . But the relationship because of the Catholic and Protestant marrying (Angelo and Dorothy) was well mellowed by the time I came along, if it had been an issue at all."

Not surprisingly, Patri was closest to Josephine, who was born when Angelo was six years old, and with whom he had shared seven years of childhood before Rose was born: "I know that whenever . . . we would visit Uncle, he would say, 'Is Jo coming?'" meaning his sister Jo, my grandmother. . . . He seemed to look forward to her visits and when she was there I specifically remember Aunt Dora being very, very kind to her, not in a condescending way, but in a loving way. . . . I remember Uncle looking forward to her visit and chatting. Neither one of them heard very well in their later years, so there would sometimes be a contest. They would both be speaking and neither would know the other was speaking and Aunt Dora would say . . . 'Leo, Leo,' and he would get the idea that his sister had something to say and was well into it."

Frank, born in 1941, of course had no memories of Rose, the second surviving sister, who died in 1936, but did remember the third sister, Jane, who married Abraham Kroll many years after Jim Reilly died. "She would visit Uncle with Abe Kroll, who was by then on the City of New York Board of Examiners; they were cordially received and there was always a good bit of school talk about what was going on with the central Board of Education in Brooklyn."

Frank recalled an evening when Patri was going to speak at Eastview Junior High in White Plains: "My mother fixed a plate for him and he said, 'I have never eaten before I speak.' Now this is in the mid-fifties and he had been speaking for 35 years at least, major addresses, and he is going to speak before a group of about 200 people and that's how he reacted to it emotionally. . . . I think it means that no matter what the group was . . . there was an inner drive for him to do his best, and along with that something to create a tension in him to achieve whatever level he was aiming for within himself. . . . I remember someone at home asking him: 'What's your topic going to be tonight?' . . . I think he said, 'The relationship of the home and the school. . . . That's so general I can talk forever.' "

Frank saw this as an illustration of Patri's consistency: "That speech was about probably an hour and a half. And for me the only difference was the fact that it was uninterrupted and . . . that he was standing on a podium as opposed to sitting in his easy chair in his own living room talking. . . . The types of stories were the same thing you'd hear for ten or fifteen minutes in his own living room. . . . The mixture of warmth and seriousness and humor was exactly what I had witnessed over and over again after that . . . ."

I can best begin my interpretation of these interviews with a discussion near the end of our talks when I said to Frank, "Well, you certainly chose an interesting family to be born into," and he replied, "It would be nice to take credit for that, wouldn't it?" I summarized my thoughts: "I get a very steady picture of Patri, in spite of the slight variation on Jeanne's part. My impression is that he was a man who was mentally and physically very healthy. In fact, the whole family was. . . . A remarkably integrated family, and you've maintained connections over the generations. It's really kind of a heartening story to hear." And when Frank told me about his uncle's speech in White Plains, I responded: "This is a perfect example of what I have been hearing in a more general way: there is no difference between the public Angelo Patri and the private, personal, family Angelo Patri: he is the same man in both situations."

The Patri I had read about in *Schoolmaster of the Great City* and in his unpublished memoir was the active educator focused primarily on his work with students, parents, teachers, and administrators. The Patri I began to know through his relatives was a man nearing the end of his school career and then a retired patriarch. The words that come to mind to describe him at these later stages of his life are "affluent and generous." In moving through geography, ethnicity, and social class, from poverty in Piaggine to prosperity in Haviland Hollow, Patri had become one of the fortunate new Americans who achieved notable financial and personal success.

I had wondered if Patri had drawn on the childhood experiences of his nieces and nephews in his speaking and writing. Dick Bause said that Patri told a story about him in one of his books, but no other family members reported similar examples. A careful reading of Patri's books of advice to parents may turn up further family stories, but it is safe to conclude that much of Patri's personal understanding of child development came from his memories of his own childhood in Italy and the United States. His parents, though unschooled, drew on centuries of accumulated wisdom as they raised Patri and his sisters with sensitivity, support, and love. His own childhood experience was then supplemented and reinforced by his extensive work with thousands of students. Helping to raise Dora's nephew and other children no doubt gave Patri firsthand knowledge of childrearing. One interviewer wrote in 1928 that Patri "and his wife have reared several children and two of their proteges are now attending college."[8] Patri's studies at Teachers College with such professors as Frank McMurry, Nicholas Murray Butler, Paul Monroe, and John Dewey, acquainted him with current thinking on child development. Through these and other influences Patri acquired a thoughtful, sensitive understanding of children that helped him become a remarkably effective principal and a widely read and trusted adviser to parents.

These interviews also gave me some insight into the Americanization of an extended southern Italian family. Although Patri became unusually well known and influential for a first-generation immigrant, some of the family story is typical and can be briefly generalized: A father comes to America, finds work, and gets a place for the family to live. The mother and her brother then come to America with her two children, one of whom dies in infancy. She and her husband have three American daughters, one of whom marries an Italian Catholic, one a German Catholic, and one an Irish Catholic. The son, moving farthest from family expectations, marries a woman from a Protestant Irish background. The youngest sister, many years after the death of her first husband, marries a Jewish educator.

The parents sacrifice to help the son complete college and a master's degree in preparation for professional work. He in turn helps his sisters and their husbands in their careers, several in education. The American public school plays a significant role in this family and in others like it. Not only do the children get free public education through high school, but several move into decent, respected jobs in those schools as teachers, administrators, special education personnel, truant officers, and secretaries. [9]

If we were to follow this family story into the next generation, we would find further educational achievement, more geographical mobility, and marriages even more distant from the Italian Catholic center. But we would find also that many of this later generation are eager to maintain strong ties with their Italian heritage and language.

Patri working on a small sculpture

(Frank Merolla)

TEN

Connecting His Worlds: Patri as Writer and Public Speaker

"I WAS ELEVEN BEFORE I WENT TO A CITY SCHOOL. ALL the English I knew I had learned in the street. I knew Italian. From the time I was seven I had written letters for the neighbors. Especially the women folk took me off to a corner and asked me to write letters to their friends in Italy. As they told me the story I wrote it down. I thus learned the beat of plain folks' hearts." This is how Patri described what we may see as the precursor of his career as a writer, four years before he enrolled in school.[1] From these small beginnings Patri gradually developed the ideas and style that would make him a successful and popular writer, with thousands of articles to his credit. He was also active as a speaker, both to live audiences and on the radio. These articles and speeches were worked into his books, particularly the advice books for parents and teachers. I will discuss some of his more important books, show how they were received by thoughtful Americans, and conclude with brief reflections on Patri's career as a writer and speaker and on the impact that career had on his life.

If Patri's memory was correct, he had acquired literacy rapidly. He came to America when he was five years old, and his mother's brother taught him to read and write Italian. He was a very bright child, so it is not impossible that he had in two short years acquired enough skill to write simple letters to his neighbor's relatives in Italy. I can only assume that Patri did, in fact, learn to write very early but that his memory for specific times may have been fuzzy.

During his five years of public school, Patri no doubt got much practice in writing. Then at City College he and his friend Anthony Pugliese took the five-year classical course in which they studied texts in rhetoric and grammar, wrote compositions, and delivered declamations. They studied the classics of Greece, Rome, and England, which gave them powerful models of classical prose, and which Patri often cited in his own later writing. They read little American literature—only selections from Irving's *Sketchbook*, Longfellow's *Evangeline*, and Webster's *Bunker Hill Orations*— but did study some American history.[2] Patri and Pugliese were both active in the Clonia Literary Society—apparently the only Italian-American members—and during their senior year Pugliese was president and Patri vice-president of the club. Clonia sponsored debates, essay contests, and entertainments and maintained a library of 2000 volumes. Their membership brought them in contact with students like Upton Sinclair, later to become a well-known radical novelist, who was editor of the Society when they were officers in it.[3]

Patri's first piece of extended writing was the master's thesis that he wrote at Columbia University Teachers College under the supervision of Frank McMurry. He wrote it in 1903–1904 while teaching school full time. This seventy-two page document showed Patri's capacity for assimilating a range of materials and applying them to urban problems. Patri raised in the thesis the same issue that recurred later in *Schoolmaster*—how best to Americanize the varied immigrant groups in New York. His response, which constituted most of the thesis, was that the public schools must take the lead and organize the work of many other agencies to assist in this process. The composition was written in formal, effective language but would have profited from careful editing.[4]

In 1907 Patri became principal of PS 4 in the Bronx, where he had large numbers of Italian students. Their need for good reading matter may have inspired Patri in 1911 to translate two Italian books into English: Bertelli's *White Patch* and Eugenio Cherubini's *Pinocchio in Africa*. *White Patch* was published as a well-illustrated nature study book intended for school use. It adapts Bertelli's story of a boy named Gigino who does not want to go to school, and says: "Rather than study grammar, I would change myself into an ant." To his surprise he is transformed into an ant, and his two companions become insects in order to avoid arithmetic and history. The rest of the book tells in detail about varieties of insect life, presented from an ant's perspective. Patri's progressive educational perspective is expressed in the preface, where he writes: "This story forms the nucleus around which direct experiences may be grouped. . . ." The author expected teachers to give students real experiences with insects and to use the text to help understand and organize those experiences.[5]

Patri then translated into English Collodi's *Pinocchio in Africa*. He summarized Collodi's original *Pinocchio*, adding: "Brought across the seas, he was welcomed by American children and now appears in a new volume which sets forth his travels in Africa." Then, in schoolmasterly fashion Patri added: "The lessons underlying his fantastic experiences are clear to the youngest readers, but are never allowed to become obtrusive."[6] It is interesting to note that both of these books involve drastic species changes in which in the first children become ants and in the second Pinocchio briefly becomes a donkey.

Patri was appointed principal of PS 45 in 1913 and somehow found time during his first four years there to write *Schoolmaster of the Great City* and to prepare it for publication by Macmillan in 1917. The book was widely read and well reviewed, and was republished in 1921 and 1925. The popularity of the book led to invitations from editors to write for their publications, and in 1919 Patri began a series of short essays called "Americanisms" for the *Red Cross Magazine*. Writing on topics such as "Democracy" and "Truth," Patri expressed a broad-minded, liberal patriotism. He went on to publish more substantial articles for the same magazine on such topics as "The Spoiled Child," and "My Country."[7]

The publication of *Schoolmaster* also led to invitations to speak to various groups. In 1920 for example, Patri gave addresses at a meeting of school superintendents in Cleveland, at the National Education Association in Salt Lake City, and at the first convention of the Progressive Education Association in Washington, DC.[8] Patri delivered his addresses rather formally in the pure unaccented English that he had learned in public school, at City College, and at Teachers College.[9] The book, articles, and speeches brought him to further public attention. In June 1920, Gary Superintendent Willard Wirt wrote a letter to Patri that attested to his growing reputation as a writer and speaker: "Many of our local teachers have been reading your Red Cross Magazine articles. . . . You certainly can write and talk and you are so genuine that you command attention. . . . Many superintendents on the way home from Cleveland commented on your appearance there. . . .You are so worthy that it is a real joy to see you come into your own."[10]

Another letter six weeks later tells of a "road not taken" in Patri's career. Arthur Morgan, soon to become president of Antioch, wrote to Patri on March 11, 1920: "Dear Sir: Would you not like the prospect of being in charge of a small teachers' training school . . . and at the same time, have direction of the school system in which a large part of these teachers would work as they had prepared themselves?" Morgan complained mildly about the current superintendent who tried to do more than he should. Patri did not reply for nearly two months, and then said: "I am glad your superintendent wants to do the whole job himself. I would not do." He closed the letter saying, "There is work ahead where we can pull together—maybe not in the same city, but surely in the same country." Morgan apparently did not read this as a rejection and on July 4 wrote: "Dear Mr. Patri: I suppose there is no other way out of it. In as much as you made it a condition of coming to Antioch that I should be in charge there, I took the presidency of the college. So make your plans for the year 1921-1922. Would you like to have charge of a school somewhat after the manner of the Moraine Park School at the College, to be a demonstration school, and a practice school? . . ."[11] Patri chose not to accept, but it is intriguing to think how Patri's career might have differed had he accepted Morgan's offer. However, instead of becoming a teacher educator, Patri continued as an administrator and went on to become a leading writer of advice for parents.

The connection with Arthur Morgan yields an intriguing footnote concerning Morgan's interest in persuading John Dewey to join the Antioch faculty. Patri encouraged Morgan to think that Dewey might be interested in leaving Columbia and talked with Evelyn Dewey about the possibility of Dewey's going to Antioch. According to Patri, Evelyn was encouraging. Morgan wrote an exploratory letter to Dewey, who was in China at the time. Dewey's reply, if any, has not been found, but is hard to believe that Dewey, after all his years in Ann Arbor, Minneapolis, Chicago, and New York, would have been tempted to give up the advantages of urban living for the bucolic pleasures of life in Yellow Springs, Ohio.[12]

After a visit from Morgan Dorothy Patri wrote him in late 1920: "We think we are going to take up the work we spoke to you about with the Evening Post. I hope it comes through. We need the job for several reasons, all equally good . . . " One of the reasons may well have been financial, as the Patris had recently bought the farm in Paradox, New York. In any case, in 1921 Patri did sign a contract with the *New York Evening Post* to write a daily column on children.[13]

Patri's column was quickly taken up by other newspapers and led to many invitations to speak. Then, drawing on his columns, essays, articles, and speeches, Patri began to assemble books for parents and teachers. The first was *Child Training*, a substantial volume of 434 pages published by Appleton in 1922. It presented practical advice on such topics as "The Child in the Home," "Building the Child's Character," "Vacation Time," and "The Child and His Country." The book sold well and was positively reviewed by progressive education writer Agnes de Lima, who already knew about Patri through her work in support of the New York City Gary

program. De Lima praised "Patri's paragraphs to parer
so long enjoyed by readers of the *New York Evening Post*
dom and real insight into child nature by one who u
and loves them."[14]

The Bell Syndicate gradually extended Patri's colu..,
to other cities so that eventually it reached hundreds of newspapers w..
millions of readers. Patri also wrote essays for *Redbook Magazine* and other
periodicals.[15] Many of his columns were written in response to questions
received from readers, and he quickly assembled some of these into a second book, *Talks to Mothers*, published by Appleton in 1923. This slender
volume of sixty four pages consisted of brief, personal, practical, supportive talks on such mundane matters as nail-biting, fighting, whining, and
reading in bed.

Patri continued to write on Americanization, as he had in *Schoolmaster.*
In 1924 he gathered his "Americanisms" and other essays into *The Spirit
of America*, a well-illustrated text for children that presented an optimistic
picture of this country. Patri began with recollections of his Italian village
birthplace, crossing to America by steamship, playing in the streets, and
eventually attending "an American school. That was where my life in the
new country began." In school he heard the stories of American heroes.
"And it happened to me, as it did to thousands of foreign-born children,
that after many years, I was graduated from an American school and then
from an American college. I became a teacher, an American teacher in an
American Public School. I belonged."[16] In all this patriotic writing Patri
reflected the pattern recently described by Robert A. George when he said
that an "immigrant . . . tends to absorb the earnest, spiritual myths of his
adopted country even more than those native-born."[17]

Patri gave his liberal interpretation of Americanism: "Every people
under the sun is represented here in America. How then can America be
a nation?" Immigrant groups keep their old-world habits, but "America
is too big to be measured by food or dress or custom. America is an idea,
a way of living." And the idea "lies at the heart of what we call America,
'Our country,'—the right to be different while being useful and happy:
free as common brotherhood allows one to be free." Patri's understanding
of democracy kept him from being a single-minded advocate of superficial
unity: "The man who leads the minority is necessary in this government
of ours. He calls attention to the things that are not as they should be. He
keeps us alive and growing."

Ignoring massive contemporary evidence to the contrary, Patri cheer-
fully asserted that majorities eventually learn that minorities "are bearing
the heart of America with them." Patri recognized that intolerance was

...d on fear, but optimistically claimed: "We have begun to learn the lesson of tolerance. . . . We are learning, as the years go by, that intolerance is but another way of saying: 'We're afraid.'" Then, in a statement much like that in Franklin Roosevelt's inaugural speech eight years later, Patri wrote: "What have we to fear? Nothing but our own fears." But Patri's fellow immigrants were currently experiencing real and justified fear of the rampant nativism which led that very year to anti-immigrant legislation directly aimed at Italians and other southern Europeans.[18]

In 1925 Patri assembled and published a third collection of his columns, this one titled *School and Home*. The relation between these two entities had been a theme of Patri's thinking ever since he wrote his thesis in 1903–04. This volume was more focused than the first two advice books, with short essays integrated into fewer but longer chapters. Patri strongly supported school taxes as sound investments in the future and presented extended arguments in support of public schools that worked closely with their communities. Perhaps drawing on the 1918 *Cardinal Principles of Secondary Education*, he assigned many tasks to the schools, including preparation for "the enjoyment of leisure."[19] He preached again his message of tolerance: "When your grandson asked you where the black man came from and where he was going the day he saw him carrying off the trunks, did you carefully explain who he was and all about him? That he was a friend who helped one go safely and comfortably on a long journey?"[20]

The anonymous reviewer for the *New York Times* understood why Patri's writing was so relevant to parents: "Mr. Patri uses the illustrative method very largely, pointing all his arguments with anecdotes of real cases of children who presented problems of one sort or another. This makes the volume readable and entertaining, although he loses no opportunity of presenting the pleas and arguments that are evidently close to his heart."[21]

Taking advantage of his current popularity, the next year Patri published *What Have You Got to Give?*, a volume of essays addressed more to parents than teachers. The title piece carried a familiar Patri question: "What have you, you busy one, struggling so hard for your share of goods and content . . . what have you to offer?" The various selections reminded readers that everyone had much to give to others. One essay, "The Lighted Candle" presented a response from Patri's own household—a reminder that Patri helped raise children in his own home as well as at school: "The Boy who lives in our house is very much like other boys save for one thing: he 'has a way with him.' " The boy skips his homework, is tardy, and just gets by in school, but "from the grandmother who adores him, to the French teacher who flunks him, everybody is his friend." The "lighted candle" of his warm personality and character will carry him through. Patri is here describing his wife's nephew, who lived with them in the Bronx apartment in an extended family that included Dora, her mother, and her sister, the boy's mother.[22]

Patri continued his speaking career, addressing teachers' associations on discipline, giving radio talks to parents and, on his 1927 trip to Europe, discussing "Moral Education" at the Third International Moral Education Congress in Geneva, Switzerland.[23] Patri had by this time translated *White Patch* and *Pinocchio in Africa* for children, written *Schoolmaster* for the general public, assembled *The Spirit of America*, and written and edited five books for parents and teachers. Some educators realized that Patri had helpful things to say to both new and experienced teachers, so Clinton Carpenter, at the State Normal School in Adams, Massachusetts, edited some of Patri's essays into a volume titled *The Problems of Childhood*. Unlike most of Patri's books, this one had discussion questions, references, and an index, presumably to make it more usable as a textbook by teachers and parents. Leta S. Hollingsworth, a psychologist at Teachers College, wrote an introduction attesting to the book's value to "parents, teachers and other guardians of the human young. . . . From long experience of Mr. Patri and his works, we have learned that he is trustworthy. . . . Thus again this Schoolmaster of the Great City has performed a service for children, by acting as interpreter for what they have no words to express."[24]

Reviewers, including one for the *New York Times*, agreed on the soundness of Patri's writing: "It is all done with the greatest simplicity, although it is all based on the results of modern investigation and scientific research. The work is, consequently, dependably scientific in its counsels, while it is simple and practical enough in its application of principles for the understanding of any parent. For teachers, its fine illumination of wearisome problems arising from the temperament of pupils and ignorance of parents will be very helpful."[25]

However, Patri's rapid publication of six books in five years attracted some criticism. Agnes de Lima, in a review of five books on childhood and education, wrote: "Angelo Patri, it appears to us, is over-writing himself. He has done all over again what he did so charmingly, so easily, and so lucidly only a few months ago. He has written a lot of quick little sketches of childhood needs and perplexities, and of adults who are skilled and unskilled in their treatment of these needs. He is always wise, but he is getting too facile, and his wisdom shows signs of wearing thin."[26] Dorothy Canfield Fisher made a similar point in an otherwise complimentary review, referring to Patri's writing as "perseveringly repetitious."[27]

. The repetition is not surprising. In his column and radio shows Patri invited parents to send him letters with their questions. Many did so, and Patri's papers in the Library of Congress include 7,000 such letters, the majority written between 1925 and 1939. Most were from mothers, but about seven percent were from fathers.[28] These thousands of letters referred recurrently to the problems that parents faced, and Patri responded to them in book after book. Equally important, he dealt with these problems in a consistent way. The encouraging, concerned, moderate, sensitive positions and attitudes one encounters in his 1904 thesis can be found throughout his writings, all the way to his final 1948 advice book, *How to Help Your Child Grow Up*. Thus some repetition was inevitable in the questions raised, in Patri's consistent answers, and in the books assembled from his responses.

Patri may have had thoughts similar to those expressed above by Agnes de Lima and Dorothy Fisher, for after the appearance of *The Problems of Childhood*, for five years he published no books for parents or teachers. He did, however join with others to help sponsor *Children, The Magazine of Parents*, a new journal promoting healthy patterns of raising children. Patri served as editor along with other well-known child advocates such as Julia Lathrop and Judge Ben Lindsey.[29]

Angelo's and Dora's trip to France, Switzerland, and Italy during spring, 1927 may have regenerated his interest in Pinocchio, and his next book was about that famous Italian boy. Patri's somewhat autobiographical *Pinocchio in America* was published in 1928 in a handsome edition by Doubleday, Doran with unusual, modernistic illustrations by Mary Liddell.[30] The next year Ginn and Company republished the book in a school edition for its "Once Upon a Time" series. The title was changed to *Pinocchio's Visit to America*, and more conventional illustrations were provided by Sears Gallagher. The book sold well, and the success of these two editions led logically in 1930 to Doubleday, Doran's publication of Patri's translation of Collodi's original *Adventures of Pinocchio*.

While working on the Pinocchio books Patri continued to write articles and essays for various magazines. "A Parent's Prayer," which first appeared in *Child Welfare Magazine* in 1927, was widely republished.[31] Patri spoke to the National Kindergarten Association that same year, calling for kindergartens for all children.[32] His column, "Our Children," appeared in *La Luce*, an Italian-language periodical.[33] In 1931 Appleton published *The Questioning Child and Other Essays*, yet another compilation of his columns. The title essay presented to adult readers the point Patri had made for children in *Pinocchio in America*: that questions are the key to learning. Patri presented sensible advice on children's questions about sex: give them enough honest, direct information to satisfy them, and be prepared for the next levels of questions. In "What is Wrong with Teaching," Patri described his own thirty-five years in the schools, starting at only twenty dollars a month. Admitting the failings of many teachers, Patri confidently asked parents to "let us know what is wrong, let us who need help for our schools and our children go out and ask for it, telling our story so as to enlighten the minds and stir the hearts of the people who make our schools."[34]

In one of the more philosophical essays in the book, "Work as Part of Education," Patri clearly showed his Deweyan pragmatic convictions. He critiqued untested book knowledge, declaring: "There's nothing in the world that teaches the value of an idea so promptly and so effectively as the doing of it and accepting the responsibility for the doing. Unless a thing 'works' for you it does not exist for you." Dewey had defined education as "that reconstruction or reorganization of experience which adds to the meaning of experience, and which increases ability to direct the course of subsequent experience." Patri made a similar point in more personal terms: "Education is something that a child must take. He takes it up from the earth and transforms it into intelligence by the experiences that he gathers through his nerves and muscles—and his hands."[35]

As usual, the book sold well and elicited positive reviews. M. L., writing in the *Christian Science Monitor* explained Patri's approach: "Mr. Patri writes always from the viewpoint of the child. It is the child that is to be considered, let the grown-ups adapt themselves as they must. From his long experiences as teacher and principal in the New York Public Schools, he has gleaned the wisdom of the sage; and he clothes his thoughts with the poetry of the artist."[36] Another reviewer, Adelaide Nichols, gives readers personal pictures of Patri as a speaker as well as a writer: "This book evokes for me the very tones of the voice which I have heard speaking to a little child standing before the principal's desk, which I have heard prophesying the new day in education to a group of private-school teachers. There is the same intimate feeling touched with quiet dignity, the same range of persuasive power from short, simple statements stark as the Ten Commandments until on a sudden wind of emotion the banners of his eloquence unfurl."[37]

While receiving the approval of readers and reviewers, Patri gained more formal recognition from respected individuals and groups. In 1931 he was awarded *The Parents' Magazine* medal "for distinguished service in parental education in the City of New York." In awarding the medal, George J. Hecht, publisher of the magazine, said: "Mr. Patri is one of the country's leading educators of children; he is certainly the leading educator of parents. . . . When Mr. Patri took over the principalship of a New York school one of the first things he did was to found a Parents' Organization. . . . He fired it with interest in his educational program. From that modest local beginning more than twenty years ago, Angelo Patri has made his influence felt in nearly every home in America. . . .

Hecht was impressed by the size of Patri's readership: "Angelo Patri has a tremendous following through his syndicated child guidance feature, appearing every day except Sunday in more than a hundred newspapers . . . with an aggregate circulation of more than five and a half million."[38] Among the readers was Harvard's former president Charles William Eliot, who said: "Whatever else Patri does, he must never stop those irreplaceable talks to teachers and parents in the newspapers."[39]

Noting Patri's career as educator as well as writer, Hecht commented: "In his public school work, Mr. Patri has always been a step ahead of the times. His greatest interest now is in the establishment of junior high schools which will allow children to experience the widest possible variety of work before they enter high school." Hecht connected Patri's origins and his commitments: "Though born in Italy, Angelo Patri came to America early enough to become thoroughly Americanized, but he has never ceased to be interested in the struggle of immigrant children, and, for that matter, the plight of all the underprivileged children in the city."[40]

Writing had been a key to Patri's own success, and he always supported writing as an important activity for students, so he occasionally took part in programs to encourage children to write for publication. In 1935 a tabloid called *The Boys' and Girls' Newspaper* appeared with a front-page letter of support from President Roosevelt, saying that its publication "should be helpful in the education and development of boys and girls." Patri was listed as an advisory editor along with several others including writer Dorothy Canfield and the unlikely sports figures Babe Ruth and Gene Tunney.[41] Six years later Patri chaired the editorial board for *Moments of Enchantment*, an anthology of writing by students from all New York City junior high schools. A *New York Times* article said that the writing was of high quality, and that "according to Dr. Patri, most of it measures up to . . . adult standards and has a professional ring. Moreover, it gives the impression of happy children, enthusiastic in their creative tasks, glorying in a job well done."[42]

Although he continued to write his newspaper column, for nine years Patri published no more books for parents. The transition of his school to a junior high in 1929 no doubt occupied much of his time, but he was also busy with speeches and radio programs. Between 1928 and 1943 he gave hundreds of radio talks and dramatizations in programs sponsored variously by the Campbell's Soup Company, Eastman Kodak, the Child Training Association, and the National Education Association. His radio experience led to his 1939 appointment by Mayor La Guardia to the New York City Radio Board and, three years later, to the Mayor's War Council.[43]

In 1940, drawing on columns published during the previous two years, Patri published *The Parents Daily Counselor.* Like *Talks to Mothers* (1923), this was a collection of two- and three-page articles, mostly dealing with specific problems like stammering. But Patri occasionally generalized for parents, as when he gave them some basic rules for raising children: "First, have a clear idea of what you want a child to be and to do. . . . Second, teach him to obey. . . .Third, use force as little as possible. . . . Fourth, don't talk and talk and talk to a child two or three years of age. . . . Fifth, keep order in the house. . . . Sixth, routine the day. . . . Seventh, teach your child to be useful." His elaborations on these principles showed yet again his Deweyan convictions: "It is nonsense to say that teaching a child obedience is robbing him of freedom. Proper obedience saves a child from the slavery of ignorance and sets him free to use his intelligence." Patri's position on freedom and obedience was consistent with Dewey's, published just two years earlier in *Experience and Education:* "For freedom from restriction, the negative side, is to be prized only as a means to a freedom which is power. . . . The ideal aim of education is creation of power of self-control. . . . [G]uidance given by the teacher to the exercise of the pupil's intelligence is an aid to freedom, not a restriction upon it." Both men claimed that children attain intellectual freedom, not through absence of restraint, but through growth in knowledge and skill developed by caring adult guidance, instruction, and example.[44]

In 1943 Patri published *Your Children in Wartime*, a small volume of patriotic essays intended to help readers deal with the challenges and stresses of World War II. Much of Patri's success and influence came through his newspaper columns, so it was appropriate for him to dedicate the book to "the Newspapers of the United States." He explained the importance of newspapers to his work: "Long ago I went to the newspapers of the country for help reaching the homes, the fathers, and mothers of the children whose welfare had become my chief interest, my life's task. To those papers I owe a great debt, for they have made it possible for me to teach, to interpret, to plead for the intelligent upbringing of our children." Patri then described how the many letters he received from parents helped him know what questions faced them. "When this war began, the letters increased in numbers and took on a note of anxiety beyond all that had gone before.

'How,' they asked, 'are we to keep the children healthy and happy, at peace within themselves, while the world burns over their heads?' " With his unfailing optimism and patriotism Patri wrote: "With a little help from us and a great deal of affection, they will come through ready for the day when peace reigns once more in the world and the United States stands like a bulwark preserving the freedom of mankind."

Patri then directed his advice to three specific groups. With the help of his endless supply of stories, he advised parents on morale, rediscovering the home, children in wartime, and home and community. He told teachers that they were part of war service, that war brought new problems, and that school and home were closer because of war. He reminded children that they were citizen soldiers, that they had war work to do, and that older children had particular responsibilities. He expressed the same kind of responsible patriotism as he had throughout his career, noting that it wasn't enough to win a military victory—that victory must promote the best in America. To the children he said: "This war is being fought for your future life. . . . You must help to win it; you must help to make that winning worth-while; you must help each other. . . It is you who must carry on the ideals of this nation."[45]

Patri retired from PS 45 in 1944, but continued to write his column, "Our Children" until May 1962, only three years before his death. He also took on other editorial and writing assignments. A typical one was with *Children's Activities*, a monthly magazine offering children "Games, Puzzles, Songs, Things to Do, Stories, Play Projects, Creative Work, Drawings." The September 1946 issue, which claimed a circulation of half a million, featured prominently in a box in the middle of the cover, this note: "We announce with pleasure the acceptance by ANGELO PATRI of a position on our staff as Editorial Adviser. Millions know and love this great American for his life of service as a teacher, author, lecturer, and practical psychologist. The welfare of children is his main concern. We are proud of our association with him."

Between ads for Heinz baby food and Fletcher's Castoria, there was on page three a preachy little Patri piece addressed to children, titled "Your Choice." School was beginning that month, and Patri described two boys who made very different choices as they returned to their classes. John did his homework promptly, with the radio turned off, before going out to play. Bob found excuses to avoid homework, and when he did it at the last minute kept the radio on. John entered high school with a good record while Bob just barely made it. Never reluctant to point the moral, Patri reminded each reader that when "he chooses wisely, he shows his strength and power and learns the true meaning of happiness, the real flavor of success."[46]

In 1948, four years after retirement, Patri published his last book for parents, *How to Help Your Child Grow Up*, a summing-up volume that drew on Patri's decades of experience as a schoolmaster and writer. While some of his earlier advice books were unorganized collections of columns, this volume profited from a careful review of Patri's many publications. His editors at Rand McNally "brought together some selections from Dr. Patri's extensive writings in a syndicated column and, with his permission and cooperation" organized them into an impressive volume.

While *Your Children in Wartime* had three distinct audiences, *How to Help* was dedicated to "the Mothers of America's Children" and addressed primarily to parents. The book responded to the needs of children and parents in what was to be soon identified as the postwar baby boom. Several of Patri's earlier books had emphasized the needs of school-aged children, but two-thirds of *How to Help* was devoted to infants and pre-school children. It advised new parents to relax about schedules and not to be anxious about normal behavior like thumb sucking. Parents should accept their children's curiosity about sex and give them sound information about it. The book updated earlier advice, organized it in usable fashion, and presented it clearly. The result was what one reviewer described as "the opinions of an educator who has worked 50 years with children and parents, and still sounds undated." Another reviewer gave it a balanced assessment: "An impressive volume. . . . As a book to read it is pretty tremendous and tedious. As a handbook for parents it is a thorough and sympathetic piece of work."[47]

Readers familiar with Benjamin Spock's *The Common Sense Book of Baby and Child Care*, published just two years earlier, might note some similarities in tone and content. Spock drew on his work as a pediatrician, while Patri applied what he had learned in decades as an educator. But, coming from these different backgrounds, both published books that comforted parents, assured them that they were competent, and gave them specific and useful advice. It may well be that Patri's book represented Rand McNally's attempt to compete with Spock's increasingly popular volume.[48]

Patri was well known and respected for his writing and was often asked to endorse books, magazines or other products. He was generally careful about such endorsements but in 1950 made one serious error when he let his name and his words be used in radio and newspaper advertisements for television. In one he was quoted as saying "It is practically impossible for boys and girls to hold their own if television is not available. . . .

Children need home television for their morale as they need sunshine and fresh air for their health." The editors of the Providence newspaper were so disturbed by this message that they announced: "The *Journal-Bulletin* will not permit supposedly independent and objective experts who appear in its columns to pervert their positions for commercial purposes. We have, therefore, permanently discontinued Angelo Patri's column." Patri's strong endorsement of television led to a series of angry letters in the *New York Times*. One parent wrote: "As for Angelo Patri, the less said about his testimonial in this ad the better. What does Patri advocate, a new generation of television-nursed brats? A new generation of video-chondriacs?" A day later an article reported that the Family Services Association condemned the ads because they pressured parents to buy televisions so their children would not feel left out by their peers. Discomfited, Patri was quoted as saying that he would return the $1,000 he had received for his endorsement and that he was "never going to advertise anything for anybody any more." The article said that "future advertisements would stress a 'more positive and cheerful' approach" and that Mrs. Franklin D. Roosevelt would replace Patri as columnist. Patri, used to adulatory evaluations of his writing and teaching, must have found this incident painfully embarrassing, but it was the only such incident in his long public career, so he was apparently able to put it aside and continue with his writing.[49]

Surveying Patri's voluminous writings, and getting some perspective on them we see one theme—childhood—expressed in two forms: books for children and articles and books for parents and teachers. This parallels the ways Patri spent his days and evenings. During the day he was talking with and listening to children in his schools, while in the evenings he was often speaking to or writing to parents and teachers. Given Patri's intense interest in childhood, it may be significant that his first and last books were for children. His first books were his 1911 translations from Italian to English of *White Patch* and *Pinocchio in Africa*. His last book, *Biondino*, published forty years later, was also for children. While there were autobiographical hints in *Pinocchio in America*, there were more than hints in *Biondino*. Here we have a collection of childhood stories, including an expanded version of the incident Patri mentioned in *Schoolmaster* when his father killed the wolf that had been destroying his livestock. We have also the sad story of the death of an infant sister after the family's arrival in America. And at the end we have the village authorities building a new school and naming it SCUOLA ANGELO PATRI.

At age seven Patri was writing letters in Italian for his New York neighbors. As a columnist he often wrote articles for the Italian-language press in America. He gave radio talks for various Italian-American stations including WHOM, sponsored by the newspaper *Il Progresso* in New York City.[50] After his and Dora's trip to Italy in 1927 he corresponded with family members there. Writing and translating the Pinocchio stories, writing *Biondino*, and doing other writing about Italy were ways of maintaining over many decades strong connections with his homeland and his first language.

Patri's publishing career spanned just over five decades, from *White Patch* and *Pinocchio in Africa* in 1911, until his final column, "Our Children," in May 1962. Patri was not widely known until the publication of *Schoolmaster of the Great City* in 1917, but after that remained in the public eye with his children's books and the series of advice books for parents and teachers produced until 1950. This is an impressive publishing history, particularly for an administrator who simultaneously led schools with thousands of pupils and hundreds of teachers, and who spoke in frequent public appearances and radio programs. Patri was able to do all this partly because he was himself an avid reader. In his columns and radio programs he often commented on books for teachers and parents. Through his reading he was able to test his own ideas, put them into meaningful contexts, and extend them into new areas.

He could achieve this also because he made efficient use of his material. Parents wrote him with questions about their children and he would respond in a column. That response would be reworked into a talk on the radio and then expanded into a chapter of one of his advice books. Patri was constantly rewriting old stories, mixing them with new ones, and producing material that parents found helpful. His advice met needs felt particularly by city parents, immigrant families, and urban teachers.

Another reason for Patri's success as a writer was his clear, straightforward style. He consciously avoided the inflated, pompous language that characterizes much educational writing. He made his approach explicit in a 1938 article in the *Journal of the National Education Association* where he wrote: "The vocabulary of professional people—I am concerned mainly about the words educational people use—has always been a grief to me. . . . One would think that those who so earnestly desire to teach the common people would use words they could understand. They do nothing of the sort." After citing dreadful examples, Patri declares that teachers and parents "will not read it; they will not listen to it; they cannot benefit by it. It kills the thing it hopes to create—public interest and cooperation in the education of the public." Then, elevating this mundane topic, he cited the example of Jesus, who told simple stories with familiar words. Patri concluded: "We teachers of lesser degree might well follow His example."[51]

Assessing Patri's impact on his readers in general is obviously impossible. We have only the testimony of those who reviewed his books like Agnes de Lima and Dorothy Fisher, of influential educators like Charles William Eliot, of psychologists like Leta Hollingsworth, and—less visibly—of families who have left records of Patri's impact. One such family was represented by Mary Bischoff, who, in writing family genealogy, kept encountering references to Patri and clippings of his writings. She found through the internet that I was studying Patri and asked for information about him, saying: "The first time I ever heard of Angelo Patri was in reading some ancestral letters of my grandmother and great aunt. Both references were with regard to child-rearing. These were written in the late 1920s or early 1930s. Later I came upon a writing by Patri titled "Beautiful Old Age. . . . " The writing has some beautiful thoughts and I wanted to know more about this man."

I sent Mary some material on Patri and she responded with an interesting set of notes and clippings. She explained that "we have handed down Angelo Patri for several generations without really knowing about him—save these few items. He has an endearing wisdom that draws you." Mary's younger sister still has two of Patri's books, presumably left by her grandmother, "a college educated woman who taught school in Ohio to support herself for years before marriage." Mary included an undated clipping from Patri's column, "Our Children," in which he urged parents not to spoil their children, but to carefully teach them to take care of themselves. Mary's greataunt Margaret had written at the top, "You children were taught this way." Mary added a 1942 note from her greataunt Mimmie, which said, "Angelo Patri writes much about the need of children being alone for a quiet period each day . . . so your children find what is good for them."

Mary also sent Patri's "Beautiful Old Age" column, published with an illustration of a handsome ancient tree, ending with these lines: "Age brings peace; and it will, if we desire it, bring to us a beauty beyond the touch of this earth." Mary added a note about some related Patri "lines that Linda wrote out . . . perhaps from a writing that Aunt Margaret had on her kitchen wall back in 1987. . . ."

"In one sense there is no death,
The life of the soul on earth lasts beyond his departure.
You will always feel that life touching yours,
That voice speaking to you—that spirit looking out of other eyes,
talking to you in the familiar things he touched . . .
Worked with . . . loved as familiar friends.

He lives on in your life
And in the lives of all others that knew him." [52]

Patri's writing and speaking bridged gaps between generations, parents and children, Italy and America, and the Italian and English languages and enabled him to reach millions of appreciative readers. His success in these areas had a strong effect on Patri himself. He took pride in his influence as a respected speaker and writer as well as an educator. But the most practical effect was that this work enabled him to live well and to share his good fortune with family and friends. His income from speaking and writing far surpassed his modest earnings as an educator. The royalties from *Schoolmaster* enabled him by 1920 to purchase a summer home in Paradox, a tiny town near Schroon Lake in northern New York. He shared this vacation property with his three siblings and their children, and here he doubtless learned more about child development as he helped his nephews and nieces grow up. As his prosperity increased, he sold the Paradox property and bought a handsome estate in Patterson, New York. Here he and his wife spent weekends, often with members of their extended family. After his retirement in 1944 Patri lived here as a "country gentleman" for twenty-one years until his death in 1965. And, as one might expect from this productive man, he continued to write and speak on behalf of the world's children.

Patri remembered in warm, idealized terms his own childhood in Italy under the benign influences of his parents, his grandfather, and Brother Felice. The death of his beloved younger sister soon after the family's arrival in America affected young Angelo deeply. He was still a wholly Italian child at that time, and he responded sadly but fatalistically as he would have if he had still been in Piaggine. Shortly thereafter his father shaved off his American beard and again became for Angelo his familiar Italian father.

Patri never became a father himself, but he learned a great deal about young people through sharing his home with them, talking with thousands of them in his schools, and reading about them in the many letters he received from parents. Out of such experiences Patri as an adult reinterpreted his own childhood, the childhoods of his extended family members, and those of the thousands of other children he encountered as teacher, principal, and parent adviser. He gradually created an informal theory of childhood that integrated his European, Italian, spiritual perspectives with the more secular, American perspectives of Dewey and other progressives. The next chapter will present a European perspective on Patri's conceptions of childhood.

Patri holding grand-nephew Frank Merolla, Jr. on Memorial Day, 1941
(Frank Merolla)

ELEVEN

Childhood in the Thought of Angelo Patri

by Luciana Bellatalla

AT THE FIRST PATRI SEMINAR IN SALERNO IN 2002, I WAS
*pleased to find European scholars who were writing and speaking about Patri. The
title of the seminar translates as "The Thought and Work of Angelo Patri," with
his ideas and his practice having equal status. American writers on Patri have
concentrated on his practical work in the schools, but some European scholars have
focused on his ideas themselves. This may be partly because in America Patri was
best known through articles about his educational activities, whereas Europeans
knew him primarily through a few of his books, some of which have been translated into Italian, French, and other languages.*

*At the seminar Dr. Luciana Bellatalla presented an earlier version of this
paper which was then published in the Proceedings of the meeting. Dr. Bellatalla,
of Ferrara University, has written books on Dewey and Jane Addams and is
familiar with the progressive context for Patri's ideas. I asked her to translate
her article into English, and she invited me to edit it for an American audience.
It helps initiate a dialogue about Patri's psychological and educational principles.
Was Patri, to use Lawrence Cremin's term, an educational "sentimentalist," ide-
alizing childhood? How does Bellatalla's European child-centered interpretation
square with a more American picture of Patri as a community-oriented educator?
There is useful perspective in the fact that this European scholar, drawing on some
of the same sources, gives a different emphasis to Patri's thought.[1]*

*Patri's broad conception of childhood is reminiscent of the ideas of Bronson
Alcott, the father of Louisa May Alcott, and one of the earliest Americans who
might be called a progressive educator. Alcott wrote in 1836: "I sit down to make
some remarks on the lives and circumstances of my children but e'er I am aware, I*

have left the consideration of them as individuals and have merged their separate lives into the common life of the spirit."[2] A century and a half later, Clark Blaise used an analogy to make a similar point: "We deny the evidence of our senses if we do not have a concept broader than our senses to enclose them. If I don't have a concept of oceans, I won't see the waves. . . . Lacking a concept of childhood, we saw children as defective adults."[3] Going beyond children, Leon Wieseltier recently wrote: "The care that we feel for people other than ourselves is the result of regarding us all, the subjects of our concern and ourselves, under a single and highly general description, which is the description of the human." Patri's concern for the individual child as well as for an ideal Childhood may be seen as a part of this broader concern for individual humans and for Humanity itself.[4]

1. From Child to Children

A story about Angelo Patri says that he once lost patience with some boys as they were trampling on a new wet cement sidewalk, disturbing his quiet work at home. His wife was surprised at his impatience, as she knew his love for children, and she reminded him of that love. Patri replied, "Yes, I love them in the abstract, but not in the concrete." This may be just a legend, but the abstract/concrete issue can help us see that Patri, an intelligent and wise teacher, understood the relationships among educational theory, instructional choices, and conceptions of childhood. He realized that "the Child" does not refer to an actual individual, but to an ideal.

A natural, effective educational situation is a process which includes on the one hand, as conditions, certain ideal general qualities of the child such as curiosity, creativity, and intellectual plasticity; and on the other, as results, these often hidden qualities preserved in particular ways in each individual child. Patri explicitly states in his 1922 *Child Training* that ideal childhood is, at the same time, both the ground on which education lies, and the goal of its process.[5] Certainly Patri was a teacher more than a theorist of education. Nevertheless, thanks to his Deweyan sympathies, his interest in ideal childhood was central. This can be clearly seen in his books, in which he frequently deals with this topic in an articulate manner and a conversational style. As a teacher, a principal, and a family counselor, he consciously tried to popularize educational issues and perspectives.

Patri always writes of children, as shown from the titles of his books, most of which include the words "child," "childhood," or "children."[6] Patri is principally interested in childhood problems from different points of view. All these perspectives are connected in planning educational and school activities, which are the greatest of Patri's concerns. He first describes the ideal child which he loves, for it is the necessary ground of all educational inquiry; after that, he deals with the actual universe of children, in all possible situations in the streets, at home, in the interrelations with parents, siblings, and friends. Finally, he studies the child in the school. According to Dewey, school and society are interacting; therefore, the actual child outside and inside the school is in a dialectical, necessary relationship, and this important relationship should not be neglected by educators. I will discuss these considerations one by one to clarify my argument. However, theoretically speaking, these matters should not be discussed separately. As a group, they define the ground on which Patri elaborates his educational strategies and finally the quality of his work.

2. Ideal Children

Patri, like all theorists of the New Education movement, takes his conception of childhood from Rousseau.[7] Thanks to the original vision of Rousseau's optimistic and positive ideal child, Patri is nearer to the *école sereine* (the European idealistic version of the learning-by-doing theory) than to American progressive education based on Dewey's philosophy of education. For Patri, children are naturally good: their natural gifts must, therefore, be preserved; their needs and their desires must be stimulated. For Dewey, education must organize and control natural human inclinations and impulses; this is simply the necessary requirement for educational work. In Patri's educational model, Nature is the necessary and sufficient condition of human growth, and, therefore, it must be defended and encouraged. By contrast, in Dewey's educational model, a continuously planned and controlled interaction among Nature, the social and cultural environment, and adult work is fundamental. Nature, by itself, cannot develop growth and improvement. On one side, the outcome is child-centeredness; on the other, children and adults, pupils and teachers are necessarily interacting.[8]

The key words in Patri's idea of childhood are goodness, freedom, imagination, and play. These are the four foundations of teachers' activity, expressed in all Patri's works, but particularly in his autobiographical tale for children, *Biondino: An Italian Reader*. Biondino is obviously Patri himself. Here he describes not only his life in Italy and his departure for the United States but tells also of his conception of childhood. Biondino is a joyful boy, loving poems and songs, playing and listening to adults, who tell stories and popular legends: "During the long evenings, Biondino lived in a world of beauty and peace. Now there was magic in the prayers, in the songs, and in the legends mingling so marvelously. For him each day was a day of enchantment and the nights brought sleep and dreams of peace and happiness."[9]

Biondino's life is marked by the rhythms of family, the cycle of seasons, and by extraordinary and often incomprehensible events like traveling to America. As in children's plays, fairy tales, and folklore, all life spreads from the cyclic and mysterious stream of Nature. This word is written intentionally with a capital letter, because it is the paradigm of life itself, nourishing the imagination. Nature is, consequently, the most important reference in Patri's educational ideas. Nature is defined as a good mother of mankind, the guardian of the principles of freedom, joy, beauty, and intrinsic moral values. At birth, children receive this natural gift; the task of education is to preserve it, as Rousseau indicated. In the same way, this positive natural heritage can also be found in the folkloric tradition, which new generations need to know and appreciate. It is obvious—and here Patri again echoes Rousseau—that children are different from adults. However, they are endowed with a moral sense and aesthetic taste, and—thanks to play and imagination—can create Beauty. This innate infusion of Truth and Beauty justifies the central role of children in the world.

Giuseppe Lombardo-Radice, Patri's Italian friend, considers the Child to be the father of mankind. Dewey, Patri's teacher, describes in *Democracy and Education* the continuity of culture in the alternation of generations.[10] Patri's Child does even more, because he nourishes and renews the spirit of life. Therefore Patri may be connected to the *école nouvelle* movement as well as to progressive education as Dewey defined and described it. When Patri talks about the duty of children in the world, he seems to refer implicitly to the philosophy and the ethics of William James and his *Will to Believe* and *Talks to Teachers* more than to Dewey.[11] Patri writes, "It was for this children were sent into the world. They renew our waning courage in the warmth of their glowing souls. Our faith is renewed by their faith in the joy and beauty and mystery of life. They warm our chill hearts and help us on. . . . That is why I am a teacher. Daily I renew my soul in the glow of childhood's reverent, joyous wonder."[12]

3. Actual Children

Nevertheless, the innocent Nature of the ideal Child does not eliminate, as the passage quoted above could suggest, individual differences or the necessary work of schools and teachers. Education is an unavoidable process which takes place, thanks to adults and to experience, both inside and outside the school. The ideal child is an abstract notion, which daily life at school and at home must approach, and to which it must be related, even if in normal life children are quite different from this ideal. Patri refers to familiar and difficult physical and psychological circumstances—to poverty, prejudice, superstition, and a diffuse coldness towards children.

Therefore, to know how and how far actual conditions have concealed the good Childhood spirit, Patri suggests an educational process aimed at bringing to light the ideal Child, which is sleeping in all children.

Patri emphasizes social, economic, and cultural conditions because he wants his readers to understand not only that education is broad and lifelong, but also that all adults (and not only teachers and educators) are morally engaged in this process of growth and change. Nobody can or should shirk this responsibility. Moreover, corrupted childish behavior generally is caused by the mistaken habits of adults. Adults used to take care of children according to common sense or tradition. Patri said, as other educators did in that same cultural milieu, that adults tend to adjust children to their own expectations, habits, and ideals, with no respect for children's needs and natural gifts.[13] Children must sometimes be scolded, but authoritarian behavior is not right.[14]

Patri accepted, though implicitly, the then current idea of parallelism between ontogenesis and phylogenesis in human development—that the development of the individual parallels the evolution of the group. Therefore, as far as children and adults, on the one hand, and early and modern humans, on the other, are connected by a similar relation, he thought that the adult's duty was to wipe out the "caveman" heritage in children. But corrective measures must not be violent or authoritarian, because the process of growth is always natural and necessary. It happens and cannot be stopped. Consequently, adults must not impose behaviors or habits, since violence and authority are in contradiction with Nature and natural needs.

Patri, looking closely at his environment, sees that the excessive authoritarianism of adults, overprotection by mothers, and the tendency to remove children from their peers kills their curiosity, astonishment, and need of movement, of play, through the imposition of unpleasant duties. Therefore, mothers' anxieties and traditions must be challenged because both prevent children from growing and their natural gifts from developing. Babies "are covered up snugly to keep them from the cold" and, by contrast, are frequently scolded.[15] Patri criticizes prohibitions and exaggerated compliance, because they usually turn a child, not into an autonomous adult, but into a spoiled child, a toy for his parents, and a poor human being, not capable in the future of self-determination.

From this point of view, children's frequent moral faults, such as idleness, tantrums, selfishness, lack of attention, and bad manners may also be explained. Patri gives interesting suggestions concerning these behaviors. He wants to show that the actual child is always the fruit of a misunderstanding of education, which does not follow Nature and the natural signs in children's minds. Teaching aims to make children's souls or spirits free.[16] Therefore teachers must plan projects to educate young pupils and their families at the same time, because only in this way will they be able to face their responsibilities and duties. Families too are custodians of values because they are the heirs of a popular culture that is close to Nature, to be handed down to posterity. Without this culture, the roots of human life and therefore of childhood will get lost.

Patri writes: "There is more philosophy—big, broad, human philosophy in the simple folk lore of some of the poorest and most distressed people than there is in most of the books that you read. It is only when you keep in constant touch with humanity that you see the child, more important than the curriculum, than the school, than the per cents, than promotions."[17] All of Patri's moral and educational commitment is summed up in these words. He became a teacher to set children free and, then, on the same grounds, became a teacher of teachers and counselor to parents, as is shown by his books, which are often handbooks for families. Moreover, he entrusts to education a demiurgical or creative duty, which he emphasizes again and again. (A demiurge is a deity who shapes the real world toward the ideal.) Patri says to the teacher: "You are a greater artist than he who paints a picture, than he who carves a statue, than he who writes a book. Your product is that wonderful thing, human conduct! You are a creator! America looks to you for her greatness, her united voice, her bigness of race!"[18]

Patri believes that this splendid duty can be accomplished and the naturally most beautiful souls saved, if adults are effectively involved in educational work and, particularly, in the reality of schooling. He claims that children are better off than in the past, having a more optimistic attitude, for the present is dominated by progress, knowledge is diffused, science is rich, and education is living its Copernican revolution. All these contribute to human, social, ethical, scientific, and spiritual amelioration.

Nowadays, children are cleverer, freer, cleaner, more conscientious, diligent, and happier than in the past. A child grows up in interaction with the environment; if it is good, the child will be good too. And no doubt the present is better than the past, not only for cultural and scientific improvement, but above all in a moral perspective. Not accidentally, his key words are freedom, tolerance, respect, and fraternity. Patri pointed out these ideas in 1926, in a period when American economic life was at a high level; however, his beliefs did not crack after 1929, in the periods of economic crisis and of World War II. His optimistic attitude is not affected by historical or economic circumstances because it is rooted in his belief in education, which he intends not just as a reconstruction of the environment and the subject (as Dewey did), but as an activity capable of bringing to light the natural, necessary, and eternal foundations of the human spirit and life.

4. Children in the School

Since education is the development of human potential, the teacher should help pupils to discover their deep and true identities. The teacher must necessarily be a loving and respectful guide in order to support a process of self-education, the only education that can provide successful development. Today's child looks to "teachers for help, but not too much help; for guidance, but not too much guidance, for he would do a better job than any of us have done, and he can only do that through freedom and through the fine appreciation that we may give him." [19]

Patri describes a school that looks like many contemporary experiments in the new education in the United States and in Europe insofar as he shares with this movement methodological strategies, love for children, and an informal social classroom climate. Democracy, learning by doing, practice, and joy are the most important characteristics of these new or progressive schools. [20] However, Patri still accepts the traditional curriculum: the child must learn writing, reading, and arithmetic, and must also learn to love art, literature, good books, folk culture, and democratic habits. If the curriculum content changes only partly from the traditional, Patri proposes to modify radically the methods of teaching and learning and the actual relationships among teachers and pupils. The educational process must be an occasion of social and ethical growth for pupils and their families too. Therefore, the school must be open to society—to families, neighborhoods, streets, and cultural institutions—as Dewey suggested in 1899 in *School and Society*. The classroom must become a social, democratic, and cooperative microcosm of society. [21]

Thus in the new schools, children are, at one and the same time, the *ends* of the process, because all activities are planned for their ethical, psychological and spiritual development; the *means*, because they must connect educational activities to their own direct experiences; the *resources*, because the school depends on the pupils; and the *links with society*, because they connect the school, the family, and the environment. Teachers have long taken special care of children who are in physical, psychological, or social difficulties, so as to give them better chances of healthy development. This is right, Patri says, but the so-called normal children need the same care as the others. Patri expresses the same position as contemporary educators: that teachers must plan more opportunities for *all* their pupils, taking care of each of them, because every child is a particular universe and, therefore, has peculiar problems and natural gifts. Consequently, Patri promotes the learning-by-doing school, planned for interaction and interrelation with the social environment, open to neighborhood needs. On the one hand, such a school becomes a social democratic enterprise; on the other, it considers children and their natural potential as the core of its plans and goals.

From this point of view, Patri says that a teacher must have not only a high level of professional competence, but must also be well disposed towards children. This is a requirement if the teacher is to pay attention to children's activities, realize their needs and desires, resolve their difficulties, promote their freedom, and encourage the expression of their imagination and their inner life.

In *Child Training* Patri wrote that God gave the child years to develop. "During those years we cannot tell what growth is being formed. We can only feed his mind and soul and wait. . . . Be patient." [22] While being patient, a teacher has to prepare the occasions of learning and growth, as Rousseau says in *Emile*. When necessary, the teacher scolds and corrects, gives direction to energies and desires, helps pupils achieve self-determination and, finally, provides to all the pupils what they naturally need, as far as every individual is different from the other. Teachers have in each pupil a guide for their work and instructional choices. Patri tells adults: "Stand back and keep hands off. Watch reverently for him to unfold. Man's awakening comes in the fullness of time." [23]

The school must be on the children's scale and teachers must believe in children's potential. This is the key to educational success, and the echo of William James in *The Will to Believe* is evident. Patri says that the child "will respond to our faith in him. Faith works miracles." [24] Patri's graduates testify that his writings are the fruit of his direct experience. He took care of the intellectual, cultural, and moral development of his pupils but was also concerned about their present and future happiness. So he talked with pupils in his office and suggested for them individual learning plans and learning by doing. This nonauthoritarian method was beneficial above all to marginal students, giving them attention, care, respect, and human dignity. Thanks to this individual counseling, the most difficult situations were resolved, and Patri's pupils were able to find their way in the world. [25]

5. Conclusion

The ideal Child is a key to Patri's work as teacher, teacher educator, writer, and parent adviser. Patri was aware that all teaching that aims at true education must be supported by theoretical principles. Patri identified this principle in the Child. The ideal Child allows Patri to accept both the European model of the New Education and the American practice of progressive education. Certainly, as he recalled, Dewey affected his instructional choices. [26] Patri refers not only to Dewey's scientific educational theses, but to his deep respect for children. When Patri first read Dewey he wrote: "I had come in contact with the personality of a great teacher, fearless, candid and keen, with nothing dogmatic in his nature. Under this leadership I came in touch with vital ideas and I began to work, not in the spirit of passive obedience, but in one of mental emancipation."[27]

Patri's interpretation of Dewey's philosophy of education emphasizes Dewey's respectful attitude towards children, perhaps because Patri first read only "Ethical Principles Underlying Education," published in 1897. Here Dewey expressed educational theses and teaching suggestions much like those in his 1916 *Democracy and Education*. But Patri does not mention, for example, *How We Think*, a complex work centered on the role of thinking and on the place of free thought in the process of human growth and education.[28] Dewey focuses less on childhood than Patri does, instead emphasizing scientific method. For him children must be respected to the same extent as all individuals who are engaged in the process of growth and of interactive reconstruction of life and environment. Interaction and interrelation are the fundamental principles of this reconstruction. Hence a static and perfect Nature is a paradox, because all is changing in a perpetual quest for an unreachable certainty. Patri proceeds from a general theory of the structure and function of thinking and experience, to the search for a principle that could justify educational choices and organization.

Therefore Patri's school integrates a Deweyan progressive model with the European *école sereine*, where the emotional aspects of children are emphasized, and the central role of children is strongly stressed. Patri knew and appreciated Dewey, but he had much in common also with educators like Pestalozzi, who saw in love (and especially in mothers' love) the prime mover of education. He may even be compared to A. S. Neill, who, in his school Summerhill, used private conversations as therapy for the most problematic of his pupils and extolled the natural virtues of the child, as Rousseau had taught.

Patri, a democratic teacher, influenced by Dewey's educational theory and a supporter of the civic culture of the United States, was more libertarian than he himself thought, in considering the Child—a naturally and necessarily perfect subject—as the paradigm for human experience and existence. In the last two pages of *Schoolmaster*, Patri writes a celebration of Children which is more revealing than any other statement of his: "The feet of men know not where to go and you show them the way. The souls of men are bound and you make them free. You . . . are the dreams, the hopes, the meaning of the world. It is because of you that the world grows and grows in brotherly love. I look a thousand years ahead and I see not men, ships, inventions, buildings, poems, but children, shouting happy children, and I keep my hand in yours and smiling, dream of endless days."[29]

Tall Eleanor Roosevelt visits short Angelo Patri
(Muriel Sherlock and Marilyn Shea)

TWELVE

Back to the Future:
Current Perspectives on Patri

AS I DISCUSSED MY STUDY OF PATRI WITH FRIENDS AND *family they asked challenging questions about him, his books, his career, and his influence. I was reminded that varying kinds and degrees of exposure to any-one, including Patri, gives different perspectives, so I began asking them to write their responses to his memoir and his books. I gave copies of* Schoolmaster, How to Help Your Child Grow Up, *and excerpts from his memoir to some adult friends and family and requested reactions from them. I also wanted responses to Patri's writing for children so gave copies of* Pinocchio in America *to three granddaughters and* Biondino *to another, and invited them to write their responses as well. In all this I wanted to know if Patri's writings, forty years after his death, still had the power to entertain, instruct, and persuade.*

My bias is shamelessly evident in my selection of respondents. The adults whom I asked to write share my progressive values, so it is not surprising that they had similar responses to Patri and his writings. I have made no effort to solicit reactions from a wider range of people and present these only as outcomes of a dia-logue I have had with friends and family concerning Patri and his ideas. All of my respondents invited me to edit their pieces, but I have only found it necessary to in-tegrate and rearrange some paragraphs and to omit or change occasional words. In a few places writers cite brief quotations from Patri that I or others have already quoted; I leave this repetition only to show that some of his words are particularly telling for several readers. I thank all my writers for their contributions and for broadening my own perspectives on Patri. I will introduce each one in italics.

Patri wrote or translated eight books for children. One of the most popular was Pinocchio in America, *published in 1928 with attractive art deco-style illustrations by Mary Liddell. (Incidentally, "Pinocchio" literally translates as "pine eyes," or, more loosely, "wooden eyes.") I enjoyed the book and found copies for three granddaughters. Jin-Mei McMahon, at that time a third grader at the Portland Montessori Earth School, chose a question and answer format for her response.*

Why did Pinocchio come to America? Because he thought that America was a place where nobody goes to school.

How did he expect Americans to welcome him? Nicely, with no school. Fairs in honor of him. Speeches about him, where they clap their hands and twirl their hats.

What was it really like, instead? Hard, and with school. No fairs. No speeches except little ones that always turned out wrong and with mad people always trying to catch him.

What did Pinocchio think about going to school? Not fun at all. Math and other things were hard.

What did the Blue fairy tell him? To find out what is behind things.

What is the important point that the Red Rooster makes in the story? Teaching, working, and paying attention to people.

What did Pinocchio finally learn? That questions are behind everything.

What happens to him in the end? He sails back home to Gepetto.

What were your favorite things in the story? I liked Patsy, his dog, because he was Pinocchio's best friend. Also Patsy was so good in school that he didn't get sent away, and he took good care of the turnips so they didn't get eaten by the blue cow. He was so faithful! I liked Pinocchio because he was funny. He really knew how to make speeches! But he was a rascal. He even ran away from school!

—◆—   —◆—   —◆—

Adrienne Vasquez Wallace was in the fifth grade at Portland's Llewellyn Elementary School when she wrote this.

This book is very funny and it is about Pinocchio and he swims to America to get away from school. But he was wrong, in America there is also school and he has to go to school and study hard. He gets into a lot of trouble because he is lying and makes up goofy stories so he won't get into trouble. He leaves Gepetto all alone and just takes off without saying goodbye. Gepetto is very worried and is looking everywhere for Pinocchio but can't find him.

Angelo Patri is a very talented person and I don't know how he thought about writing this book. I really like it and my favorite part was when Pinocchio got his dog because Pinocchio was very happy and immediately named it Patsy. Patsy goes with Pinocchio everywhere and obeys his commands. She is his best friend. My least favorite part was when Pinocchio was sad and didn't eat and wasn't happy or cheerful.

Bonnie Cramer wrote this response when she was in the fifth grade in the Silver Crest School in Silverton, Oregon:

I enjoyed *Pinocchio in America* very much. I enjoyed all the lessons that Pinocchio endured. For instance Pinocchio ran away and from that came consequences and lessons. He learns to look behind what is there and find answers. Also, the obstacles that he comes across show him that to do something, you first have to learn how. It also shows you that if you run away from your home to get away from school like Pinocchio did, you will always find that there are things you don't like in the new place.

I don't think there was much that I did not like, but I thought that Pinocchio thought too much of himself and I believe that you should not only think of yourself but also think of others, so I think he should learn to think of others in his lessons. I enjoyed reading the Roman numerals for chapter headings and I thought that the old language was very interesting. The pictures were interesting too, they matched the writing very nicely. They were blank on the back where normally in books there would be writing, and when you touched the pictures you could feel an indent from when it was put on a printing press. I thought that it was cool not only that the pictures matched the writing but the surroundings in the writing, for instance Pinocchio is a marionette and just like a marionette the drawing has little spaces at all the joints.

Each and every time I turned a page it not only looked as though I was traveling through the author's memories but it felt like it too. I noticed that the book was written in 1929, 75 years ago, I don't know much about Angelo Patri but when I read this book it made me feel as though Patri went to America just like Pinocchio. I have read very many books and I have never read a horrible book and this book was definitely not at all horrible and I recommend it.

Gwendolyn Cramer was in the seventh grade at the Silver Crest School when she read Patri's autobiographical children's book Biondino.

Biondino is a pretty good book. It isn't the kind of book that I normally read, but it was still rather well written and entertaining. It's about a young boy (Biondino, because he has blond hair) who lives in Italy and gets himself into various predicaments. He really likes the sound of big words. One of my favorite parts was when Biondino went to school, which he was way too young for. The students were learning the vowels by shouting them out, and Biondino just shouted out all the sounds he could think of. The teacher of course, got very mad, and Biondino ran all the way home crying. I also like when Biondino repeats words that people say. It's pretty funny. Biondino is an autobiographical book by Angelo Patri, about him when he was a little kid. The story starts off with Biondino as an old man and ends the same way. I kind of like it when stories go back in time like that.

Patri did a very good job of showing Biondino as a young boy. He reminded me of many other little kids I know, all innocent and easily distracted. I couldn't really tell that the story took place in Italy. I probably wouldn't have found out if I hadn't known where the book took place already. The pictures in one version of the book didn't go along with the story too well, especially the one on the cover. It's a picture of some brown-haired boys waving goodbye to a ship that looked like a cruise ship. That's not at all how I imagined any part of the story.

I think I would mostly recommend this book to young children. Although they would probably have a lot of questions, they would find it really entertaining and funny. I usually like reading books that are from the point of view of someone my age. I know that some other people like that too.

I wonder if some of the words have been changed in all the translations the book has been through. It was first written in English, then translated into Italian, and then re-translated back into English. I hope that it wasn't changed too much. It would be interesting to find an original copy in English and look for any differences. All in all, I liked this book. It was an interesting story by a good author. I learned a lot about Patri's personality. I can't honestly say that *Biondino* was the greatest book I've ever read—there weren't enough details for my liking, but it was a cute little short story. It was fun to read and never boring.

About twenty years ago I had a student named Mineko Koyabashi who had a strong interest in international education. She pursued that interest in graduate school and then returned to Japan to work, marry, and raise children. (Her married name is Yoshimura.) I recently had dinner with her, her husband, and other friends, and we discussed her activities in international education and curriculum development. In passing I made several comparisons with Patri's schools in the Bronx, and we talked about what did and didn't work in education at various times and places. Mineko and family were on their way to work in South Africa, where I sent her a copy of Schoolmaster. *I invited her to respond to it in light of her work there and in Japan. She wrote:*

It is well known that there are some serious problems in Japan's educational system, and the number of children who refuse to go to school confirms this. This number was estimated at no less than 130,000 in 2003, according to a survey by the Ministry of Education. These children range in age from 8 to 15. This statistic is based on elementary and junior high school children and does not include students who drop out of senior high schools, because that age group is past compulsory education.

The reasons for their refusal vary. Some claim that they were bullied; others point out unstable family situations. The most difficult cases, however, are students who cannot pinpoint the exact reason for their inability to go to school. Many are talented and intellectual children with caring and understanding parents. These children try to go to school during the initial stages, but later become unable, physically and psychologically, to bring themselves to go to school. Although many parents and teachers try to convince them that they are okay at school, these efforts often prove useless. Many educational psychologists or therapists now recommend that these children be allowed to stay at home. So they do stay home—behind the closed doors of their bedrooms.

Why? Many people are desperately searching for reasons for this situation. It is a threat to society that there are 130,000 children who refuse what many of us believe to be necessary. If Angelo Patri were asked to solve this, his answer would indubitably be quite simple: change the schools. During the past fifty years Japanese compulsory education has aimed at producing a mass of obedient and disciplined people to build the country to be economically successful. Teachers and schools conducted drills, enforced oppressive rules, forced students to take examinations, and in general exerted strict control over their students.

Japanese society now needs a completely new group of people who are able to think, using their both their emotions and their critical thinking skills. This means that the schools, teachers, and teacher education need to change. As Patri suggested in *Schoolmaster* more than eighty years ago, we must do all of the following: change the kind of experiences that students have in the school; improve teacher training; individualize the school; give the school over to the people; change our attitude towards the child. We need to trust the children.

It is obvious that the intelligent children who are currently refusing to attend school could be guiding lights in Japanese society. They refuse to attend school because they know they cannot get what they want or need there, unless the schools and the teachers change. They know there is more harm than benefit in attending, but they do not know how to articulate this truth. Therefore their only defense is not to go to school.

As an educator who has worked with children in Japan, the United States, Denmark, Liberia, Ethiopia, Malawi, and South Africa, I must state that what I described in Japan rarely exists in less economically developed countries. Going to school is any child's dream in Liberia torn by war, in rural Ethiopia oppressed by its own minorities, in black communities in Malawi and in South Africa victimized by HIV/AIDS. For these children the opportunity to attend school is their hope for the future, so they do not question the quality of education or the direction that they are given at school.

It is heartbreaking that many people in less developed societies aim solely at attaining economic stability from schooling, when Japanese society can't give many children a reason to attend school. Education can do more than restrict children, push unsuitable social goals, promote only economic stability. Why do we send our children to school? Patri's message—to cultivate healthy individuals in a just society—must once again be heard across the world.

———————

Marilena Risi has been a helpful friend since my first visit to Salerno and Piaggine in 2002. She has served as an interpreter in our meetings and has translated a number of papers and articles for me. She has been a thoughtful adviser, not only on language, but on educational and political matters. We have a continuous cultural friendship carried on mostly by e-mail. At my request she wrote this essay which she titles "Angelo Patri's Message for Americans and Italians."

I am an Italian teacher with a degree in Languages and Foreign Literatures from the University of Genoa. I have taught English in private and state school for more than twenty years, and have visited several foreign countries in order to know their cultures better. In the United States I admired the different, open ways of solving educational and intellectual problems. I am now an elementary instructor in public schools. Along with my fellow teachers I am working with what we call "Riforma Moratti." (Moratti is our Minister of Education, after whom the current reform program is named). I believe that all students must learn English for its cosmopolitan and communicative approach. My special objective is to help Italian and American educators to develop a new type of education, which will assist children to enlarge their cultural views and build for their families a friendly bridge between school and society.

With these intentions I worked as an interpreter at the first two seminars on Angelo Patri and began to study his work carefully. I translated *A Schoolmaster of the Great City* into Italian, and wrote chapter summaries of Patri's *Biondino*. I am now reading Patri's *How to Help Your Child Grow Up*, his last and most complete advice book for parents and teachers. As I read the book I am making connections with our current educational situation and am finding valuable solutions for daily school problems.

Patri's main advice to parents and teachers is to cooperate with each other in order to help children grow up in healthy ways, physically and psychologically. Educators become more effective when there is open communication between school and family. Patri's message to children is also persuasive; he touches the hearts of children and encourages them to act responsibly. With empathy between teachers and pupils, students become more attentive and more likely to follow where the educator leads. In *How to Help Your Child Grow Up*, Patri notes how important it is for teachers to like their students. To the teacher who likes him, the student "is all ears, all attention, all affection, and he gladly follows wherever that one leads." (234) Therefore it's necessary that teachers be secure and confident, since they are cultural mediators among family, school and society.

Patri gave sound advice to his generation, and his deep pedagogical principles can be useful in our twenty-first century societies too. Now we live with the conflicts of mobile societies and experience all the problems of family tensions, when most parents go to work, leaving their children at school a long time. Many parents are faithful in support of schools, but some need to do much more. Parents come home late from work, and have less time to listen to their children and often no time to play with them. The school must realize this and receive the children with love, understanding, and help for their growing needs and desires. Easy communication between parents and teachers is not always possible, so they must focus on specific matters when they discuss student learning and the relationships between home and school.

I don't think that there is much difference between Patri's time and ours or between our two countries in our common educational concerns. The problems of the past are the same today, but now there is no fear of speaking about them openly. Patri wrote for people from many backgrounds; in the same way, we Italian teachers must be friends of our pupils' families from different cultural backgrounds. Mass media, especially television, movies, and computers, brought progress and much communication, but they can provoke some uncontrolled reactions in children. Many parents don't manage to control these excessive stimuli in their children, and above all, in themselves.

Parents ask teachers many questions about our new and different ways of living. Can we answer their questions? Sometimes we teachers can respond supportively, but at other times we must ask our own questions. There is continuous communication in an ongoing educational dialogue. Knowing parents' families, social backgrounds, and problems can help us understand pupils' behavior better, and thus find good ways of leading them to new intellectual perspectives.

Patri said: "Teachers are trained for their work and they understand it. . . .They feel a child's mind, feel his needs, feel his responses." Parents care for their children, but they still "need the teacher's professional help because their emotions are mixed with their understanding and their actions." (*How to Help Your Child Grow Up*, 262–263.) Patri's message is similar to one adopted in Italian schools that encourages parent-school communication, and promotes peaceful living and positive objectives for our children and future generations.

References: Patri, *How to Help Your Child Grow Up*, (Chicago: Rand McNally, 1948); Patri, A *Schoolmaster of the Great City*, (New York: Macmillan, 1917.)

* * *

My second daughter, Barbara Conde, has been an elementary teacher for many years and has taken a continued interest in my work on Patri. We've had many discussions of her teaching and of Patri's experience as we have worked on her land and built her chicken house. I think that Patri would have appreciated our natural integration of hand work and head work. Barbara titles her contribution "Haunted Squiggles."

I began teaching in a suburb of Portland, Oregon, moved on to Eskimo communities in the Arctic, then to rural Vermont and upstate New York, and finally full circle back to rural Oregon. The children and parents in each community had similar hopes and dreams. Although the details differ, the challenges of belonging and inclusion, familial and cultural differences, continue to be central. Angelo Patri in New York City faced some of the same challenges.

I've been hearing about Patri for years now, and am intrigued by my father's deepening interest in him. Some time ago Dad gave me a chapter called "Adventures in Enthusiasm" from Patri's unpublished memoir. In it Patri shares, through the eyes of a visitor to his school, beliefs that he thought were central to the development of a student's education. He tells the stories of students from a variety of cultures and their transformation as they learn. He writes about a school that I would thrive in as a teacher or a student. The essence of the school was that, in Patri's words, "Children and teachers were glad to be alive and glad to share experiences with each other, with parents, with visitors, with anyone who came our way." (211; here and below, page numbers from the memoir.)

I think of the struggles and joys of trying to achieve this sense of awakening, of enthusiasm, in the many places I've taught. I currently teach a first grade class of twenty-three children, six and seven years old, in a small town about forty-five minutes from a large city. Both the economy and the culture are still deeply rural. Parents attended the same school with some of the same teachers, some students are cousins, and everyone knows one another.

As the day begins in our classroom, I am often sitting at my desk, gathering the last details and materials for the day, setting attendance sheets and fluoride on top of the pile as the children arrive. Joe is usually there early, with his endearing smile and sparkling bright eyes. He announces, "I'm the first one here!" with the same enthusiasm every morning. Other students arrive as he takes chairs down off the tables and sets up the room. There is a slowly building bustle of energy. Children's conversations center around pictures in shared books, stories being written, and what they did last night. I watch, inquire about homework and who has eaten breakfast in the cafeteria, and let the children slide easily into their day at school.

As I read Patri's descriptions of the students and teachers in his school, I'm reminded of the best of our days. "Anyone who has watched a child enthusiastic in his work has had a thrilling experience. The child seems reborn, his eyes shine, his body glows with energy, his attention is fixed, enthusiasm colors his whole being and he is somebody he never was before – exalted, transformed. He lifts all about him, his classmates, his teachers, the casual observer, his parents, anyone who is fortunate enough to touch the hem of his garment. The teacher who witnesses the transformation gathers new strength." (242) These days full of enthusiastic immersion are the reason I teach. This immersion takes time and the freedom to explore. It feels to me like nurturing a spark as it flares up. The teacher must recognize when to add fuel and when to sit back to observe.

In the classrooms Patri writes about, students of all ages are given time to develop, and encouragement to tell their stories. "There is always a story, that is the nature of man, to be a story teller. . . . Whether original or copied or paraphrased, what is written is important to the child." (217) In our classroom one day Sam came to me after I had asked students to put away their writing notebooks. He said he didn't have enough time to write, so I asked him when we could have more time, and waited while he thought. He soon suggested that we write during the time students arrive, in the half-hour before reading groups. I got the attention of the other students, he asked them if this would work, and they were enthusiastic about the possible change. Now we write for twenty minutes and share our writing for ten minutes each morning. Patri: "Always they write and read and rewrite about the thing that moves them." (218) There are so many constraints on children in the public schools now, that any freedom of choice or opportunity to control and learn from their own decisions is welcome in my classroom.

I share Patri's beliefs about testing. He wrote: "I had little patience with speed tests where the teacher stands over a child, watch in hand,

'Now everybody ready, when I say "go" you start and work as fast as you can. I'm going to time you. When I say "stop" you stop. Now—then—go, begin.' What would you say to anybody that did that to you? Suppose you were a child and helpless and couldn't say anything, couldn't do a thing but grasp a pencil in hot wet fingers and choke down your heart and try to clear the fog that fear had spread over your mind. Would you be happy? This sort of thing happens every day in some school or other throughout the land. These tests are not arithmetic. They do not teach; they exhaust children. When weariness shouts at the door of your mind, the mind stops." (230–231)

In many states there are more and more stringent requirements for graduation as well as multiple benchmarks for students to pass in certain years. This has created enormous pressure on teachers, students and parents. Even in first grade, and with my developmental beliefs, I find myself pushing children to achieve. I no longer have learning centers, but am doing more direct, product-oriented instruction. If I don't, the children struggle in the subsequent years. The children and I are rewarded with praise from colleagues, parents and administrators, but in my heart I cringe as I watch the light in some students' eyes flicker out as they wonder if they can achieve what is being asked of them.

The benchmarks in our State dictate that all children in first grade will be able to write a complete sentence with a capital letter at the beginning and a period at the end. At our level at least there are no boundaries on what to write. One day during our new writing time, as I walk about the room quietly discussing writing with individual children, I come to Ronnie. At the top of his page he's drawn a wildly curving line with one color crayon. I ask him to tell me about it and he says, "It's a haunted squiggle." He wants to write this under his picture, so I help with spelling as he writes. At sharing time he is almost gleeful as he reads, "Haunted Squiggle." The class accepts and validates his efforts. This is the beginning of many "haunted" things in his writing notebook. Other students are writing sentences in a familiar form such as: "I see…" and "I like…" All children are unique, but Ronnie shares his individuality without reserve. Ronnie embodies what Patri advises: "Make haste slowly, stop long enough to get the feel of the full flow of its rhythm. Learning is living. With it should go a quality of contentment of the soul." (231) I hope for the day when we recognize and nurture the blessed uniqueness of all children and adults in schools and communities as we live in what Patri calls, "the light of enthusiasm." (249)

Andrea Baker has been a good friend for over thirty years. She has taught in several alternative programs and has helped teachers and schools become more effective through her decades of work for the Northwest Regional Educational Laboratory. She chose to respond to Patri personally in a letter.

Dear Dr. Patri: I wish you had been with me as I sat with my morning coffee reading two articles on school reform in the Portland *Oregonian*. Forgive my boldness, but I think you might have responded with tears, both tears of joy and tears of anguish. In *Schoolmaster of the Great City*, you said, "We must keep the 3R's, but they must change with the changing social needs." Today, nearly 90 years later, *The Oregonian* echoed your thoughts in describing a school that "settled on three traits that would define their school: relationships, rigor and relevance." A new Three R's in the making. You might say: "How rewarding that they took my words to heart." But you might also ask why it took our education system nearly nine decades to truly understand how schools must change to meet the needs of all students in all classrooms.

After seven rewarding years teaching high school, I spent twenty-four years helping teachers design programs and write relevant curriculum for students at risk of dropping out of school. I worked many days with many teachers in many schools across the country, and as I left each building to begin my journey home, I was energized by the commitment of the teachers, but also saddened by the many missed opportunities in classrooms everywhere. Students were not excited about learning and it became my goal to change that by teaching teachers the essence of your book where you say: "The sacredness of the child's individuality must be the moving passion of the teacher." (*Schoolmaster*, p. 15; hereafter just page numbers).

Today some teachers say curriculum is fine the way it is; some say it must change. Some say we need more motivated students; others say we need more engaged parents. Some say we need higher standards; others that higher standards will rob some students of success. Some say we need to help students understand how school relates to their personal lives, both today and in the future. Some say we need to change how we teach, not what we teach. Listening to these statements by teachers helped me create a framework that I call "Curriculum C's the Light." Critical elements of curriculum seeing the light are: Caring, Contextual and Community Collaboration.

Caring is first. Effective education can't happen without it. My mantra became "Motivation to learn often develops out of a relationship between two people." Schools must be structured so that connections between caring teachers, parents, students, counselors and community people are strong and enduring. Only then will we, as you say, "get teachers away from subject matter, from machinery, and toward children." (45)

The successful schools in today's newspaper "invigorate ties between adults and students." You knew in 1917 that teachers are much more than imparters of knowledge; they must also be mentors, coaches, facilitators, advocates, and cheerleaders. Only the very best teachers today are willing to take on all those roles; I imagine the same was true in your school. Many people attribute a "turnaround" in a young person's life to that one special teacher or caring adult. It is our responsibility as educators to create school culture and curriculum that build those caring relationships. You affirmed that when you said "We made a point of assigning the troublesome child to a teacher whom he liked." (172)

I sense that contextual learning was a foundation of your school. You said, "I tried to improve the teaching by getting away from the accepted treatment of the three R's. . . . I began by emphasizing subjects that held emotional values, drawing, composition, music, nature, literature. . . . I wanted composition that expressed the child and was not made to order." (46)

If teachers don't have an answer to students' "Why do I need to learn this?" question, then they should perhaps rethink what they are teaching or how they are teaching it. Learning is much more than a manipulation of facts and data; I describe it as the "use it or lose it" theory of knowledge. At a new charter school described in today's newspaper, students "build web sites, weld furniture, and use defibrillators on mannequins to study information technology, engineering and health sciences." The rigor and the relevance are obvious when we hear students say that they "shift into overdrive" when they work on projects that connect with their interests, both personal and professional.

You said, "The school must open its doors," (213) and I add that the community *is* the classroom. Community collaboration is critical for schools to be successful, yet as schools and curriculum change, the burden cannot be borne by the teachers alone. You described how the garden project and having parents come to the classroom to share their life stories strengthened the web of positive connections with the neighborhood. Students in today's newspaper spoke of the power of career-related experiences in the community. One student "spent ninety hours observing and helping brokers at a local Smith Barney office. Now she is planning to go into finance, and her accounting class is meaningful, she says." This student will never again ask of her accounting teacher, "Why do I need to learn this?"

By breaking down the walls to make the entire community the classroom, students learn that teachers are not the sole source of knowledge, that they are facilitators, and it is the student who is responsible for personalizing the learning. One of my students, Scott, did "job shadows" with local community employers who were assisting in the instructional process. Scott said "I met some great people out there and, you know, I may never see them again, but I'll never forget them. They really helped me." And you, Dr. Patri, have really helped me. Reading your book validated my career path as an educator. Please join me in wishing the best of luck to those who follow us, those teachers who continue to ask your question, "What is the effect of my program on the soul growth of the children?"

Sincerely, Andrea Baker, Retired Teacher

Andra Makler, one of my valued colleagues, taught high school social studies, earned her doctorate, and then worked in teacher education for many years, helping both new and experienced teachers achieve success in the schools. She developed and taught many interesting and effective courses, concentrating in particular on the needs of social studies teachers. While doing more than her share of administrative work she carried on an active and productive scholarly life. Now that we are both retired we often exchange ideas on our research and writing. Andra wrote:

If there had been a MacArthur Foundation giving grants for creativity during Patri's time as "A Schoolmaster of the Great City," I would have nominated Angelo Patri as an extraordinary problem solver blessed with the enthusiasm and determination of a Horatio Alger hero. Patri's story got me thinking that *A Schoolmaster of the Great City* might be used as a sort of primer for those who wish schools were places of excitement, self-discovery, and learning rather than places of test-preparation and grading.

The battles Patri fought are familiar ones today: Long-time area residents near his school distrusted the new-fangled curriculum of heroic stories, literature, drama, art, and music that Patri supported. Immigrant parents struggling with a new language, landscape, and culture wanted the emphasis on familiar book-learning, rote drill, harsh discipline, and tests that they had detested in their own schooling. In a neighborhood where street gangs of older children preyed on the younger, Patri wanted a park and trees for children to plant. In an elementary school enrolling thousands of students from disparate backgrounds, he tried to build a community where people felt responsible for each other.

Were I to use this book with prospective or experienced teachers and administrators, I would want them to explore Patri's response to adverse environmental conditions and criticism: He listened to angry parents and invited them to form committees to enumerate school problems and suggest solutions. He helped organize the first parent-teacher association to get all the "stakeholders" talking with each other. Though initial attempts to bring parents to evening meetings failed, Patri kept trying, finally hitting upon a successful enticement: viewing, sharing, discussing children's work became the focus of the meeting. Slowly a group of parents became invested in the work of the school and formed committees to act upon agendas which they created. Patri wrote, "Before we knew it group opinion began to centre about children's needs, equipment, children's work, school continuity, moral training."

Angelo Patri was one of God's optimists, but he also was a realist. He recounted his frustration and disappointment when his school was unable to provide the same opportunities for 4000 children to express themselves through art and drama as were available to an enrollment of 2000. He invited parents to tell their stories, share their culture, become part of the life of the school. At the community's urging, he agreed to house a doctor and a social worker in the school, and then worried over the emerging contradiction that the welcome presence of needed professionals undermined the community's investment in self-help strategies. Pleased that teachers believed that students were "really learning," he nonetheless checked for himself, to find the children able to read only when the teacher performed their familiar word-by-word routine; they had not become the independent readers he wanted to nurture. Despite the vicissitudes of changing times and changing school populations, Patri remained hopeful that he could lead a school to support the development of children as moral beings and independent thinkers. Patri appears to have invested himself so totally in the life of his school that he had little time for a personal life. That remains a sobering reality for public school educators today.

Ruth Shagoury, (formerly Ruth Shagoury Hubbard) is another close colleague and a storyteller in the Patri tradition. She has taught language arts in the public schools and in colleges and universities, has published several widely read books, and is now the Mary Stuart Rogers Professor of Education at Lewis & Clark College in Portland, Oregon, where she coordinates the Language & Literacy Program. She titled her essay: "Back to the Future: Lessons from the Past for Today's Literacy Teachers." (I have borrowed part of her title for this whole chapter).

Reading Angelo Patri's *A Schoolmaster of the Great City* showed me a slice of early twentieth-century life in schools: the wave of immigration that was filling schools with students from many cultures speaking multiple languages; the shortage of funds so that facilities and teachers were stretched to the limit, with class sizes of 45 to 50 students; the emphasis on a "one-size-fits-all" curriculum and mandated programs of instruction; the push to turning teaching into a component-based science. I read with growing despair. Patri could be describing the situation now, a hundred years later, as schools wrestle with startlingly similar issues. But I also saw great hope in the book; we have a mentor from the past who struggled as we do today and helped create strategies of instruction that have been borne out by a century of research. In a clear, compelling, and surprisingly modern writing style, Patri shares stories from his educational experiences that contain insights for today's teachers.

As a literacy teacher and researcher, I believe that teachers of reading and writing can learn key lessons from Patri's work, lessons supported by contemporary literacy researchers, yet seldom documented in the kind of conditions in which Patri taught. The role of stories, the stress on home and school language, an emphasis on each unique child's abilities, and the importance of creating a democratic and compassionate classroom environment are crucial to Patri's philosophy—and to the success of literacy teachers today.

The Role of Story: "What was I to do? I began to tell over and over again the stories I remembered having heard. . . . When I related these stories, they listened. They hardly breathed." From this simple beginning, Patri shares with the reader the way that telling stories—and encouraging children to tell stories—became central to his teaching practice. His book is peppered with the phrase, "Tell me about it," as Patri spoke with parents, teachers, and children. He learned to draw out their stories as he shared his own. Contemporary literacy researchers such as Anne Haas Dyson and Gordon Wells stress that stories can frame literacy instruction, as children learn the value of their own stories. Their oral and written language can develop from telling, writing, and sharing their stories with one another. Angelo Patri, telling of emphasizing stories in his teaching, said it "helped me wonderfully. Through it, I gained increased confidence in the children, the power of the school, in myself."

Second Language Connections: "In the school yard, I saw an old woman, her shawl about her head. She was talking to a group of children in her own native tongue. She was telling them stories. . . . Her voice was soft, dreamy. Her eyes were far off. The story-teller had come to school. The home had come to the school." Rather than urging parents to "speak English only," Patri was ahead of his time in welcoming the home language and encouraging true bi-literacy for his second language learners. His own life experiences taught him the importance of developing the first language as a second is acquired. His stories from classrooms show ways that teachers can encourage the stories of their students' parents and weave those stories into the curriculum. For example, folk tales became central to Patri's curriculum: "We gave the children a sympathetic appreciation of people and taught them to take home these folk stories, tell them to their parents, and get the parents to tell their own folk tales. So would the children be kept close to their parents, giving and receiving values that were human."

Literacy teachers today can learn from Patri ways to bring the home language to the school, honoring the children's culture and language, and furthering their literacy development as they transfer what they learn in their first language to writing in both languages.

Belief in Each Child: "I wanted drawing that expressed the child and not drawing that was made to order. I wanted ideas expressed in color, movement, fun, and not lines, ideas, and not perfect papers, every one alike. I wanted composition that expressed the child and was not made to order." Here Patri shows his emphasis on working from the strengths of each child, and providing the tools that she or he can best use to express individual thinking. Patri's writing philosophy is surprisingly similar to that of a pioneer in writing instruction, researcher and teacher Donald Graves. In Graves's landmark study of writing he concludes: "As the study progressed, individual exceptions to the data increased in dominance. In short, every child had behavioral characteristics in the writing process that applied to that child alone. It is our contention, based on this information, that such variability demands a waiting, responsive type of teaching."

Patri would not be surprised by Donald Graves's findings. Through vignettes that describe his experiences as a teacher and principal, Patri shows varied ways to build on children's unique processes, learning more about each child as he exhibits just the kind of "waiting and responsive" teaching that Graves advocates.

A Democratic and Compassionate Classroom: "I see that the child is the one who can carry the message of democracy if the message is to be carried at all. If the child fails to make the connection between the ideals of the school and the fundamental beliefs of the people, there is none other to do it. The children are the chain that must bind people together. . . . No matter who the people are, they need the school as a humanizing force, so that they may feel the common interest, revive their visions, see the fulfillment of their dreams in terms of their children, so that they may be made young once more." Above all, Angelo Patri stressed that the culture of the school classroom must be based on respect for children, abiding respect for each member of the school as a community. In his words, school is a place to "put power and soul" into the people. Creating this circle of trust in the classroom is hard work, and often slow work, because it requires a responsiveness to the needs of each member of the community. Patri's stories are illustrative rather than didactic and help readers imagine ways to create a similar classroom and school environment, where stories—told, written, or drawn—are shared and honored.

Perhaps one of Patri's most important gifts to today's literacy teachers is a reminder that they, too, have stories to tell that can inform other educators. Those stories from the classroom can be written with grace and voice and not the educationese that we have become so used to. My hope is that other literacy teachers will discover Patri's gifts from the past—and welcome his ideas into schools of the future.

References: A.H Dyson, *The Brothers and Sisters Learn to Write: Popular Literacies in Childhood and School Cultures* (New York: Teachers College Press, 2003); G. Wells, *The Meaning Makers: Children Learning Language and Using Language to Learn* (Portsmouth, NH: Heinemann, 1985); D. Graves, *Writing: Teachers and Children at Work.* (Portsmouth, NH: Heinemann, 2003. 20th Anniversary Edition).

For about ten years John Beineke and I have carried on a friendly dialogue about educational biography and history. As we have served on historical panels together he has participated in several discussions about Patri and his work. Beineke, the author of a biography of William Heard Kilpatrick, is now Dean of the College of Education at Arkansas State University. Since he is familiar with the some of the research behind this book I asked him to comment on a chapter of Patri's memoir of PS 45.

The opening line of L.P. Hartley's novel, *The Go Between*, says, "The past is a foreign place, they do things differently there." As I read the chapter on teachers from Angelo Patri's unpublished memoir, I felt I too was in a foreign place. Not a place that I was unaware of, not even a strange place, but a place where things are done differently than they are today. And in a way, that is sad for us. The first clue I had from the memoir that I was in a pedagogue's foreign land was that students were seen as individuals, not fodder for test scores or economic units that could compete with other nations first on mathematics scores, then later in industry. But don't we believe in the individual child today? Don't our colleagues in early childhood development repeat the mantra "All children are individuals?" (And then quickly remind future teachers that all students go through the same "ages and stages" as all other students.) But Patri truly saw each child as an individual. That is why we see him encourage his students Fred and Max in their work on the harp and Fred in his activities in the print shop. Fitting a child into a larger economic scheme was never Patri's main objective.

The progressive notion of interest and effort, derived from John Dewey, was at play in Patri's world. A comparable memoir of a similar time is that of William Van Til. Placed in a situation where he could practice his progressive philosophy with his students, or ditch it for a conventional pedagogy, Van Til chose the former. In the midst of the Depression, when he asked what interested them, a group of high schoolers from Columbus, Ohio, replied "Crooks!" Crooks became the curriculum and an interdisciplinary series of experiences occurred in English, sociology, art, and other disciplines.

Patri's stories tell a related tale. The interests of the students were present, and Patri helped those interests develop and thrive. Patri utilized a young teacher's interest in puppets to reach out and engage students while transforming the educator professionally. Students in the world of the progressives and the world of Patri's school "did history" not just "read history." They grappled with real problems of their own design and interest and learned from one another. Can we still find this kind of classroom? To use our "foreign country" metaphor, it is often a long journey.

In foreign nations we often see objects just like ours but with different labels. In Patri's work I recognized his language of education, but found that it was used differently. Today we recognize an educational policy titled "No Child Left Behind." To many it is a series of assessments that rate and sort students and schools. Patri also spoke of leaving not a single child behind, but in a dissimilar way: "To (the teacher) every child counts, every failure a tragedy." In Patri's eyes not a single child can be tossed out on the waste heap of life, marked zero in the books, and forgotten. In almost Biblical terms, Patri states that ninety-nine may look good on paper, but the teacher wants to know where the last one is.

A final unfamiliar and possible foreign role for the modern educator, compared to the world that Patri lived and practiced in, is that of values and morals. Using words such as "responsibility," "a spiritual process," "an ideal to serve," and "moral reawakening," Patri identifies the moral dimension of education. Others in our time, including John Goodlad, have spoken of this component of the teacher's personality, but few have made it central to the work that teachers do. "No child must be abandoned," wrote Patri, "until he is safely on his way."

What are the lessons learned that last? Those that have meaning and are connected to the real worlds of students. Those can only occur when both student and teacher are viewed as distinct beings who bring to the school experiences and knowledge unique to them and them alone. Patri's progressive philosophy led him to this way of practice each day of his life as an educator. We can only hope to do the same in our own time and place.

Clayton Morgareidge has been a good friend and colleague for nearly four decades. He taught philosophy at Lewis & Clark College for thirty seven years and used Dewey's writings in ethics courses and general studies classes. Along with other friends he and I participated in the ups and downs (mostly the latter) of campus struggles over faculty organization and collective bargaining. Now that we have both retired we see each other occasionally at the YMCA and at the Lucky Labrador

Brewpub. During one of our talks I told Clayton about my Patri studies and asked him if he would bring his professional philosophical perspective to bear on Patri and Dewey. I was particularly interested in Clayton's thoughts on how authentically Patri applied Dewey's ideas in his work. Clayton read Schoolmaster of the Great City, *reread some of his favorite Dewey writings, and produced this succinct essay titled "Dewey, Patri and the Life of Democracy."*

For John Dewey, a philosophical source of inspiration for Angelo Patri, democracy "is something much broader and deeper than the formal practice of electing those who govern us." Democracy is "a way of life, social and individual." Dewey's rich conception of democracy illuminates what Patri was trying to cultivate in his struggles side-by-side with the teachers, students, and families of immigrant neighborhoods in New York in the first part of the last century. While Dewey himself was no ivory-tower theorizer, often actively engaged in social activism and educational experiments, Patri's work brings into focus what it means to live the life of democracy every day in school buildings and city streets.

"The keynote of democracy," for Dewey, is "the necessity for the participation of every mature human being in formation of the values that regulate the living of men together: which is necessary from the standpoint of both the general social welfare and the full development of human beings as individuals." Not only is democracy the most effective way to ensure the effective cooperation of citizens in the regulation of social life, but the life of democratic activity is the soil in which each of us can best flourish in our own way. Nothing could be further from the military recruiter's pitch that in the army, the *least* democratic of our institutions, you can "be all that you can be."

In a democratic society, citizens do much more than vote and petition their government by writing letters or protesting in the streets. Citizens in a real democracy participate "in the formation of the values that regulate the living of men [and women] together." Concretely, this means that no institution that affects us or to which we belong should be controlled by people who are not answerable to us. "[A]ll those who are affected by social institutions must have a share in producing and managing them." The fact that each person "is influenced in what he does and enjoys and in what he becomes by the institutions under which he lives" means that "he shall have, in a democracy, a voice in shaping them. . . . "

It is at least as true today as it was when Dewey wrote these words in 1937 that most of us live in and are shaped by institutions controlled by others. We are largely excluded from the board rooms and executive offices of major corporations and financial institutions and from the higher circles of government and political parties. The exclusion, Dewey remarks, "need not be physical. . . ; [it may be] economic, certainly psychological and moral. The very fact of exclusion from participation is a subtle form of suppression." It affords us "no opportunity to reflect and decide upon what is good for [us]." Lacking experience in thinking for ourselves about the values and practices by which we should live, we leave the driving to others. "Our experience is so restricted that we are not conscious of our restriction. When the direction of social and political life is left to an elite, the apathy and irresponsibility of the masses becomes a habit and a norm—confirming common sense ideas about leadership imposed from above."

These are the ideas of leadership and habits of submission that Patri confronted daily in his schools, and that educators continue to face—at least those educators who are committed to cultivating citizens who think and act. Patri found students who expected to be told what to do and how to think. Teachers taught by the books and requirements handed down by superintendents and school boards, hoping for nothing more than obedience and test-passing from their students. Parents wanted the schools to discipline their kids and teach them the three Rs by the same books from which they had learned. The crippling effect of those methods is vividly demonstrated in one of Patri's anecdotes from *A Schoolmaster of the Great City*. A group of first-graders had been taught to read a story; their performance for the principal was letter-perfect. But when asked to read a new story containing exactly the same words, the children were stumped. They knew the words, but couldn't recognize them in a new context. "But the duck always said 'quack, quack,' before," said one boy to explain his confusion.

"And after all aren't we teachers just that way? [said one of them to Patri]. . . . Haven't we been trained to give perfect results? Haven't we been trained to fear making a mistake, to fear the responsibility of working out our own ideas? This is a school world and we always say 'quack, quack,' because we have said it before, and it was right."

Patri prods his teachers to ground their lessons in the experience of their students. Instead of talking about robins in the class room, meet in the nearby park to study robins. Rather than abstract lessons about geography, talk about the backgrounds and travels of the children's families. What is found in books can then build on the curiosity inevitably aroused by observation and discussion. Democracy, for Dewey, is faith "in the role of consultation, of conference, of persuasion, of discussion, in formation of public opinion which in the long run is self-corrective." It is, moreover, "faith in the capacity of the common man to respond with common sense to the free play of facts and ideas which are secured by effective guarantees of free inquiry, free assembly, and free communication. . . ." Dewey's democratic faith is the same as Patri's trust in children to learn and grow if they are put in contact with the "free play of facts and ideas."

Democracy is the soil in which the individual grows, but the individual child lives not only in the school, but in her home and on the streets between school and home. If the conditions of democracy are failing there, the school cannot succeed. Patri and his teachers discovered that many of the immigrant families from which his students came could not adequately feed and clothe their children and sometimes took no interest in their children's education. These children disrupted the classroom and made difficult demands on teachers. Gang warfare from the streets spilled into the classrooms and playground. Patri reflects, "Home shuts the door and by that simple action closes out the world. School shuts the door and concerns itself no further. But the street roars on, its life at full tide, sweeping the children by our closed doors. . . . Is the teacher responsible for what the child does out of school? If this is not the teacher's province how can the teacher ever know that her work counts in the life of the child?"

Patri and his staff involve themselves in the larger world, seizing opportunities as they arise, enrolling families, neighbors, city officials, and local business people in projects that begin to create community out of chaos. Parents are enticed into the school to see performances by their children. A Parents Association is formed to save a nearby park, and a house is acquired to serve as a community hall where people can meet to discuss and act on common problems. A woman acting as a social worker coordinates families, teachers, doctors and nurses to work through the myriad of difficulties that face the immigrant urban poor. "The problems of my school, therefore, loomed up as the problems of our community. . . . To save the school and the home from becoming cloistered, self centered, the culture of children would have to be a co-operative effort between the people and the teachers."

This day-to-day labor of Patri and the parents and teachers around him in classrooms, playgrounds, on the streets, and in the plain homes of poor people shows us what Dewey means when he writes: "The clear consciousness of a communal life, in all its implications, constitutes the idea of democracy. Only when we start from a community as a fact, grasp the fact in thought so as to clarify and enhance its constituent elements, can we reach an idea of democracy which is not utopian. . . . Fraternity, liberty and equality isolated from communal life are hopeless abstractions." The only thing utopian about Dewey is his faith that democratic community is possible; he has no illusions about the hard work it takes to get there—work like Patri's.

References: John Dewey, *The Moral Writings of John Dewey*, edited by James Gouinlock (New York: Hafner Press, 1976); Angelo Patri, *A Schoolmaster of the Great City*, (New York: Macmillan, 1923).

—●—◆—●—   —●—◆—●—   —●—◆—●—

Doug Sherman was one of my Reed College students many years ago, and I have followed his career in alternative education, graduate school, and teacher education ever since. For over thirty years we have been members of the same men's group where, during the past few years, we have occasionally discussed Patri and his work. I asked Doug to respond to chapter 11, "Some Fundamentals" of Patri's memoir.

Lilacs and sunshine as I write, a bracing contrast to the gloom that pushes at the doors of our public schools. Teachers fight to maintain morale and to support one another as they are hammered by shrinking resources, misguided state and federal mandates, and uneven local leadership. The U.S. Secretary of Education, representing a Presidential administration that is disrespectful of teachers to the point of hostility, calls the members of their major professional organization "terrorists." Teachers may know that many attacks on the schools are simply items on a right wing scorecard, but there's little comfort there.

In a different historical context, Angelo Patri wrote in defense of teachers: "When school systems are under repeated criticism, many things go wrong and the schools in self-defense are apt to make changes for the sake of change. But changes that cannot take root in the soil where they are planted bear no fine plants and no fruit worth gathering. . . . Even changes made with good intentions may throw out the good with the bad, confuse the sure ways of learning, overlook the experience of trained teachers, ignore the natural laws of child growth." So it is, to take a recent example, when the Mayor of New York City single-handedly, and in contradiction to the solid wisdom of early childhood educators, decides that thousands of children will be held back in third grade for failure to pass a single high stakes test.

Patri describes the real torment of teachers who are forced to follow an externally determined pedagogical regimen. "You have no idea how unhappy teachers are" he quotes a teacher as saying, "I don't know what I'm doing. If only I could I would retire. I'm treated as if I didn't know anything. My experience of years in teaching primary children all out the window." I shouldn't be surprised by historical cycles, but it is still jolting to read such precise parallels in teachers' expressions of anger and frustration. In contrast, Patri refers to the teachers in his school in elevated and respectful language. One of my favorite lines is "We had learned to move slowly, and doubt held promise, for it walked on the feet of hope and experience." Patri may have been one of those treasured principals who find ways to both inspire teachers and protect them from misguided external pressures.

I have some reservations about what I find in Patri's memoir, however. The teachers he describes as reacting so strongly to outside mandates may not have had all the answers either. The direction he reports they were being ordered to move—toward active learning, student voice and work in groups—may not be the central problem. If hope and experience introduce an element of doubt about change-for-change-sake, it's also true that openness to change can nourish "fruit worth gathering."

Patri's benevolent attitude toward teachers has another troubling aspect. By casting teachers as "good" people suffering under "bad" external pressures, Patri patronizes them as merely victims and not agents of their own professional realities. And while Patri lays out elements of an educational philosophy that is both inspiring and pragmatic, he doesn't show how such a philosophy emerges from the experience and vision of his teachers. He lauds the wisdom and skill of his teachers, but suggests rather than describes a collegial process of determining educational practice, and claims for himself the sage's voice.

Patri's insights, and his limitations, are informative. Then as now, the ideal of "public education" is impossible to imagine apart from the shape-shifting ideal of "reform," and efforts that fail to both respect and challenge teachers will be sterile. While misguided in most of its mandates, for example, "No Child Left Behind" legislation acknowledges genuine problems in the schools. Constructive responses to the law can reject its proposed solutions while accepting the troubled reality supporters claim to be addressing. The challenge now, as Patri saw in the last century, is insuring that changes "take root in the soil where they are planted." When mandates distort professional practice, class size rises, and professional development is both cut back and re-directed toward test preparation, we salt the soil of the "fine plants" that we believe can best nourish children.

I sent a draft of this chapter to all the writers for final editing and was pleased to hear from several of them that they appreciated the varied perspectives. Clayton Morgareidge wrote: "Thanks for the latest version, which I've just read and enjoyed. I particularly liked what teachers had to say. That they continue to face the same problems Patri did suggests either that nothing is ever learned from the wise ones of the past, or that these conflicts between domination and liberation are part of the human condition. Or both." I hope that readers of this book will also appreciate the range of responses presented in this chapter and throughout the book. Patri integrated his Italian practicality with his American pragmatism and developed challenging approaches to teaching and learning. I think he would have enjoyed knowing that his readers, in 2005, continue to develop fresh insights as they bring their own experiences to bear on Patri's life and ideas.

Frank Merolla, Jr. visits the Angelo Patri School in 1997
(J. Wallace)

THIRTEEN

The Legacies of Angelo Patri

ANGELO PATRI LEFT LEGACIES OF GOOD WORK AND useful ideas that were much appreciated in his lifetime, but that were mostly forgotten since his death. Before describing these legacies it may provide some useful perspective to consider why he and his work have been nearly forgotten.[1] Patri was a well-known educator and writer from 1917, when he published *Schoolmaster*, until 1962, when he stopped writing his newspaper columns, but since then his life and work have been cited only in a few educational histories and scholarly articles. Thus the question: Why has this once well-known person slipped nearly into invisibility?

Susan Semel and Alan Sadovnik explore this issue of neglect in reference to the forgotten "founding mothers" of progressive schools. They note that most of the women educators they write about, "like the schools they founded, have often wound up ignored, lumped together, or as historical footnotes." Their first explanation is gender, with women generally accorded less recognition than men of similar accomplishment. This, of course does not apply to the male Patri, but his origins in a low-status immigrant group may have had a similar effect.

Semel and Sadovnik cite other reasons for the disregard of women educational leaders. The women they studied were school practitioners, almost all of them working outside of the academy. Thus they lacked the public forum that higher education provides for professors. This was also true of Patri: his statements as an elementary and junior high principal did not carry the weight of pronouncements by college faculty. The "dominance of theory over practice" is another reason for ignoring the contributions of the women practitioners. This applies as well to Patri, who wrote many stories about his educational practice but rarely generalized the stories into theories. And, just as the women educators were "lumped together" with fellow educators, Patri was often discussed only in connection with Leonard Covello, a later and better-known Italian-American public school administrator and scholar.[2] Covello wrote a dissertation that developed into a book often quoted in studies of the Italian-American experience. Thus Covello is cited as a scholar in many academic studies; Patri, the practitioner, in very few.[3]

Patri's *Schoolmaster of the Great City* has been cited and excerpted in several educational histories; if he had completed and published his memoir of PS 45 from 1913 to 1944 it would have preserved and publicized that long and important part of his life story. But Patri found that writing his speeches, advice columns, and books was relatively easy and routine, while drafting the memoir late in life was sometimes frustrating. He received thousands of letters from his readers and listeners and responded to them promptly. After writing a few such individual replies he had the material and stories needed for a speech or column. And the columns were easily stitched together into books. Patri also had regular deadlines, which helped him to continuously produce the columns and books. And, of course, giving speeches and writing columns provided immediate personal and financial rewards. Particularly after retirement Patri developed a lifestyle that required a substantial regular income. Thus Patri devoted time to these other activities that might have gone into completion of the memoir. In effect, he traded current popularity and prosperity for what might have been a more significant long-term reputation as a progressive innovator.

Patri's later reputation might have been enhanced also if he had formed alliances with other public school progressives to extend the impact of his work. Instead, he felt quite isolated from most administrators and apparently spent little time cultivating their support. He clearly saw himself as an educational reformer but publicized his reforms primarily by writing and by talking with large numbers of visitors to his school. The teachers among them may have tried out some of his ideas and practices in their own classrooms, but any such changes were nearly invisible in large urban schools. Sixty years after Patri retired, and after decades of educational research, school reformer John Goodlad wrote that there was still no proven, foolproof, transportable system of school reform: "For schools to become good, the entire culture of each must be renewed through an intensive process of inquiry."[4] Patri created a positive, encouraging, inquiring culture with his staff and students but did so primarily through the force of his own personality. This was not something easily generalized to other schools or even sustained in his own school after he retired. So, partly because his own school experiment did not survive or spread, Patri has not received the attention he deserves. When I look at his whole career as educator and writer I see a man who was too original, interesting, and decent to be forgotten.

The preceding chapters give a generally positive picture of Patri's life, so it is appropriate to note a few of his limitations before explaining and interpreting the many legacies that Patri left to later generations. Patri was intensely aware of his shortcomings and failures, but only four of them are significant enough to recount here. The first three were specific events; the fourth was a lifelong matter of self-regard.

The first event came out of his life as an educator: Patri regretted for fifty years the time he hit a young boy and then discovered that the boy was drunk. This event remained in his mind as particularly painful because it violated his own principles of respect and affection for all children. His career as a writer led to the second event: Patri was deeply chastened by having given his name to an advertisement for television that preyed on human jealousy as its motivating argument. But in this case he took immediate corrective action, so the embarrassment and pain had less of an impact. The third event was a personal one, and was especially agonizing because he saw it as an injury to his beloved wife. This was the occasion referred to earlier that he mentioned in his diary: "I am doing penance for my great sin—when I compelled my wife to sign her maiden name on the paper that the Cardinal demanded."[5]

These were all specific, isolated events, but Patri had a more continuing sense that he was sometimes guilty of the first deadly sin—Pride. This ranged from justifiable satisfaction in a job well done to occasional vanity and self-promotion. His self-regard was mild by comparison with that of most public figures (Donald Trump comes instantly to mind), but was significant enough so that Patri and others mentioned it on occasion. The earliest reference is intriguing because Patri places it in his early childhood in Italy, which he wrote about it in his seventies in his autobiographical *Biondino*. In the first chapter Brother Felice walks into Piaggine from the monastery in the mountains, stops to visit Biondino's grandfather, and asks: "And how does my Biondino behave?" Biondino replies, "I am good. I am very good. I am good, isn't it true, Grandpa?" "Yes, yes. He is good and he knows it," said the grandfather. Brother Felice added, "He knows it with certainty. We have repeated it to him so many times that he believes it too."[6] Their efforts to encourage Biondino to be good had apparently worked all too well.

After Patri's first year at PS 45, Frank Wilsey described Patri as "everlastingly self-seeking."[7] We must consider the source of this judgment—a conservative school board member who may have resented Patri's rapid rise in the schools. But the incident is worth mentioning in spite of this ambiguity, because it can be seen as part of the pattern that Patri himself occasionally worried about. An example of such concern came after Patri had devoted a decade to developing the positive spirit of his elementary school. In his patriotic 1924 children's book, *The Spirit of America*, Patri associated that spirit with America's greatest heroes. He described how people came from all over the world to visit his school. "Each time they come, they smile and say, 'There is something here in the life of your children that makes one think of Washington, of Lincoln.' And my heart throbs, 'My Country, 'tis of Thee, of Thee, I sing.'" To the degree that Patri associated himself with these two presidents and thought himself responsible for the spirit of the children and their school, we may place this at the "justifiable pride" end of the spectrum.[8]

Others see this pride taking the form of publicity seeking. Larry Swindell wrote in his biography of Garfield: "P.S. 45 got an enviable reputation in a hurry, partly because the experimentation yielded favorable results, but also because Patri himself had a flamboyant love of the limelight. He charmed the audience with his own impassioned performance of the grateful immigrant, and soon 'the Angelo Patri school' had a terrific press."[9]

Patri's own confessions of pride had a humbler tone. William, one of the school's many successes, had written Patri a glowing letter, praising the school and its workshops, and in "The Last Day" Patri wrote: "To bolster my conceit I must keep William's letter." A half-year after Dora's death and three years before his own, Patri gave in his 1962 diary an assessment of what he again called his "conceits." "Father Storm is coming this morning to give words of cheer and absolve me of my sins. I appreciate his efforts, but who can absolve my sins? I do not know what they are. I know not what a sin is now nor what a virtue is. . . . I live with my memories. I hope I have not altogether missed my way. I tried to do a worthy job—mine especially was to make as good a school out of a public school as any private school. The children of the common man—and it was them I served—were entitled to it. . . . If with it there came the conceits of success that too I could bear." Then in nearly his last diary entry, the eighty six-year-old Patri wrote: "I am a teacher—always have been—I start the day in hope and I end in prayer lest my mistakes linger too long or my successes leave me too proud."[10] I can do no better than accept Patri's humble assessment of his own life and work. Patri confessed to errors and limitations in what was by any measure a remarkably good and generous life.

Patri's legacies are pleasanter to recount. When Patri died in 1965 he left two kinds of legacies: the traditional legal one through which he distributed his material possessions to family and friends, and another consisting of ideas, examples, experiences, and writings for children, parents, teachers, and the public. There was a consistency between these two kinds of legacies that adds to our understanding of Patri.

The material legacy, as was noted above, was substantial. By the time he retired in 1944, Patri was a very prosperous man, able to afford a handsome country home and the salaries, at various times, of cooks, housekeepers, a chauffeur, and a gardener. Although retired from the schools, Patri continued to write and lecture and maintained a good income throughout his life. When I interviewed Patri's relatives years later, they expressed gratitude for Patri's life and family, and also for the helpful nest eggs he had left them. The funds had helped them buy homes, educate their children, and—cautiously invested—pay for early retirement. In each of the homes I visited relatives proudly displayed Patri's carvings and other treasured items that he had willed to them.

Patri's legacies of ideas, examples, experiences, and writings are, of course, more complicated to identify and assess. At the risk of fragmenting a generally integrated life, I'll describe Patri's legacies by working outward from his life as a family member, as a participant in the Italian-American and broader immigrant communities, as a thinker and writer, and as an educator. Patri kept incomplete records of his varied activities, so much of the evidence for his work remains only in the many awards he received from different groups during his long life. If he were here to read about these honors he would have to struggle again with the sin of Pride.

From the time of his birth in Italy, Patri lived a rich family life. He wrote often about the close, intense, extended family in which he spent his first years, both in Italy and America.[11] Patri's father lived until 1925, and his mother until 1932, so Patri had their direct and benign influence for five decades. His three surviving sisters were successively six, thirteen, and fifteen years younger than he, but since he didn't marry until age thirty-six, he shared years of life with them in the family apartment. So Patri grew up within a nurturing, supportive, generous environment, and created a similar atmosphere when he and Dora established his own homes. The Patri apartment in the Bronx welcomed family, friends, schoolchildren, and their parents. John Dacey Blonk lived with the family in the Bronx for many years and is buried in the family cemetery plot. Patri and Dora had no children but often had the children of relatives and friends in their homes. Dora's mother Sarah, her sister Anna, and Anna's son lived with the Patris for extended periods, and Anna was part of the household until her death in 1964.

When Patri bought a country place in Paradox, New York, he and Dora shared it with members of their extended family, who, years later, had fond memories of their visits there.[12] The pattern of hospitality continued when they bought their home in Haviland Hollow, New York. This all suggests, as interviews confirm, that Patri left the family not only substantial financial gifts, but more meaningful memories of healthy family life and good examples for later generations to follow.

Patri's extended family was part of a broader circle—the Italian and Italian-American communities. Patri's work in New York schools for nearly fifty years helped thousands of immigrant children to acquire a realistic education, to learn respect for themselves and their heritage, and to prepare for challenging lives in America's multicultural society. His leadership made Patri a well-known figure in the Italian-American community and in broader educational circles. To those communities he left the impact of his decades of good work with immigrant children and parents in his schools. He left also, in many books and articles, positive and insightful descriptions of life in Italy and in Italian America. He objected to the negative stereotyped images of Italians and Italian-Americans and tried to counter them through his writing and his civic activities.[13]

By 1933 Patri was well enough known politically so that Franklin Roosevelt's Secretary of Labor, Frances Perkins, appointed him to a committee to examine conditions at Ellis Island. The committee was to evaluate the facilities, medical conditions, and general "treatment of alien visitors and immigrants. . . ."[14] Patri was apparently the only Italian-American on this committee of forty-two members. Nine months later the group made various recommendations, including a reduction in the naturalization fee and the passage of "more stringent laws to reach and punish those who prey on the aliens whose interests they pretend to serve. . . ."[15]

The Works Progress Administration study, *The Italians of New York* (1938) placed Patri in the distinguished educational lineage of Johann Pestalozzi, of Italian-Swiss background, and Maria Montessori, "founder of the Montessori system for the all-around development of children." The authors reported that principles generated by these two were further developed and implemented by Patri when he became "the first Italian-born American to be appointed a public school principal in the United States. The school under his direction . . . situated in a district of the Bronx chiefly inhabited by Italians, very soon won fame as one of the country's model educational institutions. . . ." His column, 'Children's Problems' . . .

is published regularly by hundreds of newspapers in the United States, Canada, Latin America and Australia." The authors said that his book *Child Training* had been translated "into almost all languages, including eighteen dialects of India and the Bantu of Africa." [16]

Representatives of the Italian-American community recognized Patri as a spokesman for his people, and he was often invited to write for the Italian-language press. For years his column, "Our Children," was translated into Italian for the weekly *La Luce*.[17] When Congressman Fiorello La Guardia began *L'Americolo* in 1925, he invited Patri to contribute a column on education and children. Patri did so, in the good company of Attilio Piccirilli who wrote on art and Ferdinand Pecora who commented on developments in law.[18] Italian-American scholars and others have noted these contributions and, in the process, have reminded us of the several sides of Patri. Luigi Carnovale in 1923 identified Patri as "one of the greatest American educators," and Barbara Marinacci described him more broadly as a "principal who wrote many popular books on child training as well as a nationally syndicated newspaper column." [19] Leonard Covello noted that Patri was among the educational leaders who in 1931 supported the establishment of a new high school to serve the mixed population of Manhattan's Upper East Side. Covello, Patri and community members wanted a "general or cosmopolitan high school, in opposition to those who were advocating an industrial or trade school." Covello's well-known Benjamin Franklin High School was the result of these efforts.

Olga Peragallo in 1949 placed Patri in the context of the Italian-American literary community and described his career as an author and translator of books for children, teachers, and parents. With forgivable ethnic pride, she wrote that Patri was "considered to be the outstanding educator in his field in America." [20] Josef Lombardo, in his 1944 biography of Attilio Piccirilli, reported on Patri's role as a friend and supporter of this well-known sculptor. One of Piccirilli's sculptures is the centerpiece of the Patri memorial in the cemetery in Pawling, New York.[21] Patri was proud of the rich heritage of Italian art and was particularly supportive of the various art workshops and activities in his schools.

Patri's work on behalf of the Italian and Italian-American communities was further recognized in various ways: through Lombardo-Radice's writings; in 1946 by an award from the Belmont Community Center for his service to the Bronx; that same year by the naming of a Bronx Community House after him; by the station Il Progresso in 1947 for his radio addresses; by American Relief for Italy, Inc. in 1949, for his work for that group during and after the war; by a 1951 "Columbian Civic Award" for his writing and educational work; and by Mayor Fiorello La Guardia, who appointed Patri to various boards but failed to get him to accept appointment to the New York Board of Education. This last honor Patri rejected because, according to the *New York Times*, he "preferred to continue his work in progressive education."[22] One small example of recognition that Patri would have appreciated came the year after his death, with the 1966 establishment in the Bronx of the Angelo Patri Center of Job Orientation (JOIN). This organization provided job training and placement for unemployed school dropouts, youngsters for whom Patri always had a special concern.[23] And he certainly would have been pleased to know that, sixty years after his retirement there were schools bearing his name in New York, Italy, and Peru.[24] All this recognition demonstrates that Patri indeed left a legacy of good works and good words to those who shared his Italian heritage and to other immigrant groups and that they expressed their appreciation in a variety of ways.

One award warrants comment. In 1933 the Italian Minister of Education, Francesco Ercole, awarded Gold Medals for "Special Merit in Education" to Patri, Leonard Covello, and the chairs of the Italian Departments at Columbia and Yale universities.[25] It is clear that Ercole granted the awards partly to curry favor with the Italian-American community, but why did well-informed public school educators like Patri and Covello accept them? The Fascists under Mussolini had been in power in Italy for ten years, and Patri and Covello should have had no illusions about them. Neither man was sympathetic with Fascism. The honor of recognition by their home country must have outweighed their opinions of its current government. Colleagues in Italy later speculated that he was given the award because "he was a famous Italian abroad, and Patri accepted it on the ground of his love of Italy." In any case, given the source, this was the most problematic of the many awards that Patri and Covello received.[26]

In 1942 Mayor LaGuardia appointed Patri to a City War Council of twenty-five members. The Council had, according to the *New York Times*, "broad powers with respect to activities connected with civil defense, making it essentially a board for planning, coordination, and general long-range handling of defense problems."[27] Six months after America entered the war against Japan, Germany, and Italy Patri was one of two Italian-Americans on this Board. In 1944, the year he retired, he was appointed, along with Arturo Toscanini, Don Ameche, and others to the board of directors of American Relief for Italy.[28] The organization provided much-needed help to Italy during disastrous times. The initial phase of their work completed in 1949, the organization awarded a certificate "in recognition of the loyal service of Angelo Patri in the administering of relief to the stricken people of Italy during World War II and its aftermath."[29] All these activities and appointments make it clear that after only five years of childhood in Italy and one visit there in 1927, Patri still maintained strong ties with his homeland and with his fellow emigrants.

The assessments of Patri's work cited above were made decades ago, but in 2002 I was heartened to learn that there were people in Italy who were still studying Patri. I found that there was in Piaggine, Patri's birthplace, an Angelo Patri Study Center, and I have since profited from participation in conferences there and in Salerno. For some scholars in Salerno, Piaggine, Pisa, and other places in Italy, Patri is more than the local boy who went to America and succeeded; he is also a source of currently applicable thought on education, parenting, and other matters. One of the major sources used by Italian scholars is Giuseppe Lombardo-Radice's 1928 study, *Pedagogy of Teachers and Workers*. It includes Lombardo-Radice's detailed interpretation of Patri's *Schoolmaster* and his record of Patri's visit to Italy in 1927.[30] A number of my Italian colleagues also have copies of Patri's *Schoolmaster*, *Biondino*, and his books for parents. They are collecting his books for the Angelo Patri Study Center, have translated *Schoolmaster* into Italian, and in other ways are keeping Patri's memory alive.

Broadening beyond his love for his own people, Patri left a commitment to an inclusive cosmopolitanism, different from both the melting pot-approach and from ethnic separatism. As was noted in chapter two, Patri wrote in 1917 that immigrants and natives should work together to "Americanise America." By helping the country live up to its own professed ideals, reformers could create a country in which people could maintain and share their ethnic heritages while becoming Americans. Patri may have been able to reach these inclusive insights partly because in one lifetime he had traversed the stages often described as taking three generations: from immersion in the ethnic community and language in the first immigrant generation, to rejection of one's heritage in the next, and then to efforts to recover, revalue, and share the ethnic experience in the third.[31] Patri was immersed in Italian life in Piaggine and Little Italy, felt briefly alienated from his parental heritage while in school in New York, and gained a renewed appreciation and respect for his parents, family, language, and culture as he worked, studied, and matured.[32] To the Italian-American community Patri and his family left a good example of the classic, but far from universal, story of immigrants coming to the United States, working hard, investing in education, becoming productive citizens, and contributing from their ethnic heritage to the rich mixture of multicultural America.

—•—   —•—   —•—

Patri also left a tested collection of experience and ideas through his work as a writer and speaker. He wrote and translated eight charming books for children, and in other volumes, his unpublished memoir, and in hundreds of articles and speeches, left a record of his educational work and useful recommendations for others. In his nine books on childrearing he gave sound, practical, and appreciated advice to parents and teachers. These books were characterized by his calm, encouraging, optimistic, realistic, specific, and helpful ideas. Patri received frequent recognition for his school leadership and for his role in parent education. William Seabrook wrote in 1938 that Patri "has done as much in the advancement of child training and child psychology as any American alive today."[33] His influence was acknowledged three years later when the Associated Alumni of City College awarded Patri the Townsend Harris medal, presented with a rather extravagant citation: "You have taught parents to love their children and teachers to win their pupils; you have written wisely and simply of educational method; you have caused children to be happy in school. Reverently, it may be said you have suffered the children to come unto you."[34]

A recurrent theme in Patri's writing was tolerance. He promoted acceptance and tolerance among ethnic groups in his schools and in the broader community. Through multicultural celebrations and pageants he helped his students and teachers share the riches of their ancestral homelands. He was equally committed to tolerance among America's religious groups. In simple stories he encouraged his readers to appreciate other faiths, not to separate from them. In one of his first books for parents, he wrote in 1922 a simple homily about a Protestant girl who was reluctant to share her lemon drops with a Catholic friend until she saw the priest sharing his candy with the rector of her church.[35] Through such stories Patri repeated this message of tolerance and acceptance to children, parents, and teachers. In 1948, in his last book for parents, he wrote with his usual optimism: "Children are born democrats. If the grown people were as sincere, friendly, and democratic in their attitudes, there would soon be no such racial discrimination as now exists. When the people at home express feeling about other races, nationalities, and creeds, the children are quick to follow. The trouble does not lie with the children. It lies in the community itself, and it is the community that needs education, not the children." He encouraged teachers to handle racial matters calmly without emphasizing differences among children.[36]

In a conservative period when even suggesting the existence of social stratification is attacked as class warfare, it may be helpful to remember a time when writers like Patri took the reality of separate social classes for granted and discussed it in matter-of-fact tones. In 1931, recalling his first teaching job, Patri wrote: "I felt the pinch of poverty—my first month's salary was twenty dollars. . . . I met the prejudices of class and creed and race."[37] In his memoir Patri described sadly the transition of PS 45 into a junior high school, and reported his resistance to grouping students by IQ, leading to "class stratification and narrow education."[38]

Clearly related to his position on social class was Patri's strong and consistent commitment to public schools—particularly urban schools. Drawing on his long experience in education, Patri expressed what Pedro Noguera has called "pragmatic optimism" about public schools.[39] Sometimes Patri would begin an essay with praise for private schools and their smaller classes and richer materials but end with the demand that public education should be as well supported as private schools. In 1922 he wrote a note addressed "To You Who Send Your Children to Private Schools." He described the care with which such parents examine the environment, building, equipment, teachers, and health conditions of their schools. He wished them well in their search but ended with a challenge: "Can you as a good citizen of these United States feel that you have done your whole duty to the country you love if you permit the public schools to fall below the standards of what you consider a good school for your children?" And, deeply sensitive to the needs of school staffs, he turned this into a specific demand that parents support increases in teachers' meager salaries.[40]

After his retirement, and unconstrained by his administrative role, Patri was even more vigorous in his demands for support for public education. In 1947 he called on parent groups to demand "approximately three times as many classrooms to a school as we have now; three teachers for every one we have at present; a school day that starts early and ends late; a school year that is twelve months long; a camp extension of the school that offers all children a change of environment for two months or so, and offers them a fresh set of experiences—in short, the equipment that gives the teachers a chance to use the life experiences of the children for their development and training."[41]

Patri saw himself primarily as a teacher and writer, not a scholar, but he made a significant contribution to scholarship as he carefully preserved papers that now occupy ninety containers in the Library of Congress.

Researchers in education and the American family are beginning to discover the value of his writings, of the letters that advice-seekers wrote to him, and of his responses to them. I will give just two examples here—the first from an educational historian and the second from a sociologist. Kate Rousmaniere, in *City Teachers*, cites Patri's eloquent writing about New York City, the loneliness of teachers, and the challenges of lesson planning. She quotes Patri on the frustration involved in trying to follow Herbart's five formal steps: "Almost before I could make the first point of the lesson some child was bound to shout out the conclusion that should, according to my understanding of authority, have come at the end of the teaching process. This left me high and dry. The children refused to think according to the plan." But teachers were on their own and got little or no help as they struggled to teach, and Patri saw the teacher as "a lone creature in the wilderness of indifference."[42]

Philip LaRossa in *The Modernization of Fatherhood* makes strong claims for Patri's influence on parents. In a chapter titled "Dear Mr. Patri" he draws on Patri's extensive correspondence with parents. LaRossa notes the popularity of Patri's newspaper column and weekly radio show, and observes that in "the 1920s and 1930s, radio and newspapers were more of an everyday presence in people's lives, particularly among the middle class, than both books and magazines combined. . . . For Patri to have a regular radio show and newspaper column meant that he was being listened to or discussed almost continuously. Thus, as important as the Children's Bureau and *Parents' Magazine* were between the wars, it is probably fair to say that Patri advised more fathers and mothers on how to raise children than just about anyone else. He was a voice across America, a genuine Machine Age celebrity."[43]

Part of Patri's intellectual and educational legacy was his commitment to the ideas and practices of John Dewey. In many times and places Patri reported the influence Dewey had on him and expressed the hope that others would be similarly influenced. Patri acknowledged his debt to Dewey in *Schoolmaster*, in his memoir, and in his other writings, but wrote perhaps the most personal and emotional statement of his gratitude in response to Dewey's ninetieth birthday. Realizing that Dewey could not have many birthdays left, Patri wanted Dewey to know how much he appreciated him. On October 17, 1949, he wrote, with extra capital letters for emphasis: "Dear Dr. Dewey: Ninety years in the life of a great teacher IS something to celebrate. It's a milestone in the life of a man who has influenced the education of children, of the people of this country, and that's Something. I want to extend to you my gratitude for what you have meant to me. You were my teacher and still are, always will be. Like thousands of your pupils I may not see you but you are always near me and I hope that I am never far from you."[44]

Patri's expression of Deweyan ideas was a significant part of the record he left of his own experience as an educator, much of it written in hopes of improving schooling for all concerned. *Schoolmaster*, for example, was more than a record of Patri's experiences; it was also an attempt to influence schools for the better. Patri's many articles about schools had the same didactic intent. As noted above, it is unfortunate that Patri never published the memoir of his thirty-one years at PS 45, as it also includes much helpful advice to teachers and parents. While Patri's schools provided good models for others during his tenure as principal, he was disappointed that his reforms apparently eroded after he left. Six decades after Patri's retirement we may well ask: Why did reforms like Patri's at PS 45 not last in the schools? Frank Merolla and I visited PS 45 (now the Thomas Giordano School) in 1997. The educators with whom we talked were caring and hardworking, and the school appeared to be orderly and productive, but nobody claims that the school is the distinctive one it was under Patri's long leadership. We may well ask why not? Why is it necessary for us to reinvent practices that were apparently effective from 1913 to 1944? Several explanations may apply.

Patri's educational writing consists mostly of descriptions of his experiences, not formal reports on educational experiments, and it may have had no more impact on educational practice than other such books and articles. Educators even today have all-too-little-tested knowledge on what school practices are effective or how to make such practices last. Research in this area is still limited and controversial.[45] There is also in education as in other fields what appears to be a "regression toward the mean." When innovative leaders move on or retire, social and bureaucratic pressures tend to push their institutions back toward more conventional models. As Patri's experience with traditional bureaucrats and politicians demonstrated, fundamental reform always encounters resistance from groups that profit from their privileged status in our economic and social system.

Also public school reformers were often isolated (sometimes partly by their own choice) from groups that might have helped them sustain their good practices. Lawrence Cremin in *The Transformation of the School* (1961) noted Patri's early but brief involvement with the Progressive Education Association.[46] If Patri was, in fact, creating and sustaining effective progressive practices in his schools, why did he not continue to be active in the PEA and profit from association with like-minded reformers? Patricia Graham, as was mentioned in chapter three, concluded that public and private progressives worked in such different environments that they had little to offer one another and so went their own ways. The evolving progressive education movement paid more attention to those relatively few and fortunate students preparing for college than to the full range of pupils in urban schools led by people like Patri. Organized progressive education, as Graham noted, developed a "social class bias" which caused it to take refuge in private schools and college professional education programs, leaving leaders like Patri on their own to face the challenges of inner-city education.[47]

We may, nonetheless, gain some social and historical perspective from the experience of Patri, who developed and maintained child-centered, family-oriented, community-based schools, and who knew from experience that school reform had to be part of broader efforts at social, political, and economic change. Patri did not restrict his work to what happened in classrooms. As Clyde Furst noted in his review of *Schoolmaster*, Patri's parents' association "borrowed ground for a school garden, got trees for planting, protected the local park from encroachments, secured representation on the local school board, conducted family relief, appointed a home visitor, and developed a dispensary."[48] Patri lived near his schools and took part in neighborhood activities; he worked to destroy gang influence around the school and helped organize a nearby settlement house.[49]

The writings of several recent scholars may be read back into Patri's experience. His work with the school community exemplified a position like that recently described in Jean Anyon's vivid metaphor: "Attempting to fix inner-city schools without fixing the city in which they are embedded is like trying to clean the air on one side of a screen door." Larry Cuban, reviewing a book by Anyon, added that we need "social change in which school reformers join community development organizations, health care providers, and voter registration efforts. Improvements in teaching and learning can then occur within a larger and more congenial political and economic framework."[50]

Harvey Kantor and Robert Lowe recently made a similar point, writing that historians "can mine the past for examples of fine schools whose quality is more or less transcendent, and what they discover about the qualities of these institution can be used to inform the way we think about creating schools in the future. . . . Indeed, in our view, if history has anything to tell us about quality education, it is not that we must somehow try to recapture a time when schools were supposedly better than they are today, or that we must try to recreate the conditions that made possible the existence of a few truly exceptional schools. It is, rather, that we cannot create truly excellent schools without confronting the inequities that have long been deeply embedded in them or without understanding how those long marginalized by the educational system have contested such inequalities in ways that have promoted greater access and, at times, quality as well.[51]"

Yoon K. Pak recently wrote an article about educators who struggle to close the tragic gaps between racial minorities and whites. The final paragraph of the article applies equally well to educators like Patri, who worked to bring together traditional and immigrant Americans: "We cannot expect schoolteachers and administrators to change the deep structural fissures that continue to divide us. But history reveals that there were those individual progressive educators who held steadfast to the promise and possibilities afforded in our democracy, and who worked and continued to work to intersect our parallel histories."[52]

These thoughts may help us connect our time with Patri's, during the first half of the twentieth century. In many of his ideas and actions Patri appears to have been ahead of his time, but he was in fact very much a man of his own time. The important point is that in many essential respects the times themselves have not changed. Patri's life and writings provide one more reminder that basic economic, political, and educational inequities have persisted for generations. Just as Patri found his own way of dealing with these challenges, so we must find our own. The example of this good man may encourage us as we continue the struggles for justice which Patri and so many others progressives carried on in an earlier era.

NOTES

Introduction

1. Angelo Patri, *Schoolmaster of the Great City* (New York: Macmillan, 1917).
2. I thank David Tyack for encouraging me to make explicit what the book is and is not. I have taken the liberty of borrowing a few of his words from that suggestion. (E-mail message to author, April 26, 2004).
3. Jonathan Mahler, "20 Years and Five Editors Later," *New York Times Book Review*, September 26, 2004, 13.
4. Angelo Patri, Unpublished Memoir, Library of Congress, Manuscript Division, Patri Papers, Box 83. (Page 4, Preface).
5. Patri, *Biondino L'Emigrante* (Florence: Marzocco, 1950); *Biondino: An Italian Reader*, translated and adapted by Maria Piccirilli (New York: Vanni, 1951). Retranslated and edited by J. Wallace and Betty Schmidt, unpublished, 2004.
6. Gabriel Garcia Marquez quoted by Patricia Cohen, *New York Times Book Review*, March 6, 2005, 25.
7. Ruth Shagoury's title for her contribution to chapter 12 was so appropriate that I have borrowed and expanded it to the whole chapter.
8. Harry Golden, *Carl Sandburg* (Cleveland: World Publishers, 1961), 45.
9. James Banks, Foreword to Pedro Noguera's *City Schools and the American Dream: Reclaiming the Promise of Public Education* (New York: Teachers College Press, 2003), vii, x.
10. Ruben Donato and Marvin Lazerson, "New Directions in Educational History: Problems and Prospects," *Educational Researcher* 2, (November 2000): 12.
11. Adam Gopnik, "The Big One," *The New Yorker*, August 23, 2000, 79, 84–85. On the issue of lessons in history, I hope I am consistent with the pragmatic orientation of Joyce Appleby, Lynn Hunt, and Margaret Jacob in *Telling the Truth About History* (New York: Norton, 1994). The sections of that book most relevant to this study of Patri are "The Implication of Social History for Multiculturalism," 152–159, and chapter 8, "The Future of History," 271–309.

Chapter One

1. Patri, *Biondino L'Emigrante* (Florence: Marzocco, 1950); *Biondino: An Italian Reader,* Vanni edition, retranslated into English by James Wallace and Betty Schmidt, Portland, OR, 2004, chapters 11–13. I thank Anna Ferrara of Salerno for making a copy of the Italian edition, Marilena Risi for preparing chapter summaries, and Betty Schmidt for translating it into English with me.
2. Patri, *Schoolmaster of the Great City* (New York: Macmillan, 1917). Valentina Pugliese, "The Schoolmaster of the Great City," typescript, some time after 1965. I thank Frank Merolla for making me a copy of her paper.
3. It was actually about three months less than a year. Patri's father, age thirty two, sailed from Naples on the *Macedonia* and arrived in New York on March 17, 1881. The rest of the family came in December 1881. I thank Marilyn Shea for sending this information from the New York Passenger Lists, 1851–1891.

Chapter Two

1. Parts of this chapter have been adapted from my article "Angelo Patri: Immigrant Educator, Storyteller, and Public School Progressive," *Vitae Scholasticae,* 13 (Fall, 1994): 43-63.
2. Sidney Katz's article about Patri in the *Education Digest* is titled "Beloved Educator," 12 May 1947, 17–19. Virginia Irwin used the same word in "Patri—Beloved Teacher," *St. Louis Post-Dispatch,* 24 November 1946.
3. Salvatore J. LaGumina incorrectly states that Leonard Covello was "the first Italian-American principal in the city." "The Italian Immigrant Response," in *American Education and the European Immigrant: 1840–1940,* edited by Bernard J. Weiss (Urbana: University of Illinois, 1982), 69. See also: "Angelo Patri," entry by Jacob L. Susskind in *Dictionary of American Biography;* supplement 7, 1961–1965 (New York: Scribner's Sons, 1981), 600–601; and "Angelo Patri," entry in *Italian-American Authors and Their Contribution to American Literature* by Olga Pearsall, edited by Anita Peragallo (New York: S. F. Vanni, 1949), 177–182.
4. I am grateful to Giuseppe Pepe of Salerno, Italy, for finding this and other information, in Piaggine records.
5. Angelo Patri, *Schoolmaster of the Great City* (New York: Macmillan, 1917), 1. (Hereafter cited as *Schoolmaster.*) I have preserved Patri's spelling throughout; he often used "s" where we now use "z" in such words as "Americanize." I have also occasionally combined Patri's short paragraphs.
6. New York Passenger Lists, 1851–1891 (database online). I thank Marilyn Shea for finding the information about Nicola's trip to New York.
7. Andrew Rolle, *The Italian Americans: Troubled Roots* (New York: Free Press, 1980), 17.
8. Angelo Patri. "The Teacher Goes to War." Typescript, c. 1943, Box 81, file 3, Patri papers, Library of Congress, Washington, DC. (Hereafter only "Patri Papers").
9. Richard Gambino identifies Naples as Italy's largest city at this time in *Blood of My Blood: The Dilemma of the Italian Americans* (New York: Anchor Books, 1975), 64; the price of a ticket in steerage is noted by Thomas Kessner in *The Golden Door: Italian and Jewish Immigrant Mobility in New York City: 1880–1915* (New York: Oxford University Press, 1977), 26–27.
10. Bernie Bookbinder, *City of the World: New York and its People* (New York: Harry Abrams Publishers, 1989), 7.
11. Population figures are from Frederick Binder and David Reimer, *All the Nations Under Heaven: An Ethnic and Racial History of New York City* (New York: Columbia

University Press, 1995), 137, and Kessner, *The Golden Door*, 15. Kessner's first chapter gives a detailed picture of the city at just the time when the Patri family arrived. "Italian Life in New York," *Harper's Magazine*, April 1881, describes Manhattan's Little Italy at that same time. Republished in *A Documentary History of the Italian Americans*, Wayne Moquin, Charles Van Doren, and Francis Ianni, eds. (New York: Praeger, 1974), 39–44.

12. *Schoolmaster*, 2.
13. Michael Olneck and Marvin Lazerson note late school enrollment patterns in "The School Achievement of Immigrant Children, 1900–1930," *History of Education Quarterly* 14 (Winter 1974): 456. This article compares and explains, among other themes, the contrasting educational experiences of Jews and southern Italians from 1900 to 1930. The time period overlaps with that in Kessner, which covers the period from 1880 to 1915. Kessner provides a context for explaining Patri's own educational experience; Olneck and Lazerson apply persuasively to Patri's elementary students, from 1897 to 1929.
14. *Schoolmaster*, 122–123. Patri's experience was much like that of the children described in David Nasaw's *Children of the City: At Work and At Play* (Garden City, NY: Anchor Press/Doubleday, 1985), 24–25. Nasaw gives extensive attention to Italian and Jewish children and to children's lives in New York City.
15. Patri, "Biography of Angelo Patri," Typescript, 1938, Patri Papers. Patri apparently prepared this for use with his newspaper column, "Our Children."
16. Patri, *Schoolmaster*, 2. This was Gaetano Conte, Patri's mother's brother.
17. I thank my stepdaughter, Lila Guenther, for obtaining information about Valentina Perrone from Social Security on-line archives.
18. Valentina Pugliese Perrone, "The Schoolmaster of the Great City," Typescript, undated, but written after 1965. I thank Frank Merolla, Patri's grandnephew, for making me a copy of this paper.
19. Recommendation by Charles Holden, June 30, 1892, Patri Papers. PS 39 was located at 235 E. 125th Street, and Patri lived about 18 blocks from the school at 310 East 107th.
20. Rolle, *The Italian Americans*, 138, 14. Olneck and Lazerson, while describing and explaining the common southern Italian cultural resistance to education, give this important reminder: "This does not mean that each family or individual embodied all the cultural traits we discuss." *School Achievement*, 472. Clearly the Patri and Pugliese families did not fit some of the stereotypes.
21. Dominic Candeloro, "Italian-Americans," chapter 8 in *Multiculturalism in the United States: A comparative Guide to Acculturation and Ethnicity*, John Buenkner and Lorman Ratner, eds. (New York: Greenwood Press, 1992), 175.
22. Selma Berrol, "The Open City: Jews, Jobs, and Schools in New York City, 1880–1915," chapter 6 of *Educating an Urban People: The New York City Experience*, Diane Ravitch and Ronald Goodenow, eds. (New York: Teachers College Press, 1981), 108.
23. Letter to the author, May 12, 1996, from Barbara Dunlap, Archivist, City College of New York (hereafter CCNY).
24. "Classical Course," Catalog, CCNY, 1896–1897, 13–15. CCNY Archives.
25. *1997 Microcosm* (Yearbook), 35, 99, 140. CCNY Archives.
26. *Forty-eighth Annual Register*, 1896–1897, 60–61. CCNY Archives.
27. *Microcosm*, 185–186.
28. Letter from Alfred G. Compton, September 17, 1896, Patri Papers.
29. Patri, "Roses and Drums," Undated Typescript, Box 81, Patri Papers.
30. Kessner, *Golden Door*, 85.
31. I thank Marilyn Shea for sending me a copy of Patri's naturalization record.

32. This resistance to education is widely cited. See, for example, chapters by Joseph Tait and Leonard Covello in *The Italians: Social Backgrounds of an American Group*, Francesco Cordasco and Eugene Bucchioni, eds. (Clifton, NJ: Augustus Kelly, 1974), 489–565.

33. Stephen A. Lassonde, "Should I Go, or Should I Stay?: Adolescence, School Attainment, and Parent-Child Relations in Italian Immigrant Families of New Haven, 1900–1940," *History of Education Quarterly* 38 (Spring 1998): 37–60.

34. Patri's experience fits well with Harvey Graff's description of "Working-Class Paths" in *Conflicting Paths: Growing Up in America* (Cambridge, MA: Harvard University Press, 1995), 300–301.

35. *Schoolmaster*, 5.

36. Nicolas returned to this dangerous work, being listed as a hod carrier in the 1900 census.

37. Perrone, Valentina, "Schoolmaster," 2.

38. Binder and Reimers, *All the Nations*, 140; also Diane Ravitch, *The Great School Wars: A History of the New York City Public Schools* (New York: Basic Books, 1988), 102, 180.

39. Kessner, *Golden Door*, 80. Kessner includes teaching in Level I, his highest economic class. There is no record of Patri's having been employed before he began teaching. If that is the case Patri, because of his college education, began his career in Kessner's highest class. See page 117 for comparative data on Italian mobility and 123 for the role of education in mobility. Table 6 on page 83 shows that only 1.3% of New Yorkers born in Italy were at Level I by 1905, seven years after Patri began teaching. Patri would clearly have been ranked near the top of this Level 1 cohort.

40. Patri, "A Teacher Sees the Light," Typescript, c. 1955, Box 82, Patri Papers.

41. On the controversies surrounding New York's school consolidation, see David Tyack, *The One Best System: A History of American Urban Education* (Cambridge, MA: Harvard, 1974), 147–154; Ravitch, *Great School Wars*, chapters 11-14. Sol Cohen notes the consolidation of New York City itself in *Progressives and Urban School Reform: The Public Education Association of New York City, 1895–1954* (New York: Teachers College Press, 1964), 30.

42. *Schoolmaster*, 8–10. Chapter 4 of *Biondino* gives a more believable account, with Patri's father, with a club, killing a weak, sickly wolf.

43. Examination Record, Harlem Branch, Young Men's Christian Association, September 20, 1900, Patri Papers.

44. The most thorough study of the efficiency movement in education is Raymond Callahan's *Education and the Cult of Efficiency* (Chicago: University of Chicago Press, 1962). See 136–141 for the effort to install efficient "platoon schools" in New York City.

45. *Schoolmaster*, 6–13. Patri rarely gave dates or identified people, schools, or colleges by name, perhaps because he was continuing to work with many of them and did not wish to embarrass or offend them.

46. Lawrence Cremin, David Shannon, and Mary Townsend, *A History of Teachers College, Columbia University* (New York: Columbia University Press, 1954), 46–47.

47. *Schoolmaster*, 14; Dewey's essay was "Ethical Principles Underlying Education," *Third Yearbook* (Chicago: National Herbart Society, 1897. This was later expanded into *Moral Principles of Education* (Boston: Houghton Mifflin, 1909).

48. *Schoolmaster*, 14–16.

49. I am grateful to Dr. David Ment, former archivist at the Milbank Memorial Library at Teachers College, for sending me a copy of Patri's thesis. I quote from it courtesy of Teachers College, Columbia University.

50. Angelo Patri, "Educational Forces Outside of the Public School, Considered from the standpoint of School Administration," Unpublished master's thesis. (New York: Special Collections, Milbank Memorial Library, Teachers College, Columbia University, 1904), 2–3. I have added a few commas for clarity.

51. Patri, Thesis, 4–5.

52. Thesis, 6-10. Andrew Rolle wrote; "Ethnic stereotypes were also employed by immigrants themselves," and gave examples. Rolle, *Italian Americans*, 57. Patri's stereotypes parallel Rolle's very closely.

53. Thesis, 11.

54. Thesis, 16–17.

55. Thesis, 31–32.

56. Thesis, 71–72. Scholars in 2004 continued to attest to the power of parent involvement. See Beth Poitier, "A Curse on Both Their Houses: Liberal and Conservative Views on Urban School Change," *Ed: The Magazine of the Harvard Graduate School of Education*, v. 47 (Spring 2004): 30–31.

57. See, for example, Lawrence Cremin, *The Transformation of the School: Progressivism in American Education, 1876–1957* (New York: Knopf, 1961), 350; also, nearly thirty years later, his *Popular Education and its Discontents* (New York: Harper, 1990), 118–125.

58. Patri, page 10 of unpublished memoir, Patri Papers, Box 83.

59. *Directory of the School Board for the Boroughs of Manhattan and the Bronx*, (New York: 1900), 252.

60. Patri Thesis, 32.

61. Letter from Joseph A Fripp, May 3, 1904, Patri Papers; Memoir, 10; *Directory of the School Board*, 1903, 65.

62. *Schoolmaster*, 20–23.

63. Recommendation from J.S. Huoteeloss, Jr., P.S. 11, 314 W. 17th Street, May 4, 1904, Patri Papers. (The signature is obscure.)

64. I thank Marilyn Shea for sending me a copy of the relevant page of the 1920 census, indicating that Patri was naturalized in 1903. I am grateful also to Muriel Sherlock of Lisburn, Northern Ireland, for sending me census data, photographs, and other helpful information about Patri and his family.

65. A letter from Aimee Schlesinger, May 24, 1907, congratulates Patri on his planned trip to Norway. Patri papers, Library of Congress. I thank Muriel Sherlock for confirming that the trip took place and that Patri returned from this trip on September 3, 1907. (E-mail, December 30, 2003).

Chapter Three

1. I thank Lawrence Erlbaum Associates for permission to quote from my article *Schoolmaster of the Great City: Reconsideration*, *Educational Studies* 28 (Summer, 1997), 99–110.

2. "Angelo Patri," entry in *Italian-American Authors and Their Contribution to American Literature*, by Olga Peragallo, edited by Anita Peragallo (New York: S.F. Vanni, 1949), 177–182.

3. Michael McGerr, *A Fierce Discontent: The Rise and Fall of the Progressive Movement in America, 1870–1920* (New York: Free Press, 2003), 283–294.

4. Jerre Mangione and Ben Morreale, *La Storia: Five Centuries of the Italian American Experience* (New York: HarperCollins, 1992), 101.

5. J. L. More, Untitled review of *A Schoolmaster of the Great City*, *Nation*, June 21, 1917, 738–739. I thank David Smith of the New York Public Library for identifying the author of this review.

6. The founders of the Bronx House were Henry Samson, Henry Morgenthau, Angelo Patri, Rabbi Stephen Wise, and Lillian Wald. "Henry L. Samson Dies," *New York Times* November 4, 1929, 23.

7. For a broader view of such progressive activity, see McGerr, *A Fierce Discontent*, 269–274.

8. Paul Boyer, *Urban Masses and Moral Order in America, 1820–1920* (Cambridge, MA: Harvard University Press, 1978), 225; see also "The Children and the Child-Savers," chapter 10 of David Nasaw's *Children of the City: At Work and at Play* (Garden City, NY: Anchor/Doubleday, 1985).

9. Other progressives also proposed applying to normal children methods that worked in special education. See Agnes de Lima, "The New Education in the Pubic Schools," *Nation*, June 18, 1924, 702–703.

10. Guiseppe Lombardo-Radice identifies Dora as the "wiry little teacher" in "L'Opera Educativa di A. Patri," *Pedagogia di Apostoli e di Operai* (Bari, Italy: Gius, Laterza & Figli, 1952, 2nd edition), 154–155.

11. Philip Gleason, "American Identity and Americanization," *Harvard Encyclopedia of American Ethnic Groups*, edited by Stephan Thernstrom and others (Cambridge, MA: Harvard University Press, 1980), 31–58.

12. Patri gives vivid impressions of his childhood in Italy in *Biondino: L'emigrante* (Firenze: Marzocco, 1950).

13. Patri's position fits within the approach described by David Hollinger in *Postethnic America: Beyond Multiculturalism* (New York: Basic Books, 1995), 3–5 and passim.

14. A Registration Book in the Patri papers shows that Patri took Dewey's Philosophy of Education course, S 280, between July 7 and August 18, 1909, the summer after beginning his principalship at PS 4.

15. Editor's introduction to *Pragmatism: A Reader*, edited by Louis Menand (New York: Viking, 1997), xxvii. The other three strands which Menand saw emerging from pragmatism were in law, education, and philosophy itself (xxviii–xxxiv).

16. Randolph Bourne, "Trans-National America," 1916; republished in Bourne, *War and the Intellectuals: Collected Essays, 1915–1919*, ed. Carl Resek (New York: Harper & Row, 1964), 122–123. Contemporary pragmatists, drawing on Dewey, James, Kallen and other earlier thinkers, have proposed the extension of democratic cosmopolitanism beyond America to the entire globe. See *Pragmatism and the Problem of Race*, Bill Lawson and Donald Koch, eds. (Bloomington: Indiana University Press, 2004), particularly Judith Green's chapter on "Building a Cosmopolitan World Community through Mutual Hospitality," 203–223.

17. Richard Gambino, *Blood of My Blood: The Dilemma of the Italian Americans* (New York: Anchor Books, 1975), 357. See pages 362–376 for Gambino's descriptions of what he calls "creative ethnicity."

18. Joseph P. Cosco, *Imagining Italians: The Clash of Romance and Race in American Perceptions, 1880–1910* (Albany: State University of New York Press, 2003), 17.

19. Anonymous reviewer, "The Vitalization of City Schools," *American Review of Reviews* 56 (July 1917): 73–74.

20. Clyde Furst, Review of *Schoolmaster*, *Educational Review*, December, 1917, 516–518. Furst was at this time secretary to the Carnegie Foundation for the Advancement of Teaching. See *Dictionary of American Biography*, Supplement One (New York: Scribner's, 1944), 327–329.

21. J. L. More, Untitled review of *Schoolmaster*, 738–739.

22. A recent critique of progressivism is Diane Ravitch's *Left Back: A Century of Failed School Reforms* (New York: Simon and Schuster, 2000).

23. Unsigned review of *Schoolmaster*, in "Notable Books in Brief Review," *New York Times Book Review*, July 29, 1917, 282.

24. Thorstein Veblen's *The Instinct of Workmanship and the State of the Industrial Arts* had been published in 1914, and, given his use of the phrase from the title, apparently Bourne was familiar with it.

25. Randolph Bourne, review of *Schoolmaster*, *Survey* 38 (11 August 1917): 422–423.

26. *Schoolmaster*, 208.

27. *Schoolmaster*, 200.

28. Recommendation from Joseph L. Taylor, District Superintendent, May 15, 1914, Patri Papers. Presumably it was Taylor who gave Patri his annual ratings as a principal from 1909–1913. All the ratings were G (good) or H (high), and there was apparent improvement through the years. In 1909 Patri was rated good nine times and high five; in 1913, his last year at PS 4, he was rated good six times and high eight times. (Ratings form, 1909–1913, Patri Papers).

29. "To Whom It May Concern," Rev. Joseph Auhino, May 13, 1913, Patri Papers.

30. The congressman is quoted by Philip Perlmutter in *Divided We Fall: A History of Ethnic, Religious, and Racial Prejudice in America* (Ames: Iowa State University Press, 1992), 225; Coolidge is quoted by Claudia Roth Pierpont in "The Measure of America," The *New Yorker*, March 8, 2004, 58.

31. Lawrence Cremin, *The Transformation of the School: Progressivism in American Education, 1876–1957* (New York: Knopf, 1961), 246–247.

32. Patricia Graham, *Progressive Education: From Arcady to Academe. A History of the Progressive Education Association, 1919–1955* (New York: Teachers College Press, 1967), 163.

33. David Tyack, *Turning Points in American Educational History* (Waltham, MA: Blaisdell, 1967), 232, 243–247.

34. David Tyack, *The One Best System: A History of American Urban Education* (Cambridge, MA: Harvard University Press, 1974), 256.

35. Paula Fass, *Outside In: Minorities and the Transformation of American Education* (New York: Oxford University Press, 1989), 57–58. Fass was citing *Schoolmaster*, 213.

36. William A. Bullough, *Cities and Schools in the Gilded Age: The Evolution of an Urban Institution* (Port Washington, NY: Kennikat Press, 1974), 121.

37. Bullough, *Cities and Schools*, 127.

38. Rosetta Marantz Cohen and Samuel Scheer, editors, *The Work of Teachers in America: A Social History Through Stories* (Mahwah, NJ: Lawrence Erlbaum, 1997), 205.

39. Stephen Preskill, Review of *The Work of Teachers in America*, *Educational Studies* 28 (Summer, 1997): 157–161.

40. Stephen Preskill and Robin Smith Jacobovitz, *Stories of Teaching: A Foundation for Educational Renewal* (Upper Saddle River, NJ: Merrill Prentice-Hall, 2001), 25–27.

41. Howard Gardner, *Frames of Mind: The Theory of Multiple Intelligences* (New York: Basic Books, 10th Anniversary Edition, 1993). Gardner places himself in a critical progressive tradition in "Intelligences," a chapter in *Education for Democracy: Proceedings from the Cambridge School Conference on Progressive Education*, eds. Kathe Jervis and Arthur Tobier (Weston, MA: The Cambridge School, 1988), 86–102.

42. Deborah Meier, *The Power of Their Ideas: Lessons for America from a Small School in Harlem* (Boston: Beacon Press, 1995). On page 9 Meier makes explicit comparisons between the current school crisis and a similar one in 1918. See also 147–148 for parallels between her work and Patri's.

43. Tyack and Cuban, *Tinkering*, chapter 3.

44. George Wood, *Schools That Work: America's Most Innovative Public Education Programs* (New York: Plume, 1993). In chapter 7 Wood lists some of the steps required to create successful schools and some of the roadblocks to be circumvented. Patri took most of the steps listed except those dealing with school size and encountered many of the obstacles that Wood identifies.

45. Laurel Tanner, *Dewey's Laboratory School: Lessons for Today* (New York: Teachers College Press, 1997).
46. Kate Rousmaniere, *City Teachers: Teaching and School Reform in Historical Perspective* (New York: Teachers College Press, 1997), 133. Rousmaniere draws on Patri's letters and unpublished memoir on pages 29, 101, and 105.

Chapter Four

1. Much of this chapter is adapted from my Research Note, "A Gary School Survives," published in *History of Education Quarterly* 45 (Spring 2005), 96–111. (Copyright by History of Education Society. Reprinted and adapted by permission.)
2. Unpublished memoir, Patri Papers, Box 83.
3. See chapter 11, below, for Patri's diary entries concerning the memoir.
4. There are 243 references to Patri in the *New York Times* between 1897 and 1965. See the index to Patri in ProQuest Historical Newspapers, *New York Times*.
5. David Tyack and Larry Cuban, *Tinkering Toward Utopia: A Century of Public School Reform* (Cambridge, MA: Harvard University Press, 1995), 5. Patri used the same phrase as Tyack and Cuban when he told William Wirt that he wanted to "break the mold" in his program. (Memoir, 67)
6. Lawrence Cremin, *The Transformation of the School* (New York: Knopf, 1960), chapter 6.
7. Herbert Kliebard, *The Struggle for the American Curriculum, 1893–1958*, (New York: Routledge, 1995 edition), 231–252.
8. Lawrence Cremin, *The Transformation of the School* (New York: Knopf, 1960), 251–258.
9. For example, mostly private schools are described in older and more recent books: Harold Rugg and Ann Shumaker, *The Child-Centered School: An Appraisal of the New Education*, (Yonkers, NY: World Book Company, 1928); Charlotte Winsor, ed., *Experimental Schools Revisited: Bulletins of the Bureau of Educational Experiments* (New York: Agathon Press, 1973); Susan F. Semel, *The Dalton School: The Transformation of a Progressive School* (New York: Peter Lang, 1992); Susan F. Semel and Alan R. Sadovnik, eds., *"Schools of Tomorrow," Schools of Today: What Happened to Progressive Education?* (New York: Lang, 1999); Marie Kirchner Stone, *Progressive Legacy: Chicago's Francis W. Parker School, 1901–2001* (New York: Peter Lang, 2001); Laurel Tanner, *Dewey's Laboratory School: Lessons for Today* (New York: Teachers College Press, 1997).
10. Some explanations for the preponderance of progressive private school histories may be found in Semel and Sadovnik, eds., *"Schools of Tomorrow," Schools of Today*, Introduction, chapter 13, and *passim*. The issue is raised also in some of the other books listed in the preceding note.
11. The annual volumes of the *Directory of the Board of Education of the City of New York*, from 1897–1940, are rich sources of data. Through them one can identify Patri's schools and, after 1905, the numbers of classrooms, grade levels, principal, district superintendent, and even the janitor for each school.
12. Kate Rousmaniere cites this Herbart anecdote in *City Teachers: Teaching and School Reform in Historical Perspective* (New York: Teachers College Press, 1997), 101.
13. John Dewey, "Ethical Principles Underlying Education," in *Third Yearbook* (Chicago: National Herbart Society, 1897); *The School and Society* (Chicago: University of Chicago Press, 1899). Dewey's influence on Patri was deepened when Patri took Dewey's course, Logic Applied to Education, during the summer of 1909, following Patri's first year as a principal of PS 4. Columbia University Teachers College, Registration Book for Angelo Patri, Patri Papers.
14. Katz, "Beloved Teacher," *Education Digest* 12 (May, 1947), 17–19.

15. "Educational Forces Outside of the Public School, Considered from the Standpoint of School Administration," (Master's Thesis, Teachers College, Columbia University, 1904.) I thank David Ment, former Archivist of the Special Collections, Milbank Memorial Library, Teachers College, for sending me a copy of this thesis.

16. Memorandum by Joseph S. Taylor, May 15, 1914, Patri Papers.

17. Letter from Frank D. Wilsey to Stephen Wise, June 23, 1914, Patri Papers. Wilsey is identified as a member of the Board of Education of Greater New York during 1902–1904 in *The New York Public School* A. Emerson Palmer (New York: Macmillan, 1905), 432. Presumably Wise had written a letter of recommendation for Patri. Melvin Urofsky has noted that Wise was "consulted from time to time on appointments" during Mitchel's mayoralty. *A Voice That Spoke for Justice: The Life and Times of Stephen S. Wise* (Albany: State University of New York Press, 1982), 105.

18. David Tyack, in *The One Best System: A History of American Urban Education* (Cambridge, MA: Harvard University Press, 1974), describes the heavy-handed, centralized, defensive bureaucracy in New York City. Wilsey was a typical representative of this bureaucracy. Tyack (256) quotes from Patri's *Schoolmaster of the Great City* on administration through fear.

19. Selma Cantor Berrol, *Growing Up American: Immigrant Children in America Then and Now* (New York: Twayne, 1995), 69.

20. Vineland has been identified as "probably the best known and one of the most successful of the more than sixty Italian agricultural communities in the United States." *A Documentary History of the Italian Americans*, Wayne Moquin, Charles Van Doren, and Francis Ianni, eds. (New York: Praeger, 1974), 67. Agnes de Lima also supported the idea that methods used successfully with special students would be helpful to regular students. See her review essay "The New Education: in the Public Schools," *Nation*, June 18, 1924, 116–118.

21. Mitchel was elected on the Fusion ticket, running against a "Republican, a Tammany Democrat, and a Socialist." Diane Ravitch, *The Great School Wars* (New York: Basic Books, 1988), 222.

22. In this enthusiastic recollection forty years later, Patri is presumably quoting or paraphrasing from the committee's report.

23. Patri wrote from Gary an enthusiastic letter to his students, published in a PS 45 school newspaper titled *The Children*, June 1915. Patri Papers.

24. Ravitch notes the Wirt-Dewey connection in *The Great School Wars*, 97.

25. Here Patri is paraphrasing Dewey's famous statement, "What the best and wisest parent wants for his own child, that must the community want for all of its children." *The School and Society* (Chicago: University of Chicago Press, 1899), 15.

26. Patri's supervisor, Joseph S. Taylor, described in positive terms the first seventeen months, beginning in February 1915, of the Gary program in PS 45. "A Report on the Gary Experiment in New York City," *Educational Review* 51 (January 1916), 8–28.

27. Ravitch identifies the Gary school struggle as the third of her four Great School Wars, and analyzes it at length. *The Great School Wars*, 187–230.

28. Rita Kramer, *Maria Montessori: A Biography* (New York: Putnam's Sons, 1976), 21. One correction to Kramer's statement should be noted: Patri did not become a "well-known education writer" until the publication of *Schoolmaster* two years later.

29. "Bronx Likes Gary Plan," *New York Times*, May 22, 1915, 11. Another article says that the Board of Estimate granted PS 45 $170,000 to adapt the school to the Gary Plan. *New York Times*, July 4, 1915, 56.

30. Taylor, "A Report on the Gary Experiment in New York City," 8–28.

31. The superintendent was William Maxwell. Patri seems to be drawing on his memory here and elsewhere. Ravitch in *The Great School Wars* quotes the statement as it appeared in the *New York Times* (March 25, 1915), 204 and 415.

32. Patri's debt to Dewey here and elsewhere is evident. See for example, John Dewey, *The School and Society* (Chicago: University of Chicago Press, 1899), 29. Jane Addams made the same point in a speech to the National Education Association in 1897: "Italian Children in the Primary Grades." Her speech has been reprinted in *A Documentary History of Italian Americans,* 306–312.

33. "Send Dr. Muck Back, Roosevelt Advises," *New York Times,* November 3, 1917, 22.

34. The political nature of evaluations of the Gary plan is explored in "The Social Context of Evaluative Research: A Case Study," by Adeline and Murray Levine, *Evaluation Quarterly* 1 (November 1977), 515–542.

35. Ravitch describes and analyzes these political developments in chapter 20 of *The Great School Wars.*

36. "Our School," by Boys and Girls of Paul Hoffman Junior High School, 1933, 3–4. (Copy from Frank Merolla.)

37. Patri tactfully avoids identifying his administrative critics. He was defended by J. S. Taylor, his district superintendent, who supervised him during his five years at PS 4, 1908–1913, and his first four years at PS 45, 1913–1917. Among his other district superintendents were Henry Jameson in 1920, William Boylan, 1923–1925, Patri's good friend and colleague Anthony Pugliese, 1927–1935, and A.S. Taylor, 1938–1940. Opposition to Patri came largely from the central office, not from Patri's administrative district.

38. "Offer Many Courses in Summer School," *New York Times,* July 1, 1923, E1.

39. *Directory of the Board of Education,* 1917–1920.

40. John and Evelyn Dewey, *Schools of Tomorrow* (New York: Dutton, 1915), chapter VI: Randolph Bourne, *The Gary Schools* (New York: Houghton Mifflin, 1916). Willard Wirt wrote the introduction to Bourne's book.

41. Ravitch, *The Great School Wars,* 203–204.

42. Ronald Cohen and Raymond Mohl, *The Paradox of Progressive Education: The Gary Plan and Urban Schooling,* (Port Washington, NY: Kennikat, 1979), 44–45.

43. "The Vitalization of City Schools," p. 73. It takes nothing away from Leonard Covello's outstanding later work at Benjamin Franklin High School to challenge Francesco Cordasco's statement that "in many ways it was Dr. Leonard Covello who originated the community-school concept in an urban context." Introduction to Leonard Covello's *The Heart is the Teacher* (1958) reissued as *The Teacher in the Urban Community* (Totowa, NJ: Littlefield Adams, 1970), ix.

44. Randolph Bourne, Review of *A Schoolmaster of the Great City,* *Survey* (August 11, 1917), 422–423.

45. Tarbell had become famous for her 1903 muckraking expose of the Standard Oil Company. See John Tebbel and Mary Zuckerman, *The Magazine in America, 1771–1990* (New York: Oxford, 1991), 112–113.

46. *Directory of the Board of Education,* January 1929, 111. Ravitch explains that junior high schools grew during the 1920s "in part to relieve high school congestion, but also to provide a place for vast numbers of over-age elementary school children." *The Great School Wars,* 236.

47. Raymond Callahan, *Education and the Cult of Efficiency: A Study of the Social Forces That Have Shaped the Administration of the Public Schools* (Chicago: University of Chicago, 1962), 136.

48. Lawrence Cremin, *American Education: The Metropolitan Experience, 1876–1980* (New York: Harper and Row, 1988), 237; Diane Ravitch, *The Great School Wars: A History of the New York Public Schools* (New York: Basic Books, 1988), 227; and Cohen and Mohl, *The Paradox of Progressive Education,* 60, 198.

49. Dorothy Canfield Fisher, in an enthusiastic 1940 article, noted the continued use of workshops, studios, and gardens in the school. "Angelo Patri's Public School," *Reader's Digest,* June 1940, 101–105.

Chapter Five

1. Lombardo-Radice is so identified by Winfried Bohm in "Progressive Education in Italy and Spain," *Progressive Education Across the Continents*, Hermann Rohrs and Volker Lenhart, eds. (Frankfurt: Peter Lang, 1995), 91, 85–104.
2. Giuseppe Lombardo-Radice, "Una Visita di Angelo Patri Alle Scuole Italiane," Reprinted in *Pedagogia di Apostoli e di Operai* (Bari, Italy: Gius, Laterza & Figli, 1952), 142–143. Translations by John McDonald, Antonella Merolla, and Rosanna Papapietro. In notes below this document is referred to only as "Una Visita," with page numbers.
3. Patri, "Moral Education," a presentation at the Third International Moral Education Congress," Geneva, 1927, typescript, 2–3.
4. Background on the "new education" and Gentile's "reforms" is given by Winfried Bohm in "Progressive Education in Italy and Spain," 85–104.
5. Istituto Nazionale di Documentazione per L'Innovazione e la Ricerca Educativa, Giuseppe Lombardo-Radice Fund (provisional, B3, issue II).
6. Di Robilant became the manager of the Italy-America Society in 1921, a year before the Fascists took power in Italy, and was removed from that office in 1928 for being "insufficiently Fascist." John McClure Mudge, "Laouro de Bosis Between Italy and America, 1924–1930: The Making of an Anti-Fascist Mind," *Italian American Review* 7.2 (Winter 2000): 88. I thank Stefan Luconi for recommending this article. For background on this issue, see John Patrick Diggins' *Mussolini and Fascism: The View from America* (Princeton, NJ: Princeton University Press, 1972), chapter 5, "Italian-Americans and Mussolini's Italy."
7. *Child Training* was translated by Maria Luisa Rossi-Longhi for *Associazione per il Mezzogiorno Editrice*. (Rome, 1930). Some chapters of *The Problems of Childhood* were translated by A. Pons-Bounous for *L'Educazione Nazionale*, XI, (December 1929); XII, (June–July 1930); and XIII (October 1931). Lombardo-Radice had already written about Patri's educational experiences in "Il Drama dell'Educazione Moderna nella Scuola Americana," La *Tecnica Scolastica*, III, January 1926. (E-mail letter from Giuseppe Pepe to James Wallace, January 2, 2004.).
8. Article by Carmela Mungo, *L'Educazione Nazionale* IX, (April 1927).
9. Istituto Nazionale, (prov. B3, issue II)
10. In his diary for July 5, 1962, Patri recalled visiting the four places noted in northern Italy.
11. "Una Visita," 159–160. In Giacomo Cives, *Attivismo e Antifascismo in G. Lombardo-Radice* (Florence 1983), we learn that Patri's visit lasted three months.
12. "Una Visita," 160–161. Here and below we are adapting primarily from John McDonald's translation.
13. "Una Visita," 161–162.
14. "Una Visita," 161–162.
15. "Una Visita," 162–164
16. "Una Visita," 165–166.
17. "Una Visita," 166–167
18. "Una Visita," 164–169. Marcucci continued the work of G. Cena and is the author of the essay titled *La Scuola di Giovanni Cena*, (Turin: Paravia, 1948), in which on page 262 he recalls Patri's visits and describes Patri as "a great personality of the American scholastic world, of Italian origin and director of one of the most important schools in New York."
19. Felice Socciarelli, disabled in World War I and self-taught, is the author of *Scuola e Vita a Mezzaselva* (Brescia), and *La Scuola*, in which he recalls Patri's visit.
20. "Una Visita," 174.
21. "Una Visita," 175.

22. "Una Visita," 175.
23. "Una Visita," 175–176.
24. Letter from Giuseppe Pepe, citing Lombard-Radice material in the archives of the Science of Education Faculty at the University of Rome.
25. Denis Mack Smith, *Modern Italy A Political History* (Ann Arbor, University of Michigan Press, 1997), 364.
26. A January 14, 1947, letter from Leland Case to Patri refers to one bout of pleurisy. Patri Papers. Patri may well have been suffering from pleurisy as early as 1927. Pleurisy can cause difficulties in respiration and might have made Patri cautious about the climb from sea level up to Piaggine. I thank Noemy Marra of Piaggine for finding the elevations of Piaggine (2,067 feet) and Piaggine Pruno (2,884 feet).
27. "Una Visita," 143.
28. "Una Visita," 155.
29. "Una Visita," 158–159.
30. G. Pepe, "Attualità di Angelo Patri," *ATTI del Convegno: Il Pensiero e l'Opera di A. Patri* (Salerno: Buonaiuto sas Sarno: 2003), 65–82.
31. Rosa Conte's paternal grandfather Pasquale was the brother of Carmela Conte, Angelo's mother.
32. G. Pepe, "Attualita di Angelo Patri," 80–82.
33. An important educational figure and teacher from 1965–1979 in the village Patri refers to in his childhood story *Biondino l'emigrante* (1950). The new school in Piaggine Pruno was named the Angelo Patri School, presumably in 1950. In 2003 G. Pepe and F. Domani took me on a ride and hike to find the school building, now closed.
34. B. Bruno, *L'Eco del Popolo*, December 6, 1961.
35. "Angelo Patri ai Ragazzi Della Scuola Elementare," title of a typescript of text published as *Biondino*, 54 pages, Box 86, Patri Papers. The Angelo Patri School in the Bronx is located at 2225 Webster Avenue; the school in Tacna, Peru, is titled the "Colegio Particular Mixto Italo Peruano Angelo Patri;" the Angelo Patri School in Italy is in Battipaglia, just south of Salerno.
36. Angelo Patri, *Pinocchio in America* (Garden City, NY: Doubleday, Doran, 1928), 61, 65, 255.

Chapter Six

1. Diane Ravitch, *The Great School Wars: A History of the New York City Public Schools* (New York: Basic Books, 1988), 236.
2. Diane Rice, "Fate of Children in the Depression," *New York Times*, May 29, 1932, E7.
3. Lawrence Cremin, *The Transformation of the School: Progressivism in American Education, 1876–1957* (New York: Knopf, 1961), 306.
4. Ravitch, *The Great School Wars*, 235–236.
5. David Tyack, *The One Best System: A History of American Urban Education* (Cambridge, MA: Harvard University Press, 1974), 126–129.
6. Tyack, *The One Best System*, 196–197; Cremin, *Transformation*, 179.
7. "Our School," by the Girls and Boys of Paul Hoffman Junior High School, 1933, 4–6. (Copy from Frank Merolla.) The 1922 approval of Italian as a foreign language is noted in Federal Writers' Project, *The Italians of New York: A Survey* (New York: Random House, 1938), 115.
8. Letter from Patri to Mary Margaret Harrison, July 18, 1938. Appendix B of her Master's thesis, University of Oklahoma, Norman, OK, 1939. The thesis is primarily a study of four great teachers: Johann Pestalozzi, Charles William Eliot, Mark Hopkins, and Angelo Patri. Patri's letter suggests his own preferences among his books. He

particularly recommended to Miss Harrison *Child Training, School and Home*, and *What Have You Got to Give?*

9. Ruth Shagoury, "Back to the Future," chapter 12. For further connections, see the references at the end of her essay.

10. John Dewey, *Democracy and Education: An Introduction to the Philosophy of Education* (New York: Macmillan, 1916), 192–193.

11. "New School Policy Set by Campbell," *New York Times*, June 27, 1934, 1, 5.

12. Larry Cuban, *How Teachers Taught: Constancy and Change in American Classrooms, 1890– 1980* (New York: Longman, 1984), 60.

13. Theodore R. Sizer, *Horace's School: Redesigning the American High School* (Boston: Houghton Mifflin, 1992), 87.

14. This, and the similar statement in the next paragraph, anticipates President George W. Bush's slogan, "No Child Left Behind," shamelessly stolen from the liberal Children's Defense Fund and twisted to conservative ends.

15. Alice R. Bell, "A Day in Angelo Patri's School," *Virginia Journal of Education* 32 (1939): 399–400.

16. Dorothy Canfield Fisher, "Angelo Patri's Public School," *Reader's Digest* (June 1940), 101. This was condensed from an article in the *Christian Herald*, June 1940.

17. Dewey used the word "shop-work" in *The School and Society* (Chicago: University of Chicago Press, 1899), 116.

18. Letter, Dewey to Roberta Grant, April 16, 1940; Letter from Patri to Dewey, October 21, 1944. Both in the Dewey Papers, Special Collections, Morris Library, Southern Illinois University. (JDP 12/1; JDP 13/3). These letters will be published in *The Correspondence of John Dewey*, vol. 3 (1940–1952), InteLex Corp, Charlottesville, VA 2005 (forthcoming). I thank Paula Anders McNally of the Morris Library for her assistance and for permission to quote from the letters. I am grateful to Frank Merolla for confirming, from the Visitors' Book for PS 45, April 15 as the date of Dewey's visit.

19. "Good-by, Mr. Chipps-Patri," *Newsweek* (25 September 1944): 82–83. The reference here was to the hero of James Hilton's popular book about a British schoolmaster, *Good-by Mr. Chips* (New York: Little, Brown, 1934). In the text I have removed the extra "p" that *Newsweek* added to Chips' name.

20. "Do We Need the Junior High School?" *New York Times*, November 22, 1960, 34.

21. David Tyack, *Seeking Common Ground: Public Schools in a Diverse Society* (Cambridge, MA: Harvard University Press, 2003), 184–185.

22. In spite of its demise in New York, the platoon system spread to many districts, partly because of its economic advantages. See Agnes de Lima, *Our Enemy the Child* (New York: New Republic, 1925), chapter VIII; also Charles L. Spain, *The Platoon School* (New York: Macmillan, 1929).

23. Willard Wirt, letter to Patri, June 1, 1920, Patri Papers.

24. Harold Wenglinsky, "From Practice to Praxis: Books About the New Principal Preparation," *Educational Researcher*, 33 (December 2004), 36.

25. The role of immigrants in the Gary struggle is explored by Cohen and Mohl, *The Paradox of Progressive Education*, 50–60, and by Ravitch in chapter 20 of *The Great School Wars*.

26. Patri was continuing the pattern of community involvement he had begun in PS 4. Paula Fass describes his activities there in *Outside In: Minorities and the Transformation of American Education* (New York: Oxford University Press, 1989), 57. William Bullough says that Patri made PS 4 into a "community center." See his *Cities and Schools in the Gilded Age: The Evolution of an Urban Institution* (Port Washington, NY: Kennikat Press, 1974), 127.

27. Joseph L. Taylor, Recommendation for Angelo Patri, May 15, 1914. Patri Papers.

28. Information on Patri's district superintendents is from the *New York School Directories* for the years indicated.

29. I thank Kyna Hamill of the Digital Collections and Archives, Tufts University, for sending me a copy of Patri's letter of April 9, 1923; a photograph of a commencement parade; and Patri's listing among degree recipients.

30. Patricia Graham notes Patri's alienation from the private school orientation of the Progressive Education Association in *Progressive Education: From Arcady to Academe— A History of the Progressive Education Association, 1919–1955* (New York: Teachers College Press, 1967), 163. However, in 1926, Patri along with others did accept a vice-presidency in the Association. "Tells of New Aims in German Schools," *New York Times*, March 10, 1928, 18.

31. Larry Cuban, chapter 8 of *Reconstructing the Common Good in Education: Coping with Intractable American Dilemmas*, eds. Larry Cuban and Dorothy Shipps (Stanford, CA: Stanford University Press, 2000).

32. Semel and Sadovnik note that "both public and private funding sources tend to suspect the word 'progressive.'" *"Schools of Tomorrow," Schools of Today*, 356.

33. I again thank Frank Merolla, Jr., for information concerning Patri's vacation and retirement homes.

Chapter Seven

1. "Mrs. Lindlof Dropped from Board," *New York Times*, May 5, 1943, 1; "Angelo Patri Dies," *New York Times*, September 14, 1965, 39.

2. "Dr. Patri Ends 46-Year School Service," *New York Times*, September 14, 1944, 21. It was actually 47 years.

3. "A Principal Retires," *New York Times*, September 16, 1944, 12.

4. "Testimonial Luncheon to Angelo Patri," November, 1944, Patri Papers.

5. "The Last Day" is chapter 13 (pages 307–325) of Patri's unpublished memoir, Patri Papers, Box 83.

6. The Visitors' Book is now in the possession of Frank Merolla, Jr.

7. Antonio Piccirilli's bust of Lincoln is still in the principal's office at PS 45. I thank the principal, Joseph Solanto, and vice-principal, Frank Fasolino, for their hospitality when Frank Merolla and I visited the school on June 23, 1997.

8. Ralph Waldo Emerson, "Education," in *Emerson on Education*, ed., Howard Mumford Jones (New York: Teachers College Press, 1966), 226–227.

9. Larry Swindell, *Body and Soul: The Story of John Garfield* (New York: William Morrow, 1975), 13–14, 15–19, 21–22, 33–34, 132, 151. Swindell makes minor errors about Patri (p. 14), but the rest of his Garfield story is consistent with other sources, including Patri's memoir. I have combined some of Swindell's short paragraphs.

10. "Garfield: Bronx Turned His Feet to Fame," *New York Post*, May 22, 1952, 28. Patri papers.

11. Anthony Vilhotti, "Dr. Angelo Patri—The Man," in *The Making of the Angelo Patri School*, ed. Arline Weisberg, (New York: Fordham University, Teacher Corps, 1976), 9–13. I thank Principal Rose Clunie for sending me a copy of this and other material about the Patri School.

12. Louis Menand, *The Metaphysical Club: A Story of Ideas in America* (New York: Farrar, Straus and Giroux, 2001), 323.

13. Letter from Joseph Dongarra to James Wallace, March 17, 2000. I was saddened to learn later that Professor Dongarra had died on March 8, 2001.

14. Letter from Catherine Strobel to James Wallace, October 24, 2001.

15. Teresa Cerasuola, "The Arthur Avenue/Belmont Neighborhood of the Bronx, New York," *Italian Americans in Transition*, Joseph Scelsa, Salvatore LaGumina, and Lydio Tomasi, eds. (New York: American Italian Historical Association), 1990, 75–78.

16. Rocky D'Erasmo, *Memories of Fordham* (New York: D'Erasmo, 1987), 16.
17. D'Erasmo, *Memories*, 13.
18. Letters from Rocco D'Erasmo to James Wallace, May 3, May 6, May 17, 2004; *Memories*, 3–5. There was another church of Our Lady of Mount Carmel on 115th Street in Italian Harlem in Manhattan.
19. E-mail messages from Teresa Cerasuola to James Wallace, April 25 and 27, 2004.
20. "Mr. Patri's Message," included in the 1938 Graduation Announcement for PS 45. CCNY Archives.
21. Memoir, Patri Papers, 268.

Chapter Eight

1. This and much other information in this chapter comes from "Memories of Angelo Patri" by Frank Merolla, Jr., Typescript, December 2003. (Hereafter cited as "Merolla Memories.")
2. "Dr. Patri, 89, Noted Educator and Patterson Resident, Dies," *Brewster Patent Trader*, September 16, 1965. CCNY Archives.
3. Patri Diary, kept intermittently from January 1 through September 30, 1962. This entry is from June 27. I thank Frank Merolla, Jr., for permitting me to make a copy of the diary.
4. Merolla Memories, 6.
5. Merolla Memories, 1.
6. Patri spoke in Italian about George Washington on WHOM, the *Il Progreso* station. Letter from Prof. Russo to Patri, February 14, 1947, Patri Papers.
7. Letter from Richard Renoff to James Wallace, October 11, 2004. I thank Teresa Cerasuola for encouraging me to write to Mr. Renoff.
8. Letter from Lowell Thomas to Patri, February 10, 1953, Patri Papers.
9. Letter from Richard Renoff to James Wallace, October 11, 2004.
10. Patri, "The U.N." Typescript, c. 1945, Patri Papers, Box 82. Patri's descriptions of the steep country behind Haviland Hollow are similar to those he wrote in *Biondino* about Piaggine, his childhood home.
11. Valentina Pugliese Perrone, "Schoolmaster," typescript, 8–9. (Undated, but written between 1965 and 1971. The wolf story is told in *Schoolmaster* and in *Biondino*, chapter 4.
12. Merolla Memories, 3–5.
13. Frank Merolla, Jr., note for Patri Seminar, Salerno and Piaggine, October, 2003. Frank's daughter-in-law Antonella Merolla translated it into Italian. Frank was unable to attend, and I thank Marilena Risi and Giuseppe Pepe for reading it at the seminars.
14. Frank recalled later that three were abdominal surgeries and at least one was a hernia repair. E-mail to J. Wallace, March 7, 2005.
15. Merolla Memories, 2.
16. Patri was quite critical of his own carving. Frank Merolla called my attention to Patri's comments on it in his diary entry of January 15, 1962.
17. Merolla Memories, 6–10.
18. Virginia Irwin, "Patri—Best-loved Teacher," *St. Louis Post-Dispatch*, November 14, 1946.
19. Letter from Patri to Rosa Conte, August 5, 1953. I thank Antonio Conte, of Salerno, Italy, for giving me a copy of this letter.
20. Patri, *How to Help Your Child Grow Up* (Chicago: Rand McNally, 1948); *Biondino*. See chapter 1, above.
21. Patri Memoir, Chapter XIV, 2, 3.

22. A January 14, 1947 letter from Leland Case to Patri refers to a bout of pleurisy. Patri Papers.
23. The memoir is in the Patri papers, Box 83. Material on pages 78, 132, and133 of chapter XIV indicates that he wrote most of it in 1953 and 1954, ten years before his death.
24. Benjamin Fine, "Angelo Patri, School Pioneer, Retires from Education Field," Press release, North American Newspaper Alliance, May 19–20, 1962, Patri Papers. Fine wrote on education for the *New York Times* from 1938 to 1958.
25. Valentina Perrone, "Schoolmaster," 11–12.
26. Patri misdated the first page of the diary as January 1, 1961, but it is clear from the context that it was actually 1962.
27. Letter from Frank Merolla, Jr., to the author, February 12, 2004. I thank Dr. Merolla for a number of corrections and suggestions which I have incorporated above.
28. Patri is referring to Harry Krail, who had been his vice-principal at PS 45.
29. Merolla letter, February 12, 2004.
30. Merolla letter, March 8, 2004.
31. The name "Fruengloss" is unclear in Patri's handwriting. This is my best guess.
32. Mt. Carmel Day is discussed at length in *The Madonna of 115th Street: Faith and Community in Italian Harlem, 1880–1950*, by Robert Orsi (New Haven, CT: Yale University Press, 1984.) The Patris lived for some time in Manhattan's Italian Harlem near the Church of Our Lady of Mount Carmel. The feast day for the Madonna of Mount Carmel was begun by emigrants from Polla, Salerno Province, starting in 1881, the year the Patri family emigrated. See Orsi, chapter III.

Chapter Nine

1. My friend Chuck Stones was helpful in locating Frank Merolla, Jr.
2. I am grateful to the members of the extended Patri family who welcomed me into their homes, fed and entertained me, answered my sometimes intrusive questions, and gave me suggestions concerning drafts of this chapter. I thank Jeanne and Don Greco for our talk in Denver on June 18, 1997; Richard and Marjorie Bause for our discussion and lunch on June 19, 1997; and Frank and Mary Beth Merolla for their hospitality and our extended talks June 23–24, 1997. I am grateful also to the Spencer Foundation for a grant that enabled me to travel and conduct these interviews. The interviews are on audio tapes and transcripts in possession of the author.
3. I thank both Muriel Sherlock and Marilyn Shea, grandnieces of Dora and Anna, for sending me copies of the Roosevelt-Patri photograph and much other material.
4. Marilyn Shea informed me that Anna had divorced her husband. (E-mail, Shea to Wallace, November 15, 2004.)
5. Census report, 1920, Bronx district 24d. Dora and Anna's mother also lived with the Patris in 1920.
6. On Piccirilli, see Wayne Moquin, Charles Van Doren, and Francis Ianni, *A Documentary History of the Italian Americans*, (New York: Praeger, 1974), 389–391
7. 1910 Census Report, Enumeration district 1559, sheet 5, shows that Blonk lived with the Catersons at that time. I thank Marilyn Shea for providing this report.
8. Anonymous, "He Knows and Inspires Children." One-page article in the CCNY archives. The source is not indicated, but evidence in the article indicates that it may have been published in 1928.
9. Marilyn Shea sent me census data showing that just before Patri married he was living with his mother; his father, now retired at age 61; and his two younger sisters, Rose and Jennie, both employed as public school teachers. 1910 Census Report, Manhattan, Ward 12, Enumeration District 322, Sheet No. 13B. The actual address was 355 E. 116th Street.

Chapter Ten

1. Patri, *Schoolmaster of the Great City*, 2.
2. *Forty-Eighth Annual Register*, (New York: CCNY, 1897), 13–15.
3. *The Microcosm*, (1897 student yearbook, CCNY), 35, 97, 99, 101.
4. See chapter 2 for more detail on the thesis.
5. Patri, *White Patch* (New York: American Book Company, 1911), 6, iv. The American Book Company was a leading publisher of school texts. At the back of the book there are two pages of advertisements for books on nature study and agriculture.
6. Eugenio Cherubini, *Pinocchio in Africa*, translated by Angelo Patri (New York: Ginn and Company, 1911).
7. *Red Cross Magazine*, April, June, August, September, November 1919; July, August, October 1920.
8. Patricia Graham, *From Arcady to Academe: A History of the Progressive Association, 1919–1955* (New York: Teachers College Press, 1967), 32, 163.
9. Frank Merolla kindly gave me a tape of one of Patri's radio addresses. Patri's pronunciation and speaking style resembles that of Franklin Roosevelt.
10. Letter, Wirt to Patri, June 1, 1920, Patri Papers.
11. Letter, Morgan to Patri, July 14, 1920, Patri Papers. Patri's reply and subsequent letters are in the Arthur Morgan Papers, Series V, Antioch College, Box V A 1. (Hereafter only "Morgan Papers.") I thank Antioch Archivist Scott Sanders for permission to quote from these letters. Concerning the continued connection between Patri and Morgan, in 1926 both were elected (among others) vice presidents of the Progressive Education Association. "Tells of New Aims in German Schools," *New York Times*, March 10, 1928, 18. They corresponded until at least March 21, 1940, when Patri wrote a note to Morgan. Morgan Papers.
12. Letters between Morgan and Patri, September 1920–February, 1921. Morgan Papers.
13. Dorothy Patri, Letter to Arthur Morgan, November 7, 1920. Morgan Papers. Concerning the spread of Patri's columns, see, for example, the advertisement, "Do You Like Children?" *New York Times*, August 16, 1921, 13.
14. Agnes de Lima, "Our Enemy the Child," (Review of ten books on education), *New Republic*, August 6, 1923, 303.
15. Some newspapers carried Patri's column under the series title "Know Your Child." Ralph LaRossa has considerable information on Patri's publishing career in *The Modernization of Fatherhood: A Social and Political History* (Chicago: University of Chicago Press, 1997), chapter 7, "Dear Mr. Patri," 144–169 and notes, 257–266. See also *Redbook Magazine*, (July 1923), contents page.
16. Patri, *The Spirit of America* (New York: American Viewpoint Society, 1924), 1–2. The text was reprinted in 1925.
17. Robert A. George, "Conscientious Objector," *New Republic*, October 25, 2004, 23.
18. Patri, *Spirit*, 11–12, 89–90, 93. For an Italian-American perspective on restrictive immigrant legislation, see Richard Gambino, *Blood of My Blood: The Dilemma of the Italian Americans* (New York: Anchor Books, 1975), 123–127.
19. Patri, *School and Home* (New York: Appleton, 1925), 12. The influential "Cardinal Principles" may be found in many sources, including Daniel Calhoun, ed., *The Educating of Americans: A Documentary History* (Boston: Houghton Mifflin, 1969), 484–488.
20. Patri, *School and Home*, 166
21. Anonymous reviewer, *New York Times*, August 30, 1925, 14.
22. Patri, *What Have You Got to Give?* (New York: Doubleday, Doran, 1926), 1, 130.

23. "Patri Talks on Discipline," *New York Times*, May 2, 1926, 24; "Shadows of Coming Events," *New York Times*, November 1, 1928, XX15; Patri, "Moral Education," typescript in Patri papers, Library of Congress.

24. Introduction to Patri, *The Problems of Childhood* (New York: Appleton, 1926), vi, viii, ix.

25. "Brief Reviews," *New York Times Book Review*, August 29, 1926, 14.

26. Agnes de Lima, "Democracy Disposed Of," *New York Herald Tribune Books*, January 23, 1927, 16.

27. Dorothy Canfield Fisher, *Why Stop Learning?* (New York: Harcourt, Brace, 1927), 145.

28. Ralph LaRossa and Donald Reitzes, "Gendered Perceptions of Father Involvement in Early 20th Century America," *Journal of Marriage and the Family* 57 (February 1995): 223–229.

29. "A Magazine for Parents," *New York Times*, September 23, 1926, 10.

30. Patri, *Pinocchio in America* (Garden City, NY: Doubleday, Doran, 1928), 61–62, 254–255. See chapter 5, above, for a discussion of the autobiographical elements of the book. The *New York Times* carried an admiring review in "Among the Books for Children," on August 19, 1928, 62.

31. Patri, "A Parent's Prayer," *Child Welfare Magazine*, January, 1927, 210. Other versions are in Box 82 in the Patri Papers.

32. "206 New Kindergartens," *New York Times*, November 30, 1927, 22.

33. John W. Briggs, *An Italian Passage: Immigrants to Three American Cities* (New Haven, CT: Yale University Press, 1978), 219.

34. Patri, *The Questioning Child and Other Essays* (New York: Appleton, 1931), 32

35. *Questioning Child*, 118, 121; John Dewey, *Democracy and Education* (New York: Macmillan, 1916), 76.

36. M. L., *Christian Science Monitor*, April 18, 1931, 10.

37. Adelaide Nichols, Review of *The Questioning Child, Survey*, June 15, 1931, 321.

38. "Angelo Patri Honored," *The Parents' Magazine*, June, 1931, 28.

39. Quoted by Dorothy Canfield Fisher in "Angelo Patri's Public School," *Reader's Digest*, June, 1940, 101.

40. "Angelo Patri Wins Award for Book," *New York Times*, May 5, 1931, 30.

41. "Children's Paper Issued," *New York Times*, February 21, 1935, 14.

42. "New Anthology On Class Work Published Here," *New York Times*, June 22, 1941, D4.

43. Library of Congress, Manuscript Division, Papers of Angelo Patri, "Scope and Content Note."

44. Patri, *The Parents Daily Counselor* (New York: Wise-Parslow, 1940), 29–30; John Dewey, *Experience and Education* (New York: Macmillan, 1938), 74–76, 84.

45. Patri, *Your Children in Wartime* (Garden City, NY: Doubleday, Doran, 1943), viii, 110.

46. *Children's Activities for Home and School*, September 1946, cover and 3.

47. *Kirkus*, May 1, 1948, 16; *San Francisco Chronicle*, June 13, 1948, 21.

48. On Benjamin Spock's influence, see Lawrence Cremin, *American Education: The Metropolitan Experience, 1876–1980* (New York: Harper and Row, 1988), 290–294.

49. All from the *New York Times*: "Radio and TV in Review," November 10, 1950, 33; "Patri Column Dropped," November 17, 1950, 34; "Letters to the Times," November 18, 1950, 14; "Video 'Ad' Called Cruel Pressure," November 19, 1950, 40. Patri was paid $1,750 for his 200–300 word article about television. Contract, Ruthrauff and Ryan, signed by Patri on November 1, 1950, Patri Papers.

50. Briggs, *An Italian Passage*, 219. For background on the Italian-American press, see Jerre Mangione and Ben Morreale, *La Storia: Five Centuries of the Italian-American Experience* (New York: HarperCollins, 1992), 454–455.

51. Angelo Patri, "Little Words With Big Meaning," *Journal of the American Education Association* 27 (December 1938): 289. (Republished from the *New York Post*.)

52. E-mails from Mary Bischoff to James Wallace, May 11 and June 20, 2004; Patri column, "Our Children," 1928; other undated Patri clippings with handwritten notes.

Chapter Eleven

1. Lawrence Cremin, *The Transformation of the School: Progressivism in American Education, 1876–1957* (New York: Knopf, 1961), chapter 6.
2. Quoted from Alcott's diary by Honoré W. Morrow, in *The Father of Little Women* (Boston: Little, Brown, 1927), 153. Martin Bickman interprets Alcott's role in education in *Minding American Education: Reclaiming the Tradition of Active Learning* (New York: Teachers College Press, 2003), chapter 3.
3. Clark Blaise, *I Had a Father: A Post-Modern Autobiography* (New York: HarperCollins, 1993), 196–197.
4. Leon Wieseltier, "Washington Diarist," *New Republic*, June 7 and 14, 2004, 46.
5. On this matter, see my article "Bambino Ritrovato o Pedagogia Espropriata?" in *Ricerche Pedagogiche*, 144 (2002): 13–18.
6. See, for example, *Child Training*, 1922; *Problems of Childhood*, 1926; *The Questioning Child and Other Essays*, 1931; *Your Children in Wartime*, 1943; and *How to Help Your Children Grow Up*, 1948.
7. See L. Bellatalla, "Tra 'Scuola Serena' e 'Scuola Attiva': Angelo Patri," in *I Problemi della Pedagogia*, XL, 1994, 23–32.
8. See, for example, J. Dewey, *Experience and Education*, (New York: Macmillan, 1938) and "Individuality and Experience," in *The Journal of the Barnes Foundation*, 1926, reproduced in A. Barnes and others, *Art and Education*, (Merion PA: Barnes Foundation Press, 1929).
9. Patri, "Biondino: An Italian Reader", unpublished retranslation into English by J. M. Wallace and B. Schmidt, (Portland, OR: 2004), 10.
10. See, for example, G. Lombardo-Radice, *Il Problema dell'Educazione dell'Uomo*, (Firenze: La Nuova Italia, 1928); John Dewey, *Democracy and Education* (New York: Macmillan, 1916).
11. See, for example, W. James, "Is Life Worth Living?" in *International Journal of Ethics*, 1895, now in *The Will to Believe and Other Essays in Popular Philosophy*, (New York: Dover Publishers, 1956), and *Talks to Teachers on Psychology and to Students on Some of Life's Ideals*, (New York: Longmans, 1899), chapter I.
12. Patri, *Child Training*, (New York: D. Appleton), 1929, 4.
13. See, for example, R. Cousinet, *Fais Ce Que Je Te Dis: Conseils aux Méres de Famille*, (Paris: Delachaux et Niestlé, 1954).
14. *Child Training*, 6.
15. *Child Training*, 7.
16. See Patri, *The Problems of Childhood*, (New York: 1926), 16.
17. Patri, *Schoolmaster of the Great City*, (New York: Macmillan, 1923), 207.
18. *Schoolmaster*, 207–208.
19. Patri, "The Children of Today," Abridged, in *National Education Association of the United States: Addresses and Proceedings*, 1926, 27.
20. For American new schools, see J. Dewey and E. Dewey, *Schools of Tomorrow*, (New York: E.P. Dutton, 1915); for European and Italian schools, see, A. Ferrière, *L'Aube de l'Ecole Sereine en Italie*, (Neuchatel: Delachaux et Niestlé), 1927.
21. John Dewey, *School and Society*, (Chicago: University of Chicago Press, 1899).
22. *Child Training*, 115.
23. *Child Training*, 115.
24. See, for example, W. James, *Principles of Psychology*, (New York: Dover, 1950), 6–8, and Patri, *The Problems of Childhood*, 150.

25. On Patri's impact on individual students see, for example, the material by Dr. Andrew Vilhotti in chapter 7, above.
26. Patri refers only to Dewey's "Ethical Principles Underlying Education," later adapted as *Moral Principles in Education*, (Boston: Houghton Mifflin Company, 1909).
27. *Schoolmaster*, 16.
28. On *How We Think*, see my article, *John Dewey, Epistemologo della Pedagogia e della Didattica*, in G. Genovesi, *Pedagogia e Didattica alla Ricerca dell' l'Identità*, (Milano: Angeli, 2003), 113–130.
29. *Schoolmaster*, 220–221.

Chapter Thirteen

1. Some of the issues discussed here are considered at greater length in my chapter, "We Are All Multiculturalists Now: From Melting Pot to Cosmopolitanism," in *Italian Americans: A Retrospective On the Twentieth Century* (Chicago Heights, IL: Italian American Historical Association, 2001), 87–109.
2. See, for example, "Milestones of the Italian American Experience" at www.niaf.org/milestones/year_1908.asp
3. Susan Semel and Alan Sadovnik, *Founding Mothers and Others: Women Educational Leaders During the Progressive Era* (New York: Palgrave, 2002), 252. Leonard Covello, *The Social Background of the Italo-American School Child: A Study of the Southern Italian Mores and Their Effect on the School Situation in Italy and America*, edited and with an introduction by Francesco Cordasco, (Leiden: E. J. Brill, 1967).
4. John Goodlad, *Romances with Schools: A Life of Education* (New York: McGraw-Hill, 2004), 254.
5. I explain the incident with the drunk boy in more detail at the end of chapter 7, above. Patri tells the story in his memoir, 268. The second event was presented in more detail in chapter 9; the third in chapter 11.
6. *Biondino: An Italian Reader* (retranslated into English, 2004), 2–3.
7. Letter from Frank D. Wilsey to Stephen Wise, June 23, 1914. Patri Papers. I mentioned this incident in chapter 4, above.
8. Patri, *The Spirit of America* (New York: American Viewpoint Society, 1924), 2.
9. Larry Swindell, *Body and Soul: The Story of John Garfield* (New York: William Morrow, 1975), 15.
10. Patri, Diary, April 16 and August 22, 1962.
11. Patri's last book, *Biondino*, describes warmly and perhaps somewhat imaginatively, Patri's childhood in Italy and America.
12. Interview with Richard and Marjorie Bause, June 19, 1997.
13. The depth and persistence of prejudice and stereotyping is examined in depressing detail by Salvatore LaGumina in *Wop: A Documentary History of Anti-Italian Discrimination* (Tonawanda, NY: Guernica, 1999).
14. "Committee Is Named on Ellis Island," *New York Times*, June 23, 1933, 6.
15. "Legislation Urged to Protect Aliens," *New York Times*, March 28, 1934, 46.
16. Workers of the Federal Writers' Project, *The Italians of New York*, (New York: Arno, 1969; first published in 1938), 120–122. For continuity I have combined two short paragraphs.
17. John W. Briggs, *An Italian Passage: Immigrants to Three American Cities* (New Haven, CT: Yale University Press, 1978), 219.
18. Arthur Mann, *La Guardia: A Fighter Against His Times, 1882–1933* (New York: Lippincott, 1959), 252–254.
19. Luigi Carnovale, "The Non-Americanization of Immigrants," in *A Documentary History of the Italian Americans*, edited by Wayne Moquin, Charles Van Doren, and

Francis Ianni (New York: Praeger, 1974), 285; Barbara Marinacci, *They Came From Italy: The Stories of Famous Italian-Americans* (New York: Dodd, Mead, 1967), 227.

20. Olga Peragallo, *Italian-American Authors and Their Contribution to American Literature*, Anita Peragallo, ed., (New York: Vanni, 1949), 177–182.

21. Josef Vincent Lombardo, *Attilio Piccirilli: Life of an American Sculptor* (New York: Pitman, 1944), 100, 169, 196, 202, 249, and 313.

22. "Bonaschi is Named to College Board," *New York Times*, September 20, 1943, 23; "Dr. Angelo Patri Honored," *New York Times*, November 23, 1946, 13. Other documents related to these events and awards are in the Patri Papers, particularly Containers 82 and 86. See also Anonymous, "Good-by Mr. Chipps-Patri," *Newsweek*, September 25, 1944, 82–83.

23. "Job Trailer Goes Out Looking for Jobless Dropouts in the Bronx," *New York Times*, February 12, 1966, 16.

24. The schools are in the Bronx, New York; Battipaglia, Italy; and Tacna, Peru.

25. "Italy Honors Four Here," *New York Times*, March 17, 1933, 15. Francesco Ercole is identified as Minister of Education, 1931–1934 in L. Minio-Paluello, *Education in Fascist Italy* (London: Oxford University Press, 1946), 116.

26. E-mail communication, May 27, 2004, from Prof. Luciana Bellatalla concurring with the opinion of retired Prof. Giacome Cives about Patri's and Covello's motives in accepting the awards. The complex responses of Italian-Americans to Fascism are persuasively explained by John Diggins in *Mussolini and Fascism: The View from America* (Princeton, NJ: Princeton University Press, 1972), chapter 5.

27. "City War Council is Named by Mayor," *New York Times*, June 22, 1942, 13.

28. "Italian Aid Incorporated," *New York Times*, August 11, 1944, 3.

29. Patri Papers, 1949.

30. Giuseppe Lombardo-Radice, *Pedagogia di Apostoli e di Operai* (Bari, Italy: Guis, Laterza, and Figli, 1952; (first published in 1928 and in 1935). The 1935 edition includes the author's response to Patri's *Schoolmaster of the Great City* ("L'Esperienza Educativa di A. Patri nella Scuola Americana"), 125–137 and his record of Patri's visit to Italy in 1927, "Una Visita di Angelo Patri Alle Scuole Italiane."

31. One example is Thomas Wheeler's introduction to his edited book *The Immigrant Experience: The Anguish of Becoming American*, (New York: Penguin, 1972), 1–18.

32. *Schoolmaster*, 1–5.

33. William Seabrook, *These Foreigners* (New York: Harcourt, Brace, 1938), 143.

34. "Medals Presented at Alumni Dinner," *New York Times*, November 16, 1941, 53.

35. *Child Training*, (New York: D. Appleton, 1922), 277–278.

36. Patri, *How to Help Your Child Grow Up* (Chicago: Rand McNally, 1948), 215–216. Patri's position was liberal for 1948, but considerably short of some current approaches that promote the recognition and celebration of racial differences. See, for example, "How Well Are We Nurturing Racial and Ethnic Diversity?" by Louise Derman-Sparks," in *Rethinking Schools: An Agenda for Change*, eds. David Levine, Robert Lowe, Bob Peterson, and Rita Tenorio (New York: New Press, 1975), 117–122.

37. Patri, *The Questioning Child and Other Essays* (New York: Appleton, 1931), 30

38. Patri, Memoir, 177. Patri Papers.

39. Pedro Noguera, *City Schools and the American Dream: Reclaiming the Promise of Public Education* (New York: Teachers College Press, 2003), 8–10.

40. Patri, *How to Help Your Child Grow Up*, 189–190.

41. Patri, "United Parents Association: Looking Back," *Journal of Educational Sociology* 20 (March 1947), 393.

42. Kate Rousmaniere, *City Teachers: Teaching and School Reform in Historical Perspective* (New York: Teachers College Press, 1997), 101, 105. The author draws on Patri's letters and unpublished memoir also on page 29. See her notes for specific citations: 138, note 2; 144, note 21; 145, note 35.

43. "Dear Mr. Patri," chapter 7 of *The Modernization of Fatherhood: A Social and Political History*, by Ralph LaRossa (Chicago: University of Chicago Press, 1997), 144–145.

44. Letter from Patri to Dewey, October 17, 1949. Dewey Papers, Special Collections, Morris Library, Southern Illinois University. (JDP 19/7). I thank Paula Anders McNally of the Morris Library for her assistance and for permission to quote from the letter.

45. David Tyack and Larry Cuban, Comments at the Askwith Education Forums, Harvard Graduate School of Education, reported in *ED* XLVII (Fall 2003), 30–31.

46. Lawrence Cremin, *The Transformation of the School: Progressivism in American Education, 1876–1957* (New York: Knopf, 1961), 72n, 246–247.

47. Patricia Graham, *Progressive Education: From Arcady to Academe: A History of the Progressive Education Association, 1919–1955* (New York: Teachers College Press, 1967), 153, 163 and passim.

48. Clyde Furst, Review of *Schoolmaster*, *Educational Review* 54 (December 1917), 516–518. Similar points are made in chapter 3 in other reviews of *Schoolmaster*. See also Joseph Taylor's letter cited in chapter 3.

49. Patri fits the general description of the "child-savers" presented by David Nasaw in *Children of the City; At Work and At Play* (Garden City, NY: Anchor Press and Doubleday, 1985): chapter 10. However, as part of the ethnic community, Patri was more realistic and humane than some of the dogmatic, manipulative "child-savers" described by Nasaw.

50. Jean Anyon, quoted in Larry Cuban's review of *Ghetto Schooling: A Political Economy of Urban Educational Reform*, *New York Times Book Review*, October 26, 1997, 42.

51. Harvey Kantor and Robert Lowe, "Reflections on History and Quality Education" *Educational Researcher* 33 (June/July 2004): 9. Contemporary organizations promoting such approaches include the Institute for Democratic Education, the Rethinking Schools group, the National Coalition of Educational Activists, and (more ambiguously) the American Federation of Teachers and the National Education Association.

52. Yoon K. Pak, "Progressive Education and the Limits of Racial Recognition, Revisited," *Educational Theory* 51 (Fall 2001): 497.

BIBLIOGRAPHY

This bibliography includes items cited in the text and notes. It is organized as follows:

1. Writings and translations by Angelo Patri, in chronological order in each category:
   A. Books and Translations
   B. Articles and Other Writing by Patri
2. Books by other authors
3. Chapters and forewords in books
4. Articles about Patri
5. Articles about Patri in the *New York Times*
6. Book reviews
7. Documents, letters, notes, other
8. Articles and essays about Patri by James Wallace

1. Writings and Translations by Patri

A. Books by Patri

White Patch, translated and adapted by Patri (New York: American Book Company, 1911).
Pinocchio in Africa, by Eugenio Cherubini, translated by Angelo Patri (New York: Ginn and Company, 1911).
Schoolmaster of the Great City (New York: Macmillan, 1917).
Child Training (New York: Appleton, 1922).

Talks to Mothers (New York: Appleton, 1923).

The Spirit of America (New York: American Viewpoint Society, 1924).

School and Home (New York: Appleton, 1925).

The Problems of Childhood (New York: Appleton, 1926).

What Have You Got to Give? (New York: Doubleday, Doran, 1926).

Pinocchio in America (Garden City, NY: Doubleday, Doran, 1928).

Pinocchio's Visit to America school edition of *Pinocchio in America* (Boston: Ginn and Company, 1929).

The Adventures of Pinocchio, translated by Patri (Garden City, NY: Doubleday, Doran, 1930).

The Questioning Child and Other Essays (New York: Appleton, 1931).

The Parents Daily Counselor (New York: Wise-Parslow, 1940).

Your Children in Wartime (Garden City, NY: Doubleday, Doran, 1943).

How to Help Your Child Grow Up (Chicago: Rand McNally, 1948).

Biondino L'Emigrante (Florence: Marzocco, 1950).

Biondino: An Italian Reader, translated and adapted by Maria Piccirilli (New York: Vanni, 1951; Retranslated and edited by J. Wallace and Betty Schmidt, unpublished, 2004).

B. Articles and Other Writing by Patri

"Educational Forces Outside of the Public School, Considered from the standpoint of School Administration," Unpublished master's thesis. (New York: Special Collections, Milbank Memorial Library, Teachers College, Columbia University, 1904).

Letter to Students, published in a PS 45 school newspaper titled *The Children*, June 1915. Patri Papers.

"The Children of Today," abridged, in National Education Association of the United States: *Addresses and Proceedings*, 1926, 27.

"A Parent's Prayer," *Child Welfare Magazine* XXI January 1927, 210.

"Moral Education," prepared for the Third International Moral Education Congress, Geneva, 1927, typescript.

"Little Words with Big Meaning," *Journal of the American Education Association* 27 (December 1938), 289. (Republished from the *New York Post*).

"Biography of Angelo Patri," Typescript, 1938, Patri Papers.

"Mr. Patri's Message," One-page handout for students, 1938, CCNY Archives.

"The Teacher Goes to War," Typescript, c. 1943, Box 81, file 3, Patri Papers,

"The U.N." Typescript, c. 1945, Patri Papers, Box 82.

"United Parents Association: Looking Back," *Journal of Educational Sociology* 20 (March 1947).

Letter to Rosa Conte, August 5, 1953.

"A Teacher Sees the Light," Typescript, c. 1955, Box 82, Patri Papers.

Unpublished Memoir, Typescript, c. 1953–1954, Box 83, Patri Papers.

Diary, January 1, 1962–June 7, 1965. Diary in possession of Frank Merolla, Jr., and copy in possession of James Wallace.

"Roses and Drums," Undated Typescript, Box 81, Patri Papers.

2. Books by Other Authors

Appleby, Joyce, Lynn Hunt, and Margaret Jacob, *Telling the Truth about History* (New York: Norton, 1994).

Berrol, Selma Cantor, *Growing Up American: Immigrant Children in America Then and Now* (New York: Twayne, 1995).

Binder, Frederick and David Reimer, *All the Nations Under Heaven: An Ethnic and Racial History of New York City* (New York: Columbia University Press, 1995).

Blaise, Clark, *I Had a Father: A Post-Modern Autobiography* (New York: Harper-Collins, 1993).

Bookbinder, Bernie, *City of the World: New York and its People* (New York: Harry Abrams, 1989).

Bourne, Randolph, *The Gary Schools* (New York: Houghton Mifflin, 1916).

Boyer, Paul, *Urban Masses and Moral Order in America, 1820–1920* (Cambridge, MA: Harvard University Press, 1978).

Briggs, John W., *An Italian Passage: Immigrants to Three American Cities* (New Haven, CT: Yale University Press, 1978).

Bullough, William, *Cities and Schools in the Gilded Age: The Evolution of an Urban Institution* (Port Washington, NY: Kennikat Press, 1974).

Calhoun, Daniel, ed., *The Educating of Americans: A Documentary History* (Boston: Houghton Mifflin, 1969).

Callahan, Raymond, *Education and the Cult of Efficiency: A Study of the Social Forces That Have Shaped the Administration of the Public Schools* (Chicago: University of Chicago Press, 1962).

Cives, Giacomo, *Attivismo e Antifascismo in G. Lombardo-Radice* (Florence, 1983).

Cohen, Ronald and Raymond Mohl, *The Paradox of Progressive Education: The Gary Plan and Urban Schooling* (Port Washington, NY: Kennikat, 1979).

Cohen, Rosetta Marantz and Samuel Scheer, eds., *The Work of Teachers in America: A Social History Through Stories* (Mahwah, NJ: Lawrence Erlbaum, 1997).

Cohen, Sol, *Progressives and Urban School Reform: The Public Education Association of New York City, 1895–1954* (New York: Teachers College Press, 1964).

Cordasco, Francesco and Eugene Bucchioni, eds., *The Italians: Social Backgrounds of an American Group,* (Clifton, NJ: Augustus Kelly, 1974).

Cosco, Joseph P., *Imagining Italians: The Clash of Romance and Race in American Perceptions, 1880–1910* (Albany: State University of New York Press, 2003).

Cousinet, R., *Fais Ce Que Je Te Dis: Conseils aux Méres de Famille* (Paris: Delachaux et Niestlé, 1954).

Covello, Leonard, *The Social Background of the Italo-American School Child: A Study of the Southern Italian Mores and Their Effect on the School Situation in Italy and America*, edited and with an introduction by Francesco Cordasco, (Leiden: E. J. Brill, 1967).

——— *The Heart is the Teacher* (1958); reissued as *The Teacher in the Urban Community* (Totowa, NJ: Littlefield Adams, 1970).

Cremin, Lawrence, *The Transformation of the School: Progressivism in American Education, 1876–1957* (New York: Knopf, 1961).

——— *American Education: The Metropolitan Experience, 1876–1980* (New York: Harper and Row, 1988).

——— *Popular Education and its Discontents* (New York: Harper, 1990).

Cremin, Lawrence, David Shannon, and Mary Townsend, *A History of Teachers College, Columbia University* (New York: Columbia University Press, 1954).

Cuban, Larry, *How Teachers Taught: Constancy and Change in American Classrooms, 1890–1980* (New York: Longman's, 1984).

Cuban, Larry and Dorothy Shipps, eds., *Reconstructing the Common Good in Education: Coping with Intractable American Dilemmas* (Stanford, CA: Stanford University Press, 2000).

D'Erasmo, Rocky, *Memories of Fordham* (New York: D'Erasmo, 1987).

De Lima, Agnes, *Our Enemy the Child* (New York: New Republic, 1925).

Dewey, John, *The School and Society* (Chicago: University of Chicago Press, 1899).

——— *Moral Principles in Education*, (Boston: Houghton Mifflin Company, 1909).

——— *Democracy and Education: An Introduction to the Philosophy of Education* (New York: Macmillan, 1916)

——— *Experience and Education* (New York: Macmillan, 1938).

Dewey, John and Evelyn, *Schools of Tomorrow* (New York: Dutton, 1915)

Diggins, John, *Mussolini and Fascism: The View from America* (Princeton, NJ: Princeton University Press, 1972).

Emerson, Ralph Waldo, "Education," in *Emerson on Education*, ed. Howard Mumford Jones (New York: Teachers College Press, 1966), 226–227.

Fass, Paula, *Outside In: Minorities and the Transformation of American Education* (New York: Oxford University Press, 1989).

Federal Writers' Project, *The Italians of New York: A Survey* (New York: Random House, 1938).

Ferrière, A., *L'Aube de l'Ecole Sereine en Italie* (Neuchatel: Delachaux et Niestlé, 1927.

Fisher, Dorothy Canfield, *Why Stop Learning?* (New York: Harcourt, Brace, 1927).

Gambino, Richard, *Blood of My Blood: The Dilemma of the Italian Americans* (New York: Anchor Books, 1975).

Gardner, Howard, *Frames of Mind: The Theory of Multiple Intelligences* (New York: Basic Books, 10th Anniversary Edition, 1993).

Goodlad, John, *Romances with Schools: A Life of Education* (New York: McGraw-Hill, 2004).

Graff, Harvey, *Conflicting Paths: Growing Up in America* (Cambridge, MA: Harvard University Press, 1995).

Graham, Patricia, *Progressive Education: From Arcady to Academe. A History of the Progressive Education Association, 1919–1955* (New York: Teachers College Press, 1967).

Hollinger, David, *Postethnic America: Beyond Multiculturalism* (New York: Basic Books, 1995).

James, William, *Principles of Psychology* (New York: Dover, 1950; first published in 1890).

——— *The Will to Believe and Other Essays in Popular Philosophy*, (New York: Dover Publishers, 1956; first published in 1897).

——— *Talks to Teachers on Psychology and to Students on Some of Life's Ideals*, (New York: Longmans, 1899).

Jones, Howard Mumford, ed., *Emerson on Education* (New York: Teachers College Press, 1966).

Kessner, Thomas *The Golden Door: Italian and Jewish Immigrant Mobility in New York City: 1880–1915* (New York: Oxford University Press, 1977).

Kliebard, Herbert *The Struggle for the American Curriculum, 1893–1958*, (New York: Routledge, 1995 edition).

Kramer, Rita, *Maria Montessori: A Biography* (New York: Putnam's Sons, 1976).

LaGumina, Salvatore, *Wop: A Documentary History of Anti-Italian Discrimination* (Tonawanda, NY: Guernica, 1999).

LaRossa, Ralph, *The Modernization of Fatherhood: A Social and Political History* (Chicago: University of Chicago Press, 1997).

Lawson, Bill and Donald Koch, eds., *Pragmatism and the Problem of Race* (Bloomington: Indiana University Press, 2004).

Lombardo, Josef Vincent, *Attilio Piccirilli: Life of an American Sculptor* (New York: Pitman, 1944).

Lombardo-Radice, Giuseppe, *Il Problema dell'Educazione dell'Uomo* (Florence: La Nuova Italia, 1928).

——— "Una Visita di Angelo Patri Alle Scuole Italiane," Reprinted in *Pedagogia di Apostoli e di Operai* (Bari: Gius, Laterza & Figli, 1952), 138–176.

Mangione, Jerre and Ben Morreale, *La Storia: Five Centuries of the Italian American Experience* (New York: Harper Collins, 1992).

Mann, Arthur, *La Guardia: A Fighter Against His Times, 1882–1933* (New York: Lippincott, 1959).

Marinacci, Barbara, *They Came From Italy: The Stories of Famous Italian-Americans* (New York: Dodd, Mead, 1967).

McGerr, Michael, A *Fierce Discontent: The Rise and Fall of the Progressive Movement in America, 1870–1920* (New York: Free Press, 2003).

Meier, Deborah, *The Power of Their Ideas: Lessons for America from a Small School in Harlem* (Boston: Beacon Press, 1995).

Menand, Louis, *The Metaphysical Club: A Story of Ideas in America* (New York: Farrar, Straus and Giroux, 2001).

——— ed., *Pragmatism: A Reader* (New York: Viking, 1997).

Minio-Paluello, L., *Education in Fascist Italy* (London: Oxford University Press, 1946).

Moquin, Wayne, Charles Van Doren, and Francis Ianni, eds., *A Documentary History of the Italian Americans* (New York: Praeger, 1974).

Morrow, Honoré W., *The Father of Little Women* (Boston: Little, Brown, 1927).

Nasaw, David, *Children of the City: At Work and At Play* (Garden City, NY: Anchor Press/Doubleday, 1985).

Noguera, Pedro, *City Schools and the American Dream: Reclaiming the Promise of Public Education* (New York: Teachers College Press, 2003).

Orsi, Robert, *The Madonna of 115th Street: Faith and Community in Italian Harlem, 1880–1950*, (New Haven: Yale University Press, 1984.).

Palmer, A. Emerson, *The New York Public School* (New York: Macmillan, 1905),

Perlmutter, Philip, *Divided We Fall: A History of Ethnic, Religious, and Racial Prejudice in America* (Ames: Iowa State University Press, 1992).

Preskill, Stephen and Robin Smith Jacobovitz, *Stories of Teaching: A Foundation for Educational Renewal* (Upper Saddle River, NJ: Merrill Prentice-Hall, 2001).

Ravitch, Diane, *The Great School Wars: A History of the New York City Public Schools* (New York: Basic Books, 1988).

——— *Left Back: A Century of Failed School Reforms* (New York: Simon and Schuster, 2000).

Rolle, Andrew, *The Italian Americans: Troubled Roots* (New York: Free Press, 1980).

Rousmaniere, Kate, *City Teachers: Teaching and School Reform in Historical Perspective* (New York: Teachers College Press, 1997).

Rugg, Harold and Ann Shumaker, *The Child-Centered School: An Appraisal of the New Education*, (Yonkers, NY: World Book Company, 1928).

Seabrook, William, *These Foreigners* (New York: Harcourt, Brace, 1938).

Semel, Susan F. and Alan R. Sadovnik, *Founding Mothers and Others: Women Educational Leaders During the Progressive Era* (New York: Palgrave, 2002).

Semel, Susan F. and Alan R. Sadovnik, eds., *"Schools of Tomorrow," Schools of Today: What Happened to Progressive Education?* (New York: Lang, 1999).

Sizer, Theodore R., *Horace's School: Redesigning the American High School* (Boston: Houghton Mifflin, 1992).

Smith, Denis Mack, *Modern Italy: A Political History* (Ann Arbor: University of Michigan Press, 1997).

Spain, Charles L, *The Platoon School* (New York: Macmillan, 1929).

Stone, Marie Kirchner, *Progressive Legacy: Chicago's Francis W. Parker School, 1901–2001* (New York: Lang, 2001).

Swindell, Larry, *Body and Soul: The Story of John Garfield* (New York: William Morrow, 1975).

Tanner, Laurel, *Dewey's Laboratory School: Lessons for Today* (New York: Teachers College Press, 1997).

Tebbel, John and Mary Zuckerman, *The Magazine in America, 1771–1990* (New York: Oxford, 1991).

Tyack, David, *The One Best System: A History of American Urban Education* (Cambridge, MA: Harvard University Press, 1974).

——— editor, *Turning Points in American Educational History* (Waltham, MA: Blaisdell, 1967).

Tyack, David and Larry Cuban, *Tinkering Toward Utopia: A Century of Public School Reform* (Cambridge, MA: Harvard University Press, 1995).

Urofsky Melvin, *A Voice That Spoke for Justice: The Life and Times of Stephen S. Wise* (Albany: State University of New York Press, 1982).

Veblen, Thorstein, *The Instinct of Workmanship and the State of the Industrial Arts* (New York: Macmillan, 1914).

Westbrook, Robert, *John Dewey and American Democracy* (Ithaca, NY: Cornell University Press, 1991).

Wheeler, Thomas, ed., *The Immigrant Experience: The Anguish of Becoming American* (New York: Penguin, 1972).

Winsor, Charlotte, ed., *Experimental Schools Revisited: Bulletins of the Bureau of Educational Experiments* (New York: Agathon Press, 1973).

Wood, George, *Schools That Work: America's Most Innovative Public Education Programs* (New York: Plume, 1993).

Workers of the Federal Writers' Project, *The Italians of New York* (New York: Arno, 1969; first published in 1938).

3. Chapters and Forewords in Books

Addams, Jane, "Italian Children in the Primary Grades," Reprinted in *A Documentary History of Italian Americans*, Wayne Moquin, Charles Van Doren, and Francis Ianni, eds. (New York: Praeger, 1974).

Banks, James, Foreword to Pedro Noguera's *City Schools and the American Dream: Reclaiming the Promise of Public Education* (New York: Teachers College Press, 2003).

Berrol, Selma, "The Open City: Jews, Jobs, and Schools in New York City, 1880–1915," Chapter 6 of *Educating an Urban People: The New York City Experience*, Diane Ravitch and Ronald Goodenow, eds. (New York: Teachers College Press, 1981).

Bohm, Winfried, "Progressive Education in Italy and Spain," *Progressive Education Across the Continents*, Hermann Rohrs and Volker Lenhart, eds. (Frankfurt: Peter Lang, 1995), 85–104.

Bourne, Randolph, "Trans-National America," 1916; republished in Bourne, *War and the Intellectuals: Collected Essays, 1915–1919*, ed. Carl Resek (New York: Harper & Row, 1964), 122–123.

Dominic Candeloro, "Italian Americans," Chapter 8 in *Multiculturalism in the United States: A Comparative Guide to Acculturation and Ethnicity*, John Buenkner and Lorman Ratner, eds. (New York: Greenwood Press, 1992).

Carnovale, Luigi "The Non-Americanization of Immigrants," in *A Documentary History of the Italian Americans,* edited by Wayne Moquin (New York: Praeger, 1974).

Cerasuola, Teresa, "The Arthur Avenue/Belmont Neighborhood of the Bronx, New York," *Italian Americans in Transition,* Joseph Scelsa, Salvatore LaGumina, and Lydio Tomasi, eds. (New York: American Italian Historical Association), 1990, 75–78.

Derman-Sparks, Louise, "How Well Are We Nurturing Racial and Ethnic Diversity?" in *Rethinking Schools: An Agenda for Change,* David Levine, Robert Lowe, Bob Peterson, and Rita Tenorio, eds. (New York: New Press, 1975), 117–122.

Dewey, John, "Ethical Principles Underlying Education," *Third Yearbook* (Chicago: National Herbart Society, 1897. Expanded into *Moral Principles of Education* Boston: Houghton Mifflin, 1909).

Gardner, Howard, "Intelligences," in *Education for Democracy: Proceedings from the Cambridge School Conference on Progressive Education,* eds. Kathe Jervis and Arthur Tobier (Weston, MA: The Cambridge School, 1988), 86–102.

Gleason, Philip, "American Identity and Americanization," in *Harvard Encyclopedia of American Ethnic Groups,* eds. Stephan Thernstrom and others (Cambridge, MA: Harvard University Press, 1980).

La Gumina, Salvatore J., "The Italian Immigrant Response," in *American Education and the European Immigrant: 1840–1940,* edited by Bernard J. Weiss (Urbana: University of Illinois, 1982).

Lombardo-Radice, Giuseppe, "L'Opera Educativa di A. Patri," *Pedagogia di Apostoli e di Operai* (Bari, Italy: Gius, Laterza & Figli, 1952, 2nd edition).

——— "Una Visita di Angelo Patri Alle Scuole Italiane," Reprinted in *Pedagogia di Apostoli e di Operai* (Bari: Gius, Laterza & Figli, 1952). Translations by John McDonald, Antonella Merolla, and Rosanna Papapietro.

Peragallo, Olga, "Angelo Patri," entry in *Italian-American Authors and Their Contribution to American Literature,* edited by Anita Peragallo (New York: S. F. Vanni, 1949), 177–182.

Susskind, Jacob L., "Angelo Patri," entry in *Dictionary of American Biography,* supplement 7, 1961–1965 (New York: Scribner's Sons, 1981).

4. Articles about Patri

Anonymous, "Angelo Patri Honored," *The Parents' Magazine,* June 1931, 28.

Anonymous, "Garfield: Bronx Turned His Feet to Fame," *New York Post,* May 22, 1952, 28.

Anonymous, "Good-by, Mr. Chips-Patri," *Newsweek* (25 September 1944): 82–83.

Anonymous, "Italian Life in New York," *Harper's Magazine,* April 1881.

Anonymous, "The Vitalization of City Schools," *American Review of Reviews* 56 (July 1917): 73–74.

Anonymous, "Dr. Patri, 89, Noted Educator and Patterson Resident, Dies," *Brewster Patent Trader*, September 16, 1965, CCNY Archives.

Bell, Alice R. "A Day in Angelo Patri's School," *Virginia Journal of Education* 32 (1939).

Boys and Girls of Paul Hoffman Junior High School, "Our School," 1933, 3–4. (Copy of item in possession of Frank Merolla.)

De Lima, Agnes, "The New Education in the Public Schools, *Nation* (18 June 1924), 702–703.

Donato, Ruben and Marvin Lazerson, "New Directions in Educational History: Problems and Prospects," *Educational Researcher* 29 (November 2000).

Fisher, Dorothy Canfield, "Angelo Patri's Public School," *Reader's Digest* (June 1940).

Gopnik, Adam, "The Big One," *The New Yorker* (August 23, 2000, 78–85).

Irwin, Virginia, "Patri—Beloved Teacher," *St. Louis Post-Dispatch* 24 November 1946.

Kantor, Harvey and Robert Lowe, "Reflections on History and Quality Education," *Educational Researcher* 33 (June/July 2004).

Katz, Sidney, "Beloved Educator," *Education Digest* (May 1947).

LaRossa, Ralph and Donald Reitzes, "Gendered Perceptions of Father Involvement in Early 20th Century America," *Journal of Marriage and the Family* 57 (February 1995): 223–229.

Lassonde, Stephen A., "Should I Go, or Should I Stay?: Adolescence, School Attainment, and Parent-Child Relations in Italian Immigrant Families of New Haven, 1900–1940," *History of Education Quarterly* 38 (Spring 1998): 37–60.

Levine, Adeline and Murray Levine, "The Social Context of Evaluative Research: A Case Study," *Evaluation Quarterly* 1 (November 1977): 515–542.

Lombardo-Radice, Giuseppe, "Il Drama dell'Educazione Moderna nella Scuola Americana," *La Tecnica Scolastica*, III, January 1926.

——— Istituto Nazionale di Documentazione per L'Innovazione e la Ricerca Educativa, Giuseppe Lombardo-Radice Fund (provisional, B3, issue II).

Mahler, Jonathan, "20 Years and five Editors Later. . . ," *New York Times Book Review*, September 26, 2004, 13.

Mudge, John McClure, "Lauoro de Bosis Between Italy and America, 1924–1930: The Making of an Anti-Fascist Mind," *Italian American Review* 7.2 (Winter 2000).

Olneck, Michael and Marvin Lazerson, "The School Achievement of Immigrant Children, 1900–1930," *History of Education Quarterly* 14 (Winter 1974): 453–482.

Pak, Yoon K., "Progressive Education and the Limits of Racial Recognition, Revisited," *Educational Theory* 51 (Fall 2001).

Pepe, Giuseppe, "Attualità di Angelo Patri," *ATTI del Convegno: Il Pensiero e l'Opera di A. Patri* (Salerno: Buonaiuto sas Sarno, 2003): 65–82.

Pierpont, Claudia Roth, "The Measure of America," *New Yorker*, March 8, 2004, 58.

Poitier, Beth, "A Curse on Both Their Houses: Liberal and Conservative Views on Urban School Change," *Ed: Magazine of the Harvard Graduate School of Education*, 47 (Spring 2004): 30–31.

Rice, Diane, "Fate of Children in the Depression," *New York Times*, May 29, 1932, E7.

Taylor, Joseph S., "A Report on the Gary Experiment in New York City," *Educational Review* 51 (January 1916): 8–28.

Vilhotti, Anthony, "Dr. Angelo Patri—The Man," in *The Making of the Angelo Patri School*, ed. Arline Weisberg (New York: Fordham University, Teacher Corps, 1976), 9-13

Wieseltier, Leon, "Washington Diarist," *New Republic* (June 7 and 14, 2004), 46.

5. Patri-related Articles from the *New York Times*— Chronological

"Bronx Likes Gary Plan," May 22, 1915, 11.

"Send Dr. Muck Back, Roosevelt Advises," November 3, 1917, 22.

"Offer Many Courses in Summer School," July 1, 1923, E1.

"A Magazine for Parents," September 23, 1926, 10.

"206 New Kindergartens," November 30, 1927, 22.

"Tells of New Aims in German Schools," March 10, 1928, 18.

"Shadows of Coming Events," November 1, 1928, XX15.

"Henry L. Samson Dies," November 4, 1929, 23.

"Angelo Patri Wins Award for Book," May 5, 1931, 30.

"Fate of Children in the Depression," May 29, 1932.

"Italy Honors Four Here," March 17, 1933, 15.

"Committee Is Named on Ellis Island," June 23, 1933, 6.

"Legislation Urged to Protect Aliens," March 28, 1934, 46.

"Children's Paper Issued," February 21, 1935, 14.

"New Anthology On Class Work Published Here," June 22, 1941, D4.

"Medals Presented at Alumni Dinner," November 16, 1941, 53.

"City War Council is Named by Mayor," June 22, 1942, 13.

"Mrs. Lindlof Dropped from Board," May 5, 1943, 1.

"Bonaschi is Named to College Board," September 20, 1943, 23.

"Italian Aid Incorporated," August 11, 1944, 3.

"Patri Ends 46-Year School Service," September 14, 1944, 21.

"A Principal Retires," September 16, 1944, 12.

"Dr. Angelo Patri Honored," November 23, 1946, 13.

"Radio and TV in Review," November 10, 1950, 33.

"Patri Column Dropped," November 17, 1950, 34.

"Letters to the Times," November 18, 1950, 14.

"Video 'Ad' Called Cruel Pressure," November 19, 1950, 40.

"Do We Need the Junior High School?" November 22, 1960, 34.

"Angelo Patri, Educator, Dead; Pioneered in Liberal Teaching," September 14, 1965, 39.

"Job Trailer Goes Out Looking for Jobless Dropouts in the Bronx," February 12, 1966, 16.

6. Book Reviews

Anonymous, "Among the Books for Children," *New York Times*, August 19, 1928, 62.

Anonymous, "Brief Reviews," *New York Times Book Review*, (August 29, 1926), 14.

Anonymous, Review of *Schoolmaster*, in "Notable Books in Brief Review," *New York Times Book Review* (29 July 1917), 282.

Anonymous, Review of *Schoolmaster*, "The Vitalization of City Schools," *American Review of Reviews* (July 1917).

Bourne, Randolph, Review of *Schoolmaster of the Great City*, *Survey*, (11 August 1917), 422–423.

Cuban, Larry, review of *Ghetto Schooling: A Political Economy of Urban Educational Reform*, *New York Times Book Review* (October 26, 1997), 42.

De Lima, Agnes, "Our Enemy the Child," (Review of ten books on education), *New Republic* (August 6, 1923), 303.

———— Essay Review, "The New Education in the Pubic Schools, *Nation* (June 18, 1924), 702-3.

———— "Democracy Disposed Of," *New York Herald Tribune Books* (January 23, 1927), 16.

Furst, Clyde, Review of *Schoolmaster*, *Educational Review* 54 (December 1917).

More, J. L., Untitled review of *Schoolmaster*, *Nation*, (June 21, 1917), 738–739.

Nichols, Adelaide, Review of *The Questioning Child*, *Survey* (June 15, 1931), 321.

Preskill, Stephen, Review of *The Work of Teachers in America*, *Educational Studies* 28 (Summer 1997): 157–161.

Harold Wenglinsky, "From Practice to Praxis: Books About the New Principal Preparation," *Educational Researcher*, 33 (December 2004): 33–37.

7. Letters, Notes, Other Documents

Auhino, Joseph, Letter: "To Whom It May Concern," May 13, 1913, Patri Papers.

Anonymous, *Directory of the School Board for the Boroughs of Manhattan and the Bronx*, New York.

Anonymous, Examination Record for Angelo Patri, Harlem Branch, Young Men's Christian Association, September 20, 1900, Patri Papers.

Anonymous, Istituto Nazionale di Documentazione per L'Innovazione e la Ricerca Educativa, Giuseppe Lombardo-Radice Fund (provisional, B3, issue II).

Anonymous, Rating form for Angelo Patri, 1909–1913, Patri Papers.

Anonymous, Registration Book, CCNY, Patri Papers.

Anonymous, "Scope and Content Note," Papers of Angelo Patri, Library of Congress, Manuscript Division.

Anonymous, "Testimonial Luncheon to Angelo Patri," November 1944, Patri Papers.

Archives, City College of New York, "Classical Course," Catalog, 1896–1897; *Microcosm* (Yearbook, 1897); *Forty-eighth Annual Register,* 1896–1897; "Mr. Patri's Message," One-page handout, 1938.

Bellatalla, Luciana, E-mail communication to author, May 27, 2004 and later.

Case, Leland, Letter to Patri, January 14, 1947, Patri Papers.

Cerasuola, Teresa, E-mail messages to James Wallace, April 25 and 27, 2004.

Compton, Alfred G., Letter, September 17, 1896, Patri Papers.

D'Erasmo, Rocky, Letters to James Wallace, May 3, May 6, May 17, 2004.

Dongarra, Joseph, Letter to James Wallace, March 17, 2000.

Dunlap, Barbara, (Archivist at City College), Letter to the author, May 12, 1996.

Fine, Benjamin, "Angelo Patri, School Pioneer, Retires from Education Field," Press release, *New York Times,* May 19–20, 1962, Patri Papers.

Fripp, Joseph A., Letter, May 3, 1904, Patri Papers.

Girls and Boys of Paul Hoffman Junior High School, "Our School," (1933).

Holden, Charles, Recommendation for Angelo Patri, June 30, 1892, Patri Papers.

Huoteloss, J.S, Recommendation for Patri, Patri Papers.

Merolla, Frank, Jr., Letters to James Wallace, February 12, 2004; March 8, 2004 and later.

——— "Memories of Angelo Patri," Typescript in possession of James Wallace, December 2003.

——— Note for Patri Seminar, Salerno and Piaggine, October 2003.

Morgan, Arthur, Letter to Patri, July 14, 1920, Patri Papers.

Perrone, Valentina Pugliese, "Schoolmaster," typescript. (Undated, but written between 1965 and 1971).

Renoff, Richard, Letter to James Wallace, October 11, 2004.

Russo, Prof., Letter to Patri, February 14, 1947, Patri Papers.

Ruthrauff and Ryan, Contract, signed by Patri on November 1, 1950, Patri Papers.

Schlesinger, Aimee, Letter to Patri, May 24, 1907, Patri Papers.

Strobel, Catherine, Letter to James Wallace, October 24, 2001.

Taylor, Joseph L., Recommendation for Angelo Patri, May 15, 1914, Patri Papers.

Tyack, David, and Larry Cuban, Comments at the Askwith Education Forums, Harvard Graduate School of Education, reported in *ED* XLVII (Fall 2003), 30–31.

Wilsey, Frank D., Letter to Stephen Wise, June 23, 1914, Patri Papers.

Wirt, Willard, Letter to Patri, June 1, 1920, Patri Papers.

8. Articles, Chapters, and Essays on Angelo Patri by James Wallace

"Angelo Patri: Immigrant Educator, Storyteller, and Public School Progressive," *Vitae Scholasticae*, 13 (Fall 1994; actual publication date, 1996): 43–63.

"Reconsideration: *Schoolmaster of the Great City*," *Educational Studies* 28 (Summer 1997): 99–110.

"The Last Day," by Angelo Patri, Introduction by James Wallace. *Vitae Scholasticae* 16 (Fall 1997): 23–37.

"Angelo Patri," *American National Biography* (New York: Oxford University Press, 1999), volume 17, 122–123.

"Angelo Patri," *Historical Dictionary of American Education*, Richard Altenbaugh, ed., (Westport, CT: Greenwood, 1999), 278–279.

"We Are All Multiculturalists Now: From Melting Pot to Cosmopolitanism," Chapter 5 of *Italian Americans: A Retrospective on the Twentieth Century*, Paola Sensi-Isolani and Anthony Tamburri, eds. (Chicago Heights, IL: American Italian Historical Association, 2001).

"L'Istruzione Progressiva, Angelo Patri e la Scuola Pubblica 45," *Atti Del Convegno: Il Pensione e l'Opera di Angelo Patri* (Salerno: AIMC, 2002).

"A Gary School Survives: Angelo Patri and Urban Education," *History of Education Quarterly* 45 (Spring 2005).

INDEX

HISTORY OF
SCHOOLS &
SCHOOLING

THIS SERIES EXPLORES THE HISTORY OF SCHOOLS AND SCHOOLING in the United States and other countries. Books in this series examine the historical development of schools and educational processes, with special emphasis on issues of educational policy, curriculum and pedagogy, as well as issues relating to race, class, gender, and ethnicity. Special emphasis will be placed on the lessons to be learned from the past for contemporary educational reform and policy. Although the series will publish books related to education in the broadest societal and cultural context, it especially seeks books on the history of specific schools and on the lives of educational leaders and school founders.

For additional information about this series or for the submission of manuscripts, please contact the general editors:

Alan R. Sadovnik
Rutgers University-Newark
Education Dept.
155 Conklin Hall
175 University Avenue
Newark, NJ 07102

Susan F. Semel
The City College of New York, CUNY
138th Street and Convent Avenue
NAC 5/208
New York, NY 10031

To order other books in this series, please contact our Customer Service Department:

800-770-LANG (within the U.S.)
212-647-7706 (outside the U.S.)
212-647-7707 FAX

Or browse online by series at:

www.peterlangusa.com